Masculinity
The Hoax Enslaving Men

Books by Russell S. Dynda

From *PULPLESS.COM, INC.*

Masculinity: The Hoax Enslaving Men
Regulus (forthcoming)

From Other Publishers

Screw: The Truth About Walpole State Prison by the Guard Who
Lived It (New Horizon Press, 1989)

Masculinity
The Hoax Enslaving Men
by Russell S. Dynda

PULPLESS.com, inc.
775 East Blithedale Ave., Suite 508
Mill Valley, CA 94941, USA.
Voice & Fax: (500) 367-7353
Home Page: http://www.pulpless.com/
Business inquiries to info@pulpless.com
Editorial inquiries & submissions to
editors@pulpless.com

First Pulpless.Com™, Inc. Edition August, 1999.
Library of Congress Catalog Card Number: 99-62029
ISBN: 1-58445-108-4

Book and Cover designed by CaliPer, Inc.
Cover Illustration by Billy Tackett, Arcadia Studios
© 1999 by Billy Tackett

Acknowledgement

Although the vast majority of work in this book was carried out in a private world of tedious research, analytical thought, introspection and continuous revision, one other person played a major role in bringing the project to a successful conclusion.

Without Kate O'Neal the project would have been more crude in presentation, more tedious in production, and significantly less insightful. Her prudent, accurate and sensitive editing and proofreading gave significant polish to the style. Her encouragement and enthusiasm at each step of the way provided inspiration and fortified my sources of energy. Her willingness to quarrel with me on certain issues was invaluable in that it persuaded me to reexamine my views on several of them. On some I actually shifted. On others I modified my presentation. And on others, I was forced to strengthen and clarify my arguments in response to her insightful critique. (Here it is only fair to her to acknowledge that she had unwavering doubts regarding my views on homosexuality and recommended that I leave out the section devoted to it.)

Finally, Kate inspired me as an example of a strong, independent woman, devoted to the proper raising of her daughter even as she overcame some difficult times to become a successful careerwoman. I honor her for what she has made of herself and hope that she will soon receive the acknowledgment due in her second career as a music composer.

To all women, past and present, most of whom have remained unconscious to the horrible sacrifice of potential that has been forced upon them by us men, as we blindly act out the insensitive, ruthless, self-destructive masculine role designed for us by our society.

Table of Contents

Foreword

As a young boy I was raised to view my father as a hero and to seek to emulate him. Although my father often bragged about his many "successful" life experiences, the person most responsible for canonizing him was my mother.

She had many legitimate reasons to admire him. He was a dedicated breadwinner. He rose to the occasion during family crises. He stood for his principles and spoke up for them. He held respect in his community. He was generally talented, intelligent, athletic and reasonably successful in his occupation.

Then, as he would today, my father stood as a prime example of manhood. No matter that he lacked warmth when dealing with wife and children. No matter that he ruled his house tyrannically. No matter that he held in contempt those who opposed him. And no matter that he embraced violence as the ultimate means to settle disputes.

In order to earn my father's approval I tried to emulate him. I became a successful student and athlete. I doggedly kept my word and stood up for my childhood principles. But in the process I looked down upon other children (particularly girls) and tried to dominate them. As a result I made few friends and, like my dad, found myself often alone. But that was okay because being alone with my feelings indicated I was masculine.

The one area in which I faltered badly was in manifesting myself through violence. On a viscereal level violence frightened and repulsed me. This caused a serious internal conflict because on a conscious level I equated manhood with being able to manifest physical superiority through violence. If you couldn't "take" the other guy you were his inferior. And my dad, based upon his numerous stories of having punched out some adversary, had never been "inferior" to anyone in that way. I therefore was expected, and expected of myself, to come home occasionally with stories of how I too had punched out some jerk who had wronged me.

The problem was that in spite of my being physically capable of handling myself, I was scared—particularly of the prospect of losing a fight and thereby destroying my self-image. At the same time I didn't like physical pain, another weakness in my own eyes because I had seen my father act steel-willed in the face of pain.

Long into my adulthood, through thirty years of intense athletic team competition, the same feeling of insecurity regarding violence haunted me. In spite of a passionate sense of fair play, I avoided fighting at times when fighting seemed to be the only way to effect justice on the court. And often I would feel guilty because of it. In spite of all my reasoning to the contrary, my subconscious still embraced violence as a necessary characteristic of legitimate manhood. To this day I still wrestle with that concept, although my intellect has gradually begun to strip my childhood conditioning of its influence.

This awakening, however, has made me feel more isolated than ever. Violence is still accepted by the vast majority of men. Most of those who deplore violence either have not been successful using it or have been conditioned to fear it. I have not found a sense of camaraderie with either group.

Until recently I held a sexist view of women and was homophobic. I thought that because I didn't physically mistreat women and rather sought to protect them, that I was honoring them. I thought that because I had accepted homosexuality as invalid that it was necessary to shun homosexuals. It was by pure fortune that I suddenly came to see how narrowminded my view had been and how, by accepting the bulk of patriarchal views, I had indeed added to the abuse of women and homosexuals under our system.

Upon seeing this I began looking further into my misbehavior and its motivations. Miraculously, by doing so I began to feel free of the burden of "masculinity" I had been carrying since boyhood. I threw off the shackles of identifying myself as a man and began to identify myself as hu-man—a joyful, fulfilling, cleansing experience.

In this book I hope to point the way for other men to share this same experience even as I encourage women to throw off their patriarchal conditioning and seek their true potential.

Introduction

"Whenever Richard Cory went downtown,
We people on the pavement looked at him;
He was a gentleman from soul to crown,
Clean favored and imperially slim.

And he was always quietly arrayed,
And he was always human when he talked;
But still he fluttered pulses when he said,
'Good morning,' and he glittered when he walked.

And he was rich—yes, richer than a king,
And admirably schooled in every grace:
In fine, we thought that he was everything
To make us wish that we were in his place.

So on we worked, and waited for the light,
And went without the meat and cursed the bread;
And Richard Cory, one calm summer night,
Went home and put a bullet through his head."

It was a poem written near the turn of the century, but many men today feel the same despair. Since the dawn of civilization men have been subject to caste systems of various design. They have given their bodies in war and sacrificed their personal dreams in peacetime to work at meaningless jobs in support of families. Often, the only rewards they can hope for are love, admiration and respect from those they have so dutifully served. But instead, in the past four decades women have subjected them to withering attacks. In addition to all the other burdens men must face they see themselves being "bashed" by the other gender.

Most men don't respond to their exasperating situation by blowing their brains out. Instead, many repress their frustration until their bodies break down. Many sedate themselves by turning to substance addictions and recreational activities. Some who still have difficulty coping, turn their wrath upon their wives and children in harassment that often degenerates further to domestic violence.

As men, where are we? What have we become? What does the future hold?

Most men never address these questions. It's difficult to admit that the life you've been leading is largely a sham. Just the thought will often elicit rushes of anxiety or even terror.

To combat these unsettling flashes of insight, men defend the role that's been forced upon them by seeking fortification from each other. Even those who abhor domestic violence will sit in front of a TV, rabidly identifying with frenzied men who are battering each other in a violent sporting event. They'll beat their chests and exult as our armed forces kill thousands in some questionable foreign war. They'll tingle with a sensation of power as they caress their favorite firearm, justifying their possessing this death-dealing device by claiming a right to defend themselves against the ever-present menace of vicious criminals. They'll indulge in all these activities heedless of the harm being done to those children in formative years who see them as role models.

Those who haven't escaped in this manner or even further dulled their senses by retreating into drink, drugs, or other addictions, do occasionally ask: "Is this all there is? Is this the fulfilled promise of manhood? What happened to the heroic images we experienced as boys? Were our expectations wrong, or have we somehow gone wrong?"

A few have gone so far as to question the traditional focus of manhood—the pursuit of machismo. They have formed into men's groups to share experiences and forge a new path. Some are even willing to seek access to inner, softer emotions usually frowned upon in most cultures when experienced by men. And in the process, some even shed tears.

Certainly men cannot be criticized for being frustrated by the restricted role Western Society has designed for them. Structured responsibility within a technological culture isolates them from nature and the pursuit of instinctual interests. They seem to have few choices if they intend to succeed socially and financially. At the same time, their women seem to have lost appreciation of the burdens they face. Is it any wonder that in response men either weep or lash out in frustration?

Is it?

Whoa! Let's look more closely at what men are crying about.

In the recent TV movie "Gettysburg," General Robert E. Lee sat with tears in his eyes before a campfire the evening of his defeat. 43,000 men had fallen in three brutal days of fighting. Half of them were his, most having hurled themselves in blind obedience into a torrent of bullets which promised little prospect other than death or maiming. 43,000 men, with feelings, values and identity, whose loved ones would not see them again and might well face destitution because of their absence—slain because of Lee's decision to attack. And there he sat shedding tears.

But what did these tears represent? When Lee conveyed his feelings to his subordinate, General Longstreet, he did not lament the loss of these men as human beings. He swore no oath to seek an end to the carnage so that such a pitiful waste could be avoided in the future. No, with teary eyes he took blame for the defeat and stated, "The spirit of the army remains high. We will do better."

The bulk of his tears had been shed for having wasted soldiers, not human beings. He had lost comrades bound to him by common cause. His comments indicated that he did not see them as husbands, fathers, lovers, or creative men whose humane talents had dribbled out with their blood on the field at Gettysburg. No, they were soldiers whose lives were his to spend. His grief was over having spent them without having furthered their cause. In that, he had misused them, much as if he had abused horses. Would as many tears have been shed had the carnage brought victory? Not likely.

The tears of modern men are just as suspect.

The following question may annoy men, but it is a fair one. Who has been running this world for the past six thousand years? Who sculpted "Western Culture" and advanced it to the point where men are exploited? Certainly not women.

Until recently women have been men's property. While men were being exploited by the factory owner (higher class men), those very same workers were returning home and dominating their wives. If men had little choice and mobility within the industrial system, women had none. Her career potential was defined by her sexual apparatus the moment she was born. If indeed a woman was accepted to work, it was on the lowest rung of the industrial scale. Most were relegated to a life of the domestic, serving their men even as these same men (fathers and husbands) exercised property rights over them.

If men have been forced to periodically sacrifice their bodies in war (in response to the ambitions of higher class men) women have been eternally forced to sacrifice their bodies during war and peace by undergoing unwanted pregnancies (to serve the needs of men). In both cases responsibility can be laid at the feet of men.

Between 1890 and 1920 over 300,000 American women died in childbirth. Some of these deaths were unforeseen—seemingly healthy women beset by sudden complications. But many others occurred after several previous pregnancies had injured the woman's reproductive tract and doctors had warned of the dangers of a future pregnancy. Even then, with these women haunted by fear for their lives, they submitted to the relentless sexual demands of their husbands and eventually died.

What choice did they have? Cut their husbands off from sex and risk abandonment in a world where an unattached woman could look forward to little more than economic destitution? Even if they were granted a divorce, with unprotected sex forbidden they could hardly expect to attract another man (few of whom had interest in contraception) to support them. They could either risk a likely death by remaining married, or face virtually certain pauperhood for themselves and their children (if indeed these had not been awarded to the husband) by divorcing. Most remained married, a choice that left them with a life of terror as they closely monitored their monthly cycle for the telltale blood that would tell them they had been granted another month's reprieve from a death sentence.

300,000 pregnancy related deaths! What does this say about the men responsible for these pregnancies? Many of them would have bemoaned their own "misfortune" at having to face exploitation in work and death in war. And while lamenting their own fate, many of them, in effect, killed their wives.

The horrible tally of deaths only covers a thirty year period, and that in the United States. It does not include the countless millions of women who suffered the same fate throughout history and throughout the world. Nor does it address the millions of women who survived the ravages of numerous pregnancies, only to find that their weakened, misshapen bodies were now vulnerable to any number of maladies that radically reduced their life span. As much as these women may have enjoyed motherhood, they were still sexual slaves.

What option did their men have? Were they supposed to give up sex, too, after already having surrendered their freedom to the military/industrial hierarchy? Apparently they didn't think so. Somehow the issue of placing the lives of their wives in jeopardy just didn't seem to be important enough to modify pursuit of personal sexual needs.

What does this say about the privilege of gender in those times? Why didn't men push to develop birth control methods that would have saved their women untold anguish? This was the era of discovery for the automobile, the airplane and the machine gun. Was the mass produced condom so far beyond the capacity of Western science? Why didn't men call for its development and distribution? Indeed, why, until the advent of AIDS, has the use of condoms generally been avoided by men, making birth control the primary responsibility of women? If women wanted to avoid pregnancy they had to invade their bodies with devices and hormones. They endured this intrusion so that they could be protected even as men experienced unrestricted pleasure.

Yes, many men found themselves restricted in their approach to birth control by the dictates of religion. But who organized these religions and composed their doctrines? Certainly not women. A male religious hierarchy conceived and disseminated the dictates of male gods which, of course, vociferously supported patriarchal views demanding the subordination of women ("love, honor and obey").

While women of those times were forced to live under male domination, no army of social workers existed to monitor widespread physical abuse. The frequent instances of domestic violence remained undocumented. In fact, the use of force to control wives was often considered a male privilege, as evidenced by the old English "Rule of Thumb" law which limited the thickness of the rod a man could use to legally beat his wife.

Today the threat of unwanted pregnancy has vastly diminished, but domestic violence still runs rampant. Extensive studies have tried to unravel the reasons behind and extent of this scourge. Suffice it to say that in spite of outrageous claims to the contrary by male excuse makers, women suffer to a far greater extent than do men.

What men don't seem to comprehend is the physical vulnerability women face in this world of men. A physically able man can feel reasonably safe outdoors at any time as long as he avoids areas notorious for crime. A woman, unless she's earned a black belt in a martial art, never feels completely safe alone, anywhere, especially at night.

Why? Because of men.

If a woman knew that upon going outdoors she would encounter nothing but women, her physical fear would be no greater than that experienced by the average man. But knowing she will encounter strange men suddenly heightens her state of apprehension. She can never be sure that the next man she meets will respect her verbal rejection of his overture or will not misread her body language. In either case she is virtually powerless to resist physical attack.

When men's casuist, Warren Farrell, suggests that men are imposed upon when asked to provide physical escort to women, he conveniently ignores the fact that escort is being provided against the assaults of his fellow men. Almost exclusively, it is men (not other women) who pose a physical threat to women.

Throughout recorded history few women have had the power to control their own destinies. Only when men recognize this can they begin to understand the underlying terror that must haunt all women. Many men may see themselves as helpless in our culture, but this "helplessness" is sociologically imposed. They face no discrimination—no domination imposed by a prejudicial view of a genetically determined nature. Most of them, because of gender privilege, have options within their society and the power to affect sociological views. Culturally, women are sentenced to an inferior role as soon as their sex is determined.

How many men truly recognize women's plight, now and historically? Have men ever shed tears over it? Few men at most. Thus, are men really suffering bashing at the hands of women?

True, most women have fallen in line with men and shut their eyes to the tyrannical approach that has structured our society over the past several millennia. The vast majority of women have conformed to roles assigned to them within the system.

But what options did women have? As men's property they had little economic freedom, were deprived of higher education and were conditioned to accept the status quo. In those circumstances what else could they do but play the game? They learned to wield those natural skills unique to them (feminine sexuality and reproduction) to leverage themselves within the male system and carve out a place in a world dominated by male physical force. To this day, feminine conditioning as initiated by male culture, controls most women. In effect, as men, we have made women what they are. Modern Eve, the tempting manipulator men so detest, grew from modern Adam's rib.

The truth is that women's urgent voices have unsettled us because their charges contain a frightening truth. They've not only awakened us to our mistreatment of women, but they've resurrected deep feelings of insecurity we've labored so hard to bury.

Some of these charges may be outlandish, but many are absolutely justified. We, as men, have the responsibility to address them and correct any wrong we've heaped upon women. Women may have closed the gap, but we men still have far more power over our society than they. It's time to stop hiding behind claims of man-bashing. Our lives may not be easy, but we've made theirs a lot tougher. We still have the power to lighten their load even as we seek to address the wrongs in a system that has victimized us as well. We are a party to that system by buying into it. Only when we change our attitude toward the system and our behavior becomes impeccable are we justified in castigating women for any of their misbehavior toward us.

As the book proceeds it may seem to the reader that I have joined the man-bashers and placed all responsibility for gender disharmony at the feet of men. That is true only to a degree. Two realizations have sculpted my view.

First, men have had a stranglehold on the power within human communities since the dawn of history. They chose to exalt themselves and separate the genders. They established the rules and guidelines within which women had to function. Many of those rules were cruel and oppressive but women were forced to live with them.

Since women are as clever as men, many learned to conform to men's rules and still wield a certain degree of power. But once having bought into the game they became as ruthless as men. Men have recognized this and used it to justify their own approach. If those women who have attained power wield it just like men, then women have no right to criticize men's traditional behavior.

What men refuse to acknowledge is that only those women who are willing to buy into the male system have any chance of achieving power. At the same time, to be successful within the system a certain ruthlessness is required. That's the nature of the system. In this way it victimizes men as well as women. But to try to justify the system (which promulgates male superiority) by pointing to the ruthlessness of female participants cleverly twists reality. Women's choice has always been either participate and gain a small measure of power by acting ruthlessly, or remain powerless.

Men complain that women use sex as a weapon and thus are far from powerless. While this is absolutely true, what other options do women have? Woman was not created to be a subservient being. Just like man, she seeks to exercise power in her life. When man restricts her power it is only natural for her to use the power he leaves her. The bottom line is that men have forced women to use sex against them. The result has been to intensify the ugliness of the relationship between men and women. Men try to exert control through outward domination. Women, generally being less powerful in the physical context, seek control through manipulation. Both tactics are loathsome.

But then doesn't that indicate that women have as much responsibility as men for gender conflict? Hardly. First of all, men established the rules to the game. When the game got dirty, favoring men, women were not allowed to protest the rules. So women started playing dirty too.

Doesn't that indicate that if women had established the rules men would have been disadvantaged? Perhaps. Which brings me to my second realization.

It seems to be a majority view across this planet that as long as the other guy is doing something wrong we can justify our own wrong behavior. If a person is caught committing a murder and then beaten up by bad cops, somehow the murderer's crime is not as serious. If women use sex to manipulate men, then male abuse of women is more acceptable. So many of us try to justify our bad behavior by finding some justification in the behavior of those we affect. Until we accept that our personal misbehavior is our full responsibility no matter what misbehavior on the part of others triggered our actions, we are less than human.

Thus, being a man and the forced member of a polarized gender—the dominant gender—I do not see myself as having any right to blame women for our gender conflict. Perhaps women among themselves can identify areas in which they have aggravated the struggle. If so, they have a responsibility to address those areas. In any case it is my responsibility and that of my gender to identify and eradicate those areas of conflict—and there are many—which we have initiated and continue contributing to. Only when we have cleaned up our act as a gender do we have the right to examine our counterpart with a critical eye.

I believe that women's "misbehavior," as seen by men, would largely cease once men ceased trying to dominate her and welcomed her not only as an equal, but as an indispensable partner. Even if I'm wrong, the only constructive approach to resolving gender disharmony is for me and my fellow men to focus upon and address our own transgressions. This will serve the human species enormously, no matter what women do.

In the process of making my case I will, from time to time, point a finger at women as bearing a measure of responsibility for various issues that plague them. I do this in the spirit of finding truth, trying to paint a clear picture as to how we've reached this level of gender conflict. Women have made their own mistakes and added to their dilemma. Only by recognizing this can they adjust their approach to gain the status they deserve. At the same time, by acknowledging women's part in this conflict I hope to establish credibility to objective male readers who are open to change.

At times I will attribute certain viewpoints to "feminists." I recognize that the term covers a wide range of views, many of which are in conflict. Not all feminists accept the views I attribute to some. I use the term loosely simply to facilitate the narrative and forego lengthy explanations each time I refer to one of these feminist viewpoints.

The challenge I face in this book is comparable to trying to stop an old western bar room brawl and restoring order. Men and women have been hitting each other with verbal bottles and chairs for the past few decades. Reason seems to have been long lost in this conflict. How the conflict started seems to be of little concern. Everyone's focus seems to be on getting even with the last person who slugged them. Passions run so high, bruises sink so deep that both sides seem determined to blame the other for starting the brawl and have no intention of seeking an end without achieving domination.

The fact that genetics has cast me on one side in this issue complicates my task. Although I've sought to observe gender conflict objectively I must address the corresponding issues from the perspective of a man. In a brawl it's a lot easier to persuade the guys on your side to stop fighting than those on the other. For that reason I must focus on men even though I'm a strong advocate of the depolarization of the sexes.

Throughout the narrative I will hold gender relationships up to idealistic standards. I expect that even those men who are dissatisfied with their plight under the system will scoff and complain that these standards are unattainable and too much to expect of anyone trying to survive in the "real" world. I admit a certain merit to this argument. One cannot expect aeons of patriarchal conditioning and the survival demands of a rigid social structure to be cast aside in the face of ideas presented in a single book.

Yet at the same time, if we fail to aspire to the ideal by first defining it, then we can never overcome gender disharmony and all the problems it causes. When you are sick you can ingest a pain killer to allow you to endure the discomfort. But that does nothing to cure the condition. Indeed, the condition may worsen because the victim fails to heed the warning signs and take corrective action. To effect a cure the illness must be correctly diagnosed. Then, sometimes major surgery or other long and arduous cures which demand sacrifices are necessary. It is only those who fear enduring the cure who also fear the diagnosis.

Men must begin to display the courage to look at what they've done to women. They may not be able to change all at once, but small steps will help. These steps can only be taken when one recognizes the ultimate goal—the ideal. Then they will serve as examples paving the way for other men—especially younger men and boys—to build a new, constructive relationship with women.

As men, in order to find fulfillment as human beings we face two challenges simultaneously. We must lift the yoke we've placed upon women while at the same time accessing our deeper selves and learning what true manhood really is. We cannot ignore either goal to pursue the other for they work hand in hand. We cannot become fulfilled, authentic men while maintaining a position of domination over women. Nor can we completely emancipate women unless we've accessed the truly compassionate side of ourselves.

The most expedient way to begin this two-fold quest is to take a cold, hard look at what has happened to the human species since our advent. How did patriarchy and male domination of women come to pass? What did we, as men, sacrifice when we assumed the role of patriarch? Why has it not been fulfilling and why has the world, under our domination, come to the brink of ecological disaster?

Chapter One
Our Physical Nature

Male supremacy theorists such as Stephen Goldberg believe that hormonal differences make males more aggressive than females and have throughout history naturally and justifiably placed men in the role of patriarchs. Feminists such as Riane Eisler, Elizabeth Gould Davis, Elizabeth Fisher and Marilyn French denounce this aggressiveness and counter with theories of ancient matriarchies which, they claim, were superior cultures to those dominated by men.

The Feminist Movement itself can be divided into two wings: "difference" and "equality" feminists. The distinction rests on how each wing views the physical differences between men and women. "Difference" feminists acknowledge the physical differences between the sexes and maintain that our society must make allowances for women so that they can compete on an equal footing with men. "Equality" feminists claim that any physical differences between the sexes do not handicap women and that women have the capability of doing anything men can do and need no special treatment.

Nearly all gender theories look back to primitive humankind in their attempt to unravel the current gender tangle. This is a logical approach since our primitive ancestors lived simple lives in cultures of limited complexity and therefore faced far less confusing cultural pressures. This allowed them to live far closer to their natural instincts than us.

Examining the natural instincts is the key to understanding why we lack gender harmony. Although it is obvious that gender roles needed to change over the centuries in order to best serve the species, we must not lose sight of the basic instincts upon which those roles were founded. Nature, during billions of years of trial and error weeding out less successful creatures through the evolutionary process, provided us a panoply of instincts which serve our best interests in an impersonal world filled with physical threats. Had we ignored these instincts (as we have attempted to do during the past few thousand years) we would not likely have survived. For survival is often a close call, as anthropological studies of extinct flora and fauna can attest.

As our living conditions changed we were faced with choices concerning our gender roles. Technology gradually eased survival pressures and gave us the latitude to tune out our instincts, at least for a time, and still survive. Thus we could make role choices without considering instinctual imperatives. But were these role choices in our best interests?

Today, although human lifestyles have vastly changed, evolution has not yet had time to alter our instincts. We possess the same innate programming as our ancestors of ten millennia ago. However, the complexity of our modern culture has desensitized us to our instincts. These constantly try to guide us but for the most part we ignore or suppress them in order to pursue agenda entertained solely by our intellect. Gender harmony has fallen victim to this process.

In order to reestablish the bond between genders that nature intended, we must recognize how cultural pressures have controlled and blinded us to the instinctual path laid out for us. To do so we must follow the lead of other gender theorists and examine humankind in simpler times.

To begin, I must emphasize the obvious—that we live in a physical universe. Although seemingly elementary, many of those wrestling with the gender issue seem to lose sight of this axiom, even as they contemplate the physical differences between men and women. Often they allow subjective concepts of morality to cloud their analysis of the differences.

Although morals serve an important role in guiding our behavior toward others and thereby establishing harmony in our lives, they seem to have little influence on the decisions of nature. It may not appear right, or fair, that the drought destroyed the crops, but we go hungry anyway. Whether or not supernatural beings, or parallel universes, or extrasensory planes of perception exist, we must eat, drink, breathe, defecate and copulate if we are to survive in this world long enough to seek out the others. We can try to ignore the implications of the physical restrictions placed upon us, or interpret them in whatever manner best serves our particular agenda, or declare them "unfair" and thereby immoral. But nature is our ultimate authority and an unbending disciplinarian.

In allowing our creation nature has dictated that we must seek bodily sustenance from and protection against the elements—or die. It also demands that members of the two sexes pair up for at least a brief amount of time in order to reproduce. And, it requires that our offspring receive constant attention for several years if they are to survive to adulthood. These same basic commands have governed us since the advent of Homo sapiens.

Nature may seem like a cruel taskmaster but it has given us all the necessary equipment and instincts to survive. Had it not done so we would have expired eons ago. The fact that we currently find ourselves facing the threat of extinction from overpopulation and environmental destruction indicates that we have wandered off track. The solution to our problems—particularly those relating to gender—seems to lie in our returning to the path originally set for us.

Most modern thinking stands in opposition to this view. Primitive man looks so unattractive. Why would we want to return to a life motivated by primitive impulses when mastery of the environment through the application of scientific knowledge seems to offer so much more?

The answer of course is that nature's directives need not be at odds with science. We need not return to caveman days. Science is the study of nature and can help us rediscover the path nature set for us, smoothing our journey.

But we have not used science in this manner. When we have passed from our study of theoretical science into the realm of applied science we have tended to trash our respect for nature's dictates and attempted to defy them. In spite of grasping but a minute fraction of nature's secrets, we have tried to seize control of the environment. Our few and varying successes encourage us to believe that we have risen so far above our primitive ancestors that we don't have to obey nature's laws as they once did. Furthermore, somehow we can bend these laws and perhaps in time, through new scientific discoveries, cast them off and create our own. By ignoring our glaring failures and worshiping science and technology we worship ourselves even as we steadily make Earth uninhabitable.

Amazingly, we embrace this egocentric dream even as we sip water from a glass, shop for groceries, dress ourselves against the evening's chill, and retreat to dwellings which protect us from wind, rain and snow. We ignore the significance of the fact that while our discoveries have simplified our pursuit of the necessities of life they have not altered our basic physical needs. And if these needs remain the same it must follow that our basic instincts as provided by nature to pursue fulfillment of them are still valid.

While technology has altered our approach to fulfilling physical needs and in the process desensitized us to the call of our instincts, it has also altered the conditions which determined gender roles. Technological advances have allowed women to achieve parity in some, and near parity in other, of those areas once defined by physical demands as exclusively male. Today's woman can effectively assume many responsibilities once denied, with some justification, to her ancient sister.

But in the process of exercising her newly acquired power, woman has fallen into the trap with man of trying to deny her instincts and enter into a power struggle with him. Intensified gender disharmony has resulted.

Perhaps true gender harmony never existed. And yet one cannot help but believe that it must have been much closer to reality in prehistoric times when survival was so tenuous. How could humankind have survived if the genders were constantly in conflict and arguing over responsibilities?

To begin our examination of primitive humankind and our search for gender harmony there, we must keep in mind that daily physical survival dominated life in those times. In the process of obtaining food, shelter and the other necessities, humankind had little opportunity (if indeed it had the awareness) to concern itself with the issue of equality of gender. Its members hunted and gathered and huddled in whatever shelters they could find or contrive to protect themselves from the elements and/or enemies.

The realities of the world weren't all that complicated but they were ruthlessly harsh. Find food regularly or die. Eat well and you remain strong, capable of greater efficiency and stamina in your next hunting or gathering quest as well as able to sustain a longer period without food should that next quest prove less abundant. After all, you couldn't put the leftover meat and veggies in the frig. And if you weakened you just might not be able to catch up with the herd you were tracking; or you might not have the strength to cast a lethal projectile or deliver a fatal blow with your club. Survival was often determined by a narrow margin.

In those circumstances, a bright creature like Homo sapiens sought efficiency in its daily tasks. Its degree of success was graded by nature who tested all its creatures daily and killed those who couldn't pass. With that threat ever lurking, Homo sapiens by necessity assigned its members to the tasks best suited for them.

Since the adult male was generally larger and had greater physical strength, he was better designed for activity related to the external aspects of survival—wresting the means of survival from the environment. Although the female shared the same needs, she had been delegated the additional vital responsibility of bearing the offspring, and to carry out this purpose had been given a physique different from her counterpart.

The biological systems required for this miraculous process necessitated breasts and wider hips. These tended to store fat which made the fat-to-muscle ratio higher in women. In addition, the wider pelvis made the female thighs descend at a somewhat sharper angle, producing both a distinctive female gait and a slightly less stable female knee. At the same time the male physique featured generally broader shoulders and stronger muscles in the upper body. The disparity in physique tended to restrict the female's experiencing the same level of strength and physical movement enjoyed by the male.

Since human survival techniques, unlike those of most of its animal competitors, depend greatly on hand and arm usage the male upper body strength advantage played a significant role in determining survival task delegation. So even though a female was quite capable of performing most of those physical tasks performed by the male, those that depended purely on physical strength (particularly upper body) and mobility she generally performed with less efficiency.

Let me say here that exceptions to this rule likely existed then just as they do now. A small percentage of women probably possessed stronger, more agile physiques compared to those of a small percentage of men. At the same time, the wide disparity in physical strength we are accustomed to seeing today may not have existed. Consider the work of Margaret Mead and her observations on Balinese men:

The arms of the men are almost as free of heavy muscle as those of the women, yet the potentiality for the development of heavy muscle is there; when Balinese work as dock-coolies their muscles develop and harden. But in their own villages they prefer to carry rather than lift, and to summon many hands to every task. If we knew no other people than the Balinese we would never guess that men were so made that they could develop heavy muscles.

As we already know from the gym fad sweeping this country, muscles are there to be built in both men and women. Prehistoric cultures certainly existed where men were not asked to develop their considerable upper body strength potential. Thus they would not have experienced a vast superiority in strength over their women.

At the same time, considering the strenuous physical life facing prehistoric women, it is likely that generally they used their muscles to a much greater extent than do modern women. It would then follow that they experienced greater muscle development and consequently experienced less of a disparity than do modern women when comparing physical strength to their respective men.

However, a disparity still would have existed, especially in upper body strength. And that would have tended to give men priority on those tasks which required it. In short, the potential strength disparity between men and women is nowhere as drastic as patriarchal opinion would have us believe. But it does still exist.

Even so, when prehistoric women were not hampered by pregnancy or child rearing duties they certainly could have performed physical tasks more effectively than the weaker men and with equal proficiency to many others. Whether they were allowed to do so we'll probably never know. Smart male leaders would have allowed these exceptionally gifted women to participate in order to enhance general community effort. However, jealousy, ritual, superstition, etc., might have relegated these women to what we see today as traditional duties.

In any case, when I speak of men being superior physically I'm referring to strength and mobility as related to strenuous tasks. And, I do so in a general sense, recognizing that a small percentage of women are physically capable of handling all but the most strenuous of tasks traditionally assigned to men. In the best interest of the species, gender stereotyping should not have precluded women from performing any task at which they were effective, especially if their performance was equal or superior to that of men.

Now, there is still a great deal of controversy about whether humankind depended more upon hunting or gathering. But there can be little doubt that of the two genders man had the superior potential as a provider of food.

Feminists will quickly point out that a wide range of scientific opinion supports the theory that women, as the primary gatherers, actually provided more food to the primitive human community. In many regions this may well have been true. But even that does not refute the reality of man's superior food gathering potential based on his greater strength. If men provided less food than women it was likely because either men focused on hunting and much of the time hunting was less productive than gathering; or men were lazy; or men had assumed a role of dominance and chose to force women to labor so that they (men) could pursue interests more to their liking.

Whatever the case, hunting remained important. It not only provided food, but also skins for clothing, hides for shelter, and other products to enhance survival. Attempts by some feminists and anthropologists to downplay the importance of hunting would seem unjustified considering the number of primitive societies that practiced it.

These primitive societies certainly evolved with men as the primary hunters. It may have been men's first career. Being generally faster and stronger, they would likely bring home more and larger carcasses. And when your life hangs in the balance you send out the first team. Women certainly could add to the catch, but they were not likely to do as well, especially when they were pregnant or lactating, conditions they probably had to endure most of the time.

Superior male effectiveness would also have demonstrated itself in gathering, where the bigger and stronger members of the species would have had an advantage. With a larger physique and more muscle tissue, men could reach higher, more easily climb trees, dig more effectively and carry more. Again, the female could do a creditable job gathering (and may have done most of it) but was not as likely to do as well as a male who had dedicated himself to gathering.

In times when the tribe had to be defended from a predator or from another tribe, once again the greater physical strength of the male would prove more valuable. Once more, when your life is on the line you want your first team in there.

In summary, the average male physique was superior to that of the average female for dealing with the harsh environment. Yes, women could do nearly everything physically a man could do. But a man, because of a physical strength advantage, could do many things better.

Even before men used their greater strength to forcefully subjugate women, it would have become apparent to both genders that men's physical strength was a vital commodity in determining their standard of living—indeed, whether many of them would survive. Men's physical strength would have been highly valued much like money is today. Even when it was absent or misspent, its potential would always have been appreciated. In fact, in primitive times it is likely that a family with a man who used his strength to protect it even while brutalizing its members would have fared better than a family with a weak man or without any man. Man's greater physical strength potentially served a crucial, positive purpose.

Based on that by itself, it would seem that men could lay legitimate claim to being superior and justifiably assume the dominant role. But not so fast. Such a claim might have held validity if human survival as a species depended solely on wresting sustenance from the environment. But since all humans ultimately died, human existence also demanded reproduction. And in this, males played a decidedly subordinate role.

True, the male sperm was just as crucial to fertilization as the woman's egg (a fact not recognized by primitive man until later). But once impregnation had occurred, the male could act only as an observer and provider. Only a woman's body could host the unborn young, and only her body could provide the necessary sustenance to the helpless infant. Even with all his muscles and macho bravery, without woman, man was a dead end.

This should have made it apparent that neither gender was more important nor could either perform their instinctual prime directive—survive and advance the evolution of the species—without bonding with the other. Unfortunately, primitive humans lived in conditions which did not allow them the leisure to focus their intellect on philosophical matters. Few if any primitive men likely would have said, "I've got to take care of the wife and kids so that we can evolve as a species."

At the same time it's hard to accept the view of feminists who claim that most men cared little about nurturing (it naturally being a female trait) and instead concerned themselves primarily with preserving their own necks. This seems like a harsh judgment, considering that the vast majority of men throughout history have provided for their families.

But even if so, men would have sought to protect the young, seeing them as future providers and procreators—an insurance policy against old age when their own physical capacities had diminished. They would have recognized the indispensable role played by women as both bearers and nurturers of the young. They would also have seen that what matters most in the regulation of population growth is not the number of males, but rather the number of females. If the number of females was not maintained, the tribe's ability to reproduce would be seriously impaired. Motivated by these realizations, men would most certainly have valued the role of women, protecting and providing for them.

The natural reproductive difference between the sexes led directly to the first division of labor into gender classifications. Without birth control women were slaves to their biology, finding themselves frequently physically impaired and therefore dependent on men during periods of pregnancy and lactation. In addition, the human young took much longer to mature, drawing even more of women's attention. So if the young were to survive, women needed to attend to them, allowing men to assume their most effective role as primary providers.

I have just described the need for each gender to play specific roles in order to foster survival. The word "role" scares many feminists. Throughout history men have used the "role" concept to create a hierarchy from which they could dominate. Women were placed into a straightjacket defined by specific roles, many of which had no pertinence to physical differences between genders. Men laid claim to many of the more desirable roles in spite of the fact that women could just as capably have filled them. Many of the roles forced upon women were demeaning. Thus, men used roles to create a gender caste system.

In the process of trying to throw off the yoke imposed upon their gender, many feminists reject the entire concept of role playing as fostering and fortifying patriarchal attitudes. Their argument has merit. But just because men have twisted the concept of roles and used it against women does not invalidate the importance of assuming roles. The feminist response is an overreaction covering over their own inner insecurity which has driven many of them to resent their biological femaleness and the biological roles most suited to females.

Role playing became a problem when men forced roles upon women that went beyond the parameters defined by physical difference. The different physiques of men and women have much to say about the roles best suited for each. Yet roles need not necessarily be classified as exclusively male and female. If a woman had a superior physique for a task usually performed by men, then the species would have been best served if she had led. If she had possessed superior knowledge in an area ordinarily relegated to men, it would have been in everyone's best interest had she taken charge.

This rational approach has obviously not been followed as humans rose from their primitive state. Physical advantages had allowed men to assume the abundance of power, which they stubbornly clung to even as women gained physical parity through technology. As destructive as this attitude has been, particularly over the recent centuries, in primitive times conditions seemed to dictate that men assume leadership most of the time. The one ultimately responsible for protecting and feeding the family would seem to have first claim on decision-making.

Back then, had humans been as bright intellectually as we are today, the females might have demanded equal rights in being able to play any role they chose. When animal products were in need they might have demanded to be part of the hunting effort, leaving some male hunters behind to care for the children. As part of the hunting party they might have demanded that they be given an equal chance to fell the quarry. Of course that might mean that the hunting party would be slowed sufficiently to allow the quarry to outdistance them or the beast to shake off a lighter blow from a female and escape.

Over time reason would almost certainly have set in. Even the females would have seen that it was in the best interests of the tribe for its strongest members—almost always the males—to be assigned the hunting. In addition to offering greater strength, these males, unburdened by pregnancy or child rearing tasks, would have been able to focus upon and hone hunting instincts more effectively than women, whose attentions would have been periodically split.

At the same time it would have become apparent that in any inter-tribal confrontation, a force made up of the tribe's strongest men would fare much better than one consisting partially of physically weaker women.

Those tribes that succumbed to the female demand for "equality" in all areas of responsibility, if indeed there were any so foolish, likely lived less successfully, perhaps even suffering extinction. More likely, the males, fearing extinction, used their greater strength to physically subdue any females inclined toward sharing tasks which were more physically suited to men. This was probably rarely necessary for most of the women would likely rather have survived than died "equal."

Unfortunately, while any irrational demands on the part of women would likely be vetoed by men's greater physical strength, women had no reciprocal power when men acted irrationally. The uncompromising physical nature of living conditions gave brute force the right to resolve all disputes. And nature had given males a significant advantage in manifesting brute force.

Was man's decision to dominate forced upon him by circumstances, as some men's advocates would suggest? Certainly he made the decision with his primitive intellect which had little if any exposure to formal logic—the tool most frequently used to form modern concepts of morality. It must have been difficult for a man, whose entire focus was on surviving and who recognized the preeminence of physical force in his world, to share his authority with a woman whom he saw as markedly inferior physically. He was used to leading, a seeming imperative of that time. But there is a fine line between leading and dominating and apparently primitive man could not see the distinction.

As humankind gained a certain control over its environment (particularly through agriculture) the need for men to maintain their position of authority diminished. Still, for the most part men did not surrender even a fraction of their power. Rather they institutionalized it, creating governments and priesthoods to sustain their position. As we proceed we will examine how and why this happened.

In primitive times both men and women likely had little conscious awareness of their prime directive. They aligned themselves out of necessity into a social structure that met the demands for survival. It was a structure that could often be oppressive, especially to women. But for primitive humankind it was likely the most workable system in a world of harsh physical imperatives. We can draw that conclusion because nature allowed primitive humankind to survive and multiply.

However, because a male dominated hierarchy may have been the most practical social structure when humankind wore skins and made fire with flint, does not validate it for the present day. To determine what system best serves humankind today we must keep in mind our basic human nature and instincts passed down to us from primitive times.

Gender conflict today is fueled by stubborn men clinging to hierarchical attitudes valid hundreds of millennia ago contesting with resentful feminists seeking to deny basic human nature. A vast spectrum of moderate opinion exists between but virtually all of it clings to one erroneous premise—that the two genders are vastly different by nature and that gender identity is more important than human identity. This conflicts with the best interests of the human species because we function best as two genders bonded together. With both sides advocating positions that would destroy the bonding process we face unrelenting gender animosity that drains our vitality and helps push us along the road to extinction.

Chapter Two
Patriarchy/Matriarchy

In the harsh physical conditions of the prehistoric world with technology very crude, men, by virtue of their muscular strength, were given the power to decide who should govern. They chose to retain that authority for themselves, justifying the privilege by pointing to their role as primary providers and defenders. But as tools improved, even this faulty justification carried less merit and over time it became viable to share power with women. Men, however, still refused. They clung to sole governing power, turning their leadership role into one of domination. Thus began patriarchy.

Is patriarchy the natural order of things, as some male supremacists maintain? Is it an obscenity, as most feminists contend? Has it been universal in all but the most primitive societies? Or, as some feminists maintain, have there been advanced societies which were matriarchies?

Arguments still rage over these questions. Sexists of both genders, psychologists and anthropologists align themselves on various sides. Male sexists deny matriarchy because to admit its existence in any advanced society, current or historical, refutes their theory that patriarchy was inevitable and universal—a genetic, hormonal directive. For that same reason feminists go out of their way to prove the prior existence of matriarchy.

What both sides fail to see is that determining governing power by gender is counterproductive to the species. In defending a gender-centered viewpoint, advocates of both patriarchy and matriarchy ignore the characteristic that sets us apart from all other earthly creatures—higher intelligence. Whereas most other creatures depend on specialized physical characteristics to survive, we have always depended mainly upon our intelligence. It therefore follows that intelligence, rather than physical characteristics, should be the determining factor in who should lead.

Since men and women are equally intelligent, neither gender can legitimately lay claim to exclusive access to leadership. Circumstances should dictate who leads. Whichever individual can most intelligently guide the community through the situation confronting it is most qualified to lead. This may vary as situations and circumstances change. For any individual to wrest away a leadership role because of superior physical strength sets back the community. Sadly, however, physical strength has nearly always prevailed over intelligence in determining leadership and we see the fruits of this usurpation in the thousands of years of war and enslavement humans have wreaked upon each other.

Why did one gender of an intelligent species find it necessary to exalt physical strength over intelligence when the latter was its key to success? The answer is that patriarchy evolved from a perception distorted by humankind's psychological insecurities.

Even in the most primitive times men, had they possessed an inner sense of self worth, would have shared power to take advantage of the vast resource of female intelligence. The fact that man selfishly clung to authority is proof that feelings of insecurity dominated him, driving him to dominate woman. With fifty percent of its intelligence resource ignored, the human species could not help but suffer.

All of us, men and women, instinctively seek power—the ability to affect our environment. Human nature prods us to seek as much control over our lives as possible. We don't wish to feel helpless before the elements. Unfortunately, this planet presents physical conditions that often defy our efforts to tame them. Some of us may be able to maintain control to varying degrees, but most of us are regularly victimized by circumstances around us.

The manner in which we deal with situations where we can exercise no control indicates how well we are adjusted. In these situations it's natural to feel insecure. But how do we react to these feelings?

We can maintain our rationality and make the most of situations where we feel powerless, gaining the feeling of confidence that we can ride out such storms in the future. Or we can allow our healthy concern for the future to burgeon into an all consuming anxiety which brushes aside rational approaches and turns our thinking completely subjective. In this state we begin to see other human beings—whom we identify as competitors and thereby components of this outside environment—as a threat to us. We begin plotting to exercise control over them to reduce this perceived threat.

This dynamic led to the inception of the hierarchical approach to leadership practiced by humans. It has taken the form of patriarchy because men have wrested control of those positions at the top of the power pyramid.

Patriarchy attempts to cleverly rationalize its self-oriented focus. It pays lip service to being charitable, hospitable and patriotic ("family values?"), even as it pursues and thereby advocates ruthless competition for power positions from which leaders can control underlings. It is the underlings, of course, who are encouraged to embrace and exhibit charity, hospitality and patriotism—the first two to assuage each other's misery; the last to sustain patriarchy. Hierarchies, particularly patriarchy, foster pursuit of security at the expense of others.

I walk a tightrope here for I recognize that a state of constructive selfishness does indeed exist. Our motivation for living is to experience personal pleasure. Each of us has an inner conscience that acts as our final authority in choosing those actions which enhance our pleasure. To maintain our integrity as individual human beings we must feel that our voluntary actions enhance our self-interest. To some this may mean stealing from others. For others this may mean devoting one's life to charity and self-sacrifice. The latter approach is just as selfish as the former in that it is performed for self-satisfaction. Thus, selfishness need not be in conflict with having a strong social conscience. It can be both positive and negative.

Most studies indicate that human beings have always sought to maintain strong social bonds. This has enhanced our survival prospects, especially in primitive times. We experience this social proclivity particularly in our attachment to family and, to a lesser degree, to our affinity to tribe or clan. Most, if not all of us, feel strong emotional attachments for those related to us, and many of us would sacrifice our well being for theirs. This is innate or instinctual, not the dictates of intellectual reason.

If indeed a man cannot be fulfilled without maintaining harmonious contact with others of his kind, then it is in his selfish interests to see to the best interests of society as a whole rather than seeking to dominate it. This may mean sacrificing some of his individual interests to the well being of others. He may find it fulfilling to earn less so that those who work for him can earn more. He is thereby compensated by seeing them advanced.

This shows us how the demands of patriarchy conflict with natural human instinct. Patriarchy sets individuals in competition with each other in seeking to establish superiority rather than to enhance the status of everyone. We can see the resulting conflict all over the world, even today. Most human beings advocate the unique view among animals that we should preserve the lives of all of our members. And yet large segments of humanity practice genocidal politics or preserve human life only to subject it to poverty and slavery. These practices result from hierarchical approaches to leadership, virtually all of them currently patriarchal.

In general, both genders have always dealt with their feelings of insecurity irrationally. We can make allowances for primitive men and women because of the very real precarious nature of existence facing them virtually every moment of their short lives. Human beings constantly threatened with extinction and without sufficient leisure, stimulation or life span to develop an intellectual understanding of their situation, would have difficulty coping with their inner fears.

We have all felt the terrors of anxiety, even here in modern Western society which is relatively free of serious physical danger. We have all observed, if not practiced, the many bizarre techniques people use to maintain their sanity in the face of stubborn anxieties whose intensity seems to have no basis. Primitive humankind faced the same psychological crisis, except that many of its fears were justified by its having to face relentlessly pressing threats to survival.

Unfortunately, even as humankind gained survival skills that reduced some of the threat, it failed to shed its insecurities. Reason that took into account the value of all human beings remained underdeveloped. Instead, the growing intellectual abilities were used to fortify the old power-sustaining techniques.

Having seen that physical prowess was the determining factor in surviving, males ritualized and glorified physical activities to exalt themselves. In particular, the ability to employ violence, which was often necessarily used in an amoral sense to ensure survival, took on special significance. In this atmosphere women could only look inferior, an ideal situation for insecure men to take advantage of. Men combated their insecurities not only by gaining a measure of control over their environment, but by exercising unbending authority, threatening violence within their community.

Possessing limited physical capabilities compared to those of most men, women found their pool of insecurities expanded. In addition to sharing the survival fears of their males, they also had to deal with an imposed inferior status. They not only faced the survival threat imposed by the physical environment, but also physical domination by the other gender.

What feminists fail to acknowledge is that even if we end male domination, both genders will still be burdened with psychological insecurities and our tendency to address them counter-productively. Men's misbehavior in response to his insecurities is blatant, as characterized in machismo and its ramifications—war, environmental destruction and domestic violence. Women's response to her insecurities remains more concealed in a deep shadow cast by the misbehavior of men.

Feminists would like us to believe that most of women's insecurities are caused by men. The truth is that women suffer from the same basic insecurities as men but manifest them differently due to imposed subservience. Comparatively, aggression and the competitive spirit seem to be lacking in women. But can that be attributed to genetically programmed hormonal factors or is cultural conditioning responsible? We might believe the former if we did not see so many examples of women acting aggressively.

We have all heard of numerous cases where women have fought tooth and nail to protect their young. We see super aggressiveness on display every day in women's athletic competitions. And on occasion women go even further. At a recent legislative meeting in an Asian country a fistfight broke out between two women members which rapidly spread to other women. The resulting major physical brawl could only be broken up by men.

The above would seem to undermine the theory that hormones are responsible for aggressiveness. This brings to mind a pertinent observation by Marilyn French:

> If hormones were responsible for aggressiveness and passivity, people from different cultures would have to have different hormonal structures.

Why then do women seem so much less aggressive than men? Because on a purely physical plane they cannot in most situations compete successfully with men. They could never succeed using brute force in acts of aggression to wrest what they want from men. For women trying to deal in the world of men, aggression and confrontation most often leads to negative results. Therefore many have sought to fulfill their needs using those techniques that do work— the more passive approaches so resented by men like guile and manipulation.

Women often act out their aggression in a more subtle manner through what has been referred to as "harem politics." In this situation under an invulnerable master, women aspire to power by becoming close to the master. Resentment, rage and bitterness at their lot cannot be directed against the master (who could only be overpowered physically), so it is directed at other concubines who are the living embodiment of one's own degradation. A pecking order establishes itself, dependent upon one's influence with the master. Concubines typically act out on each other their repressed rage against the master, as well as internalized hatred of those "sisters" they see as competitors. If this aggression is less often manifested physically than among males, it is only because most women have been conditioned from childhood to avoid physical conflict.

In cases where individual women have risen to ruling status, they have generally practiced the same ruling style as men. Immediate examples coming to mind are: Margaret Thatcher, Indira Ghandi and Golda Meir, all of which used an approach toward carrying out their duties that would be classified as masculine. All handled foreign affairs aggressively, using war as a tool to reach their goals. These women only reached their status by rising through a male hierarchy and playing by its rules, so they may not be typical of the feminine leadership spirit. Nevertheless they proved themselves to be just as aggressive as men.

If women have a legitimate claim to being less destructive in response to their insecurities it's partially because they have been restrained by men from following men's destructive path. Women have therefore been forced to expend a great deal more effort coming to grips with insecurities than men, who can vent their frustration and hostilities upon those weaker.

If we are to accurately evaluate our past in an effort to understand how we have arrived at our current state of gender confusion, we must keep in mind the role of humankind's insecurities. Environmental imperatives limited our choices. But we nevertheless were given choices. We made them with judgment clouded by feelings of inadequacy triggered by our insecurities.

For a man whose self-esteem has been eroded by feelings of insecurity, perhaps those choices were the only ones he was capable of making. But that doesn't validate those choices even if they were made over and over again by succeeding generations. A man who did not allow his insecurities to dominate him and evolved in response to them would view his alternatives differently.

For example, secure white men did not feel threatened by allowing women or people of color to vote. However, it took centuries for this to occur, indicating that the vast majority of white men during that period felt insecure in regards to that issue (and probably numerous others). Those men vociferously defended their discriminatory points of view, often with compelling, twisted logic. The same holds true today regarding the gender issue.

So, unless we accept psychological insecurity and the tendency to respond irrationally to it as the natural, optimum mental state of humankind, we are forced to admit that a number of choices made for the species by its dominant gender have been questionable. Just because patriarchy has existed in society after society through the ages does not validate it as the system best suited to governing us.

John Stuart Mill makes this pertinent observation:

> The anxiety of mankind to interfere in behalf of nature, for fear lest nature should not succeed in effecting its purpose, is an altogether unnecessary solicitude. What women by nature cannot do, it is quite superfluous to prevent them from doing. What they can do, but not so well as the men who are their competitors, competition suffices to exclude them from.

The fact that men chose to institute a system which precluded women from ruling indicates that women did not lack ruling capability, but rather that men feared it.

Some male supremacists maintain that whatever man's mental state, he had no choice but to dominate. Hormones, particularly testosterone, demanded it. This theory places free choice in a role subordinate to hormones.

The role of testosterone is still being evaluated in laboratories. The results are still inconclusive. Some scientists claim that an infusion of testosterone increases aggressiveness. Other experiments have shown that men lacking testosterone were unusually aggressive and that an infusion of the hormone quieted them. The significance of these discoveries is still the subject of much debate. At this point, however, it appears that testosterone is only one part of a complex interacting system of hormones shared by both men and women. This system is vastly affected by social factors.

Whatever future research tells us about chemical and biological imperatives, we still must admit that volition plays a major part in humankind's behavior. Many people who, according to genetic theory, have a propensity toward alcohol abuse do not become drunks. Perhaps chemists will eventually concoct a chemical explanation to invalidate volition in these cases as well. But for now, human volition seems to be a pretty powerful tool, especially to those of us who make use of it.

If you believe that two men pumped up with testosterone are compelled to fight no matter how strongly they wish to avoid it, then you need not read on. I intend to proceed on the assumption that humans, even in the face of strong biological urges, have had the power to make choices. And, I believe they must be held responsible for those choices.

Regarding gender issues, sometimes the choices were dictated by environmental circumstances. Sometimes the choices were wrought by ignorance. Sometimes the choices were contrived and cruel. Some of the cruel choices were even well meaning. But in all cases these choices no longer need to bind us. We can and should reexamine these choices so we can comprehend how patriarchy came to pass and if it has had any validity. This will allow us to overturn negative past decisions and ensure that similar destructive choices are avoided in the future.

As I stated before, the path to patriarchy lay open because of men's superior physical strength. In primitive times one issue likely protected women at least partially from complete subservience. For much of prehistory men's function in the fertilization of women remained unknown. Reproduction, that process so vital to humankind's survival, remained mysterious.

Men could overpower women, but they could not birth a child. Without recognizing their own role in the process, men, to at least some degree, must have held women in awe. Yes, they may still have dominated. But likely they held their women in higher esteem before the crucial discovery was made. Once man's role in the fertilization process became common knowledge women's status must have drastically slipped, plunging humankind down the road toward full blown patriarchy.

In their mania to maintain power over their women and influence with their fellow men, men sought to establish lineage. To do so a man needed a woman to whom he had exclusive sexual access. His own sexual exclusivity was not demanded, the only restriction being that he did not trespass upon another man's exclusive rights with another woman.

In this way men maintained their rule. Woman rulers would occasionally arise, but purely as a stopgap measure to protect the male lineage when a suitable male offspring was not available. Usually the next generation would provide a male who would regain control for the male gender. Rarely, if ever, did female rulers seek to retain ruling power for their gender. To be sure, they often plotted to retain power, but not for gender purposes. They were quite satisfied to reserve power for their sons instead of trying to advance daughters.

I don't intend to discuss here all the inequities and cruelties of patriarchy. Many feminists have already covered that subject very effectively. They've described to us how women were treated as men's property. How, in that capacity, they were used as sexual slaves, were deprived of education, property rights and earning power, and, were generally treated as lesser beings. For the most part I have no quarrel with the feminist assessment. I would, however, like to touch on a few points that could use more emphasis.

Men under patriarchy have inflicted many outright brutal punishments and restrictions upon women. Some have been physical, some psychological. What is perhaps the most tragic of all is the imposed conditioning which has destroyed women's self-worth and convinced many of them to accept—and in many cases advocate—their fate under patriarchy.

Young girls have always had the same drive to self-actuate and achieve, as well as the same potential, as boys. But as the years pass they are subjected to a withering barrage of signals telling them that they are expected to play an inferior role to boys. Feminists Elizabeth Debold, Marie Wilson and Idelisse Malave point out in *Mother/Daughter Revolution* that as adolescence approaches girls come to see themselves viewed as flesh by males. They come face to face with an invisible wall which they can only scale by pleasing men. The authors write:

> When girls become aware of the value society places on their 'looks,' they lose their connection with the world of doing, which is the essence of personal power.

This assessment was validated by the American Association of University Women (AAUW) which, in a recent report concluded:

> Between ages 11-16 girls experience a dramatic drop in self-esteem which in turn significantly affects their ability to learn and achieve.

In spite of this, a high percentage of women today argue in favor of male supremacy. The conditioning has won out. They doubt their efficacy as beings capable of making their own way. They fear the drastic shift necessary to assume responsibility for themselves in a male-dominated world. Indeed, their fear may be justified for it is more difficult for a woman to support herself in our society. They therefore find it much easier to allow men to support them. They serve as allies to those men who have dominated them—a "Macho Man's Women's Auxiliary." Marilyn French astutely calls them "Caryatids," i.e., women who passively act as a primary support for male privilege.

These women deserve compassion, for men under patriarchy never really gave them a chance to find their true identity as women. Nor do men in general help women make the transition from subservience to self-sufficency. Nevertheless, one of the biggest obstacles to overturning patriarchy is the vast number of women who have been so deeply conditioned that they are either oblivious to their enslavement, or don't care.

Feminist Andrea Dworkin describes this conditioning well.

> It is as if our oppression were cast in lava eons ago and now it is granite, and each individual woman is buried inside the stone. Women try to survive inside the stone, buried in it. Women say, 'I like this stone, its weight is not too heavy for me.' Women defend the stone by saying that it protects them from rain and wind and fire. Women say, 'All I have ever known is this stone. What is there without it?'

In times past the conditioning of females began at birth. Both mother and father participated. Without a female role model of equal status to men to show the youngster alternative attitudes, how could the girl resist? In addition she lived in a male-dominated culture which sent constant messages regarding the ascendancy of physical force. If she resisted she would likely undergo physical punishment in addition to castigation. She might very well be cast out, leading to destitution or even death. To maintain her position within her family and community she had to embrace patriarchal views.

Likely a few women had the courage to retain their own views, even as they played the part. But for the vast majority, the onslaught of conditioning won out. They actually came to believe much of the nonsense they were fed. This destroyed virtually all resistance to patriarchy down to recent times.

If indeed patriarchy has been universal, as men's advocates assert (in order to authenticate it as natural and inevitable), that does not mean that genetic imperatives have been responsible. As feminist Janet Radcliff Richards points out:

> If women's subjugation was in the natural order of things (instinctual), there would be no need for a colossal superstructure of law and convention to keep them in their place.

No, the drive to impose patriarchy could not have been programmed into our genes. Rather, environmental factors linked with male psychological insecurities likely brought the onset of patriarchy and the system was able to maintain itself by strict conditioning of all members of society.

As humankind grew in numbers, the most vital tasks in maintaining a tribe or village were the procurement of food and the protection of the community from attack. Anthropologists accept that it is the seeking of ecological and demographic advantages, not genetic imperative, that has repeatedly triggered warfare between expanding band-and-village peoples. Furthermore when men and women are equally capable of contributing to the military needs of the community and producing food, then women's status rises to parity. But if vital aspects of production or warfare are more effectively performed by men, then women's status will be lower. We've already discussed how man possessed greater food producing potential. Few would argue that he wasn't a more effective fighter.

Man's natural superiority of status would only hold true as long as food was relatively difficult to come by. In times when food existed in abundance egalitarianism or even matriarchy was viable. The advent of agriculture would have brought about those times more frequently.

Agriculture evolved over time. Those humans who underwent the transition from a hunting/gathering community to an agricultural one would have encountered a governing as well as economic cross-roads. The hunter had governed by force. This had been natural and acceptable because physical brute strength provided much of the food. Competing with the prey, then violently conquering it, fortified men's romance with domination. Although hunters developed a sense of brotherhood through cooperation on the hunt, their respect for each other developed outside community life where the needs of women and children were manifest. The hunter-turned-farmer had only the experience of governing by domination to draw upon. He had no experience of sharing power with his women.

How then could women have possibly risen to power and initiated a matriarchy? It's not likely they could have physically thrown off men's yoke. Might male supremacists be right after all when they claim that an advanced matriarchy never existed?

Anthropologists are still aligned on both sides for the archaeological findings can be interpreted in different ways. The classic case often cited by feminists is the settlement at Catal Huyuk in Asia Minor some 8,000 years ago. Excavations have unearthed structures, artifacts and human remains that can be interpreted to represent a society ruled by matriarchy. Many anthropologists dispute this conclusion although most do not unequivocally claim that a patriarchy existed there. In any case, what is interesting is the feminist view of hypothetical matriarchy as they see represented at Catal Huyuk.

Feminists contend that ancient matriarchies were advanced egalitarian societies. The feminine spirit under the auspices of Goddess worship fostered a peaceful, fruitful lifestyle for all. Without male gods to advocate war and aggression, men became docile, productive creatures.

A typical description of matricentic societies has both men and women worshipping "The Goddess." Women lived separately with their children in the center of society, determining the direction and the activities. They also provided the bulk of the food. Men meanwhile lived on the periphery, restricted by the female leadership as to what important activities they could participate in. They were isolated from the children they had sired and, for the most part, other than for mating purposes they were physically kept at a distance from women. According to feminists, being free to hunt and socialize among themselves while avoiding major responsibility made men's lives bliss.

If this was indeed the case, then there is little wonder why men revolted and overthrew this system to create a patriarchy. First of all, this would have been a classic case of using sex to manipulate men and could only have bred deep resentment. At the same time, even in patriarchies, where men can choose to shift most of the work upon women, many men do their share of constructive work.

Perpetual, voluntary idleness does not appeal to most men. Well adjusted men find their focus for living in providing for their families and engaging in community activities. True, a high percentage overstep and seek to dominate both. But the opposite extreme—being forced to remain on the fringe of the community—would only breed resentment and eventual rebellion. "Egalitarian" societies as hypothesized by feminists would have oppressed men as badly as modern "patriarchal" societies oppress women.

How could such a matriarchy have formed in the first place? Why would men have allowed women such power?

If indeed such a society did exist the most likely reason is that ignorance of the reproductive process allowed women to create mystique around themselves as the apparent sole creators of life. Whereas the advent of agriculture reduced the need for men's brute force, it still demanded that the species reproduce itself. And as long as women appeared to be the sole instrument for creating children her power must have increased enormously over hunting/gathering days. She could have made the most of this by creating Goddess worship, surrounding reproduction in mystery and the supernatural. Men likely looked upon women's "mothering power," as represented in the Goddess Cult, in awe. Women themselves probably never understood men's role in reproduction.

We do know from figurines unearthed at various ancient sites that Goddess worship did exist. Whether it reflects a full blown matriarchy is for someone to prove. Until then we should keep in mind the following point, made by Sarah B. Pomeroy:

> To use the mother goddess theory to draw any conclusions regarding the high status of human females of the time would be foolhardy. Later religions, in particular Christianity, have demonstrated that the mother may be worshiped in societies where male dominance and even misogyny are rampant.

Whether or not matriarchies ever existed, the first important thing to remember is that both matriarchy and patriarchy are hierarchies. Patriarchy has been justly charged with using, in addition to physical force, the dissemination of a morality of fear, obedience, a sense of personal worthlessness, and awe and respect for authority to maintain power. If we scratch physical force, then this sounds suspiciously like the same technique that must have been used to maintain the power structure in matricentric societies. Both are gender based ruling orders which create castes and a class system which allows domination.

Those who believe in male supremacy claim that patriarchy evolved as a valid social structure, taking full advantage of male physical strength in a harsh physical environment. Even as conditions eased over time, it was only natural for this protocol to prevail. This view would seem to be biased and grossly unfair, failing to consider women's vital role in species survival. And yet it's not that simple.

Even in the most egalitarian situations, if people disagree over an important decision, a choice must be made. Sometimes decisions must be made immediately, without time for discussion or study. The situation demands that someone take charge, most logically the person with the most experience dealing with similar situations. Once this happens we find ourselves operating in a simple hierarchy—a leader dispensing instructions to obedient followers. This is not necessarily detrimental as long as the hierarchy dissolves when the crisis passes. Perhaps a new hierarchy with a new leader will form when the next crisis occurs. Reasonable people are always willing to defer to those who are more knowledgeable in crisis situations. When decisions are not crisis driven a democratic approach is feasible.

A rigid hierarchy—one which maintains itself over periods of time—is seriously flawed because it allows certain individuals to make all decisions regardless of their level of expertise. We have experienced this for eons to our great detriment. Back when physical survival was extremely precarious man's greater physical strength may have justified his gender assuming leadership roles more frequently than women. But that time has passed. Raw physical strength means little in modern society. Considering man's insecurities, it may be "natural" that he clings his patriarchal position of leadership, but it is not in his best interests. For intelligence is by far the most important prerequisite for effective leadership. And 50% of our intelligence pool resides in women.

Feminists claim that the patriarchal bonds restraining women became even stronger with the advent of the industrial age. In prior times wealthier men could completely subjugate their women because as men they held complete control over their wealth and provided all sustenance. Women of the lower classes, however, escaped complete subjugation because necessity demanded that they perform heavy physical work, often beside their husbands. This allowed them to demonstrate their worth in areas of physical prowess that males venerated.

Industrialization, however, split up the families of lower classes. While the men took employment in factories and thus provided virtually the entire means for family sustenance, the women were left to tend the home and children exclusively. To men, who worked long hours, women's contribution looked feeble in comparison to theirs. This seemed to justify wielding even more power over women.

Yet even though industrialization seemed to enslave women, it inadvertently set in motion forces that provided them the escape route to freedom. The new system focused on developing technology which substituted for muscle power. This narrowed the physical gap between the genders. As technology advanced, women could do more and more jobs that men could do. Man's physical strength, his only viable claim to superiority, gradually had less and less significance. Industrialization has undercut man's justification to keep women in subjugation. Yet men still thrash about concocting wild rationalizations which they hope will somehow allow them to cling to power.

It took a long suffering Feminist Movement to inflict cracks in man's armor over the decades. What began in the 1800s erupted into a full scale revolution during the 1960s and has snowballed. The movement has grown many heads with many diverse opinions and agenda. Some advocate conservative changes; others spew out venomous attacks designed to drive the genders even further apart.

For many years men endured this barrage, not taking it all that seriously. But as women gained ground in their quest for equality, men began to perceive the threat to their exclusive control of power. Even those who were relatively powerless among other men resented feminism because they fell under its criticism. Men finally began to gather together and resist the bashing. Thus gender enmity intensified.

Both sides could find legitimate targets for their attacks and counterattacks. Feminists had thousands of years of oppression from which to draw ammunition. Men obviously still held power in government and business. For men to claim that women possessed anything near equality would have been ludicrous. So feminists appeared to have men at a serious disadvantage in the debate.

But women's frustration after so many centuries of being dominated bred a small percentage of radicals who advocated preposterous points of view and bashed men mercilessly even in areas undeserving of criticism. This gave men an opportunity and they struck back by branding all feminists with the views of the radicals. By pointing out the absurdity of some of these positions while ignoring the merit of the majority, they justified their position and thereby justified clinging to power. This is where we find ourselves today, both genders polarized, one seeking to retain control while the other seeks to wrest it away. Little discussion is directed toward coming together, sharing power in a true bonding and together addressing the world's problems.

Chapter Three
Patriarchy Today

Who benefits from patriarchy? It would certainly seem that men have by far gained the most. And yet we see a large portion of the male gender discontented with the "rewards" patriarchy has bestowed upon it. Lack of fulfillment in career, frustration in relationships, mid-life crises, and no relief from the heavy burden of family/financial responsibilities are only a few complaints we commonly hear from men, even after they've achieved financial success and social status. If we examine these closely we can see that all have to a large degree been induced by our patriarchal system.

Lack of career fulfillment and mid-life crisis often go together. From youth men are conditioned to embrace the system. This tells them that establishing themselves in a "career" is essential to their future well being and demands that they begin focusing on career selection some time around the onset of puberty. Naturally, at this age the boy lacks insight into the ramifications of choosing a particular career and the responsibilities that accompany it. Nevertheless he is mercilessly pressured by the system to choose his weapon—his career—and begin honing it through education for the coming battle for wealth, power and position.

Society forces males to make these crucial, lifelong-impacting decisions at a time when they lack the insight that comes from life experience. As a natural consequence, later in life many men find themselves dissatisfied with the career decisions of their youth and experience one form of mid-life crisis.

But what is "society" and how is it to blame here?

A "society" forms around and is sustained by common mass views and opinion. A handful of individuals can sell a program to the masses, but not force it upon them. Ultimately it is the masses who decide what shape their society will take. Their weight of opinion provides heavy momentum which maintains their society on a predetermined course.

Our society, which evolved from patriarchal roots, has chosen as its focus the aforementioned pursuit of wealth, power and position.

The vast majority of men, all of whom have other choices, have accepted this focus and bought a ticket on the ride. To reject this option takes insight and enormous courage, qualities most boys on the verge of manhood lack. So they buy in, and once doing so not only become pawns of the system but become passive advocates of it, making it that much more difficult for those who follow to resist its pressure.

Even as young men struggle to pursue careers, most find themselves facing decisions concerning relationships with women. Biological and psychological needs, which exert an even stronger influence than patriarchal ideology, demand that men and women bond. Men feel this pulling but fear acknowledging its full significance. To do so would acknowledge the importance of women, a truth that patriarchal influence has encouraged them to deny in order to bolster their sagging self-esteem. Their self-esteem, of course, has fallen prey to the relentless, haunting sense of insecurity passed down through generations and now depends greatly upon feeling superior to women and in control of all dealings with them.

In addition to the internal psycho-biological pressures to mate, young men face pressure from society to marry and raise families. Most men would choose this path anyway. But many succumb to the pressure before they comprehend the emotional consequences and physical responsibilities. Lacking the maturity to recognize crucial elements of compatibility, they nevertheless select a partner. Thus they soon find themselves bearing debilitating family/financial burdens and enduring intimate, unfulfilling relationships with wives.

To further add to the frustration, these men often find their wives refusing to play by the rules established by the male power game. Instead of dutifully playing the role of accessories to men's lives, women flaunt their sexual appeal and wield their intelligence to undermine men's power. Since men already have difficulty maintaining control over their natural impulses, this "assault" from without poses a grave threat to their tediously sculpted view of themselves.

Society increases the pressure on husbands by painting them as unmanly for being unable to control their wives. Our patriarchal system also increases men's burden by discouraging them from allowing their female partners to share equally in decision making and wage earning. Once again, as the years pass a mid-life crisis often develops, this one relationship oriented.

I have just painted a picture of men as victims. But victims of whom or what? "Society"—the sum of mass public opinion?

The pressure from "society" may be relentless, but the individual does have choices. A man will not be beaten or thrown in jail if he rejects the pursuit of wealth and status. He will not sacrifice his ability to earn his own way if he refuses to marry. Men choose career, marriage and family responsibilities because they believe these pursuits benefit them.

Still, we can't ignore the overwhelming effect of societal pressure on maturing young men. To a large degree, what they believe is shaped by their conditioning under the system. The question is, at what point does a man, in a society which offers free choice, bear responsibility for the choices he makes? Does he have a right to complain when he had the chance to say "no" to the system that now abuses him?

If men can claim victimhood to any legitimate degree, it is to a far lesser extent than can women. The patriarchy game is the only one in town. If most men are pawns in that game, women aren't even on the board. For the game dictates that men play a superior role to women.

As an illustration, let's say a boy and a girl are forced against their wishes to play house. The rules of the game, established by those who are forcing the boy and girl to play, say that the girl must serve the boy in any way he wants. In effect the boy determines the direction of the game. He could, of course, determine that they will play balanced roles—neither dominating. But no, since he isn't happy with having to play he chooses to make it easy upon himself. He sits back and makes her serve him and satisfy all his needs, ignoring hers and thus degrading her status in the game. The boy will complain about being forced to play, but he ignores the plight of the girl who not only is forced to play, but is made further miserable by not being able to determine her role in the game.

Similarly, although modern society victimizes both men and women, men have been appointed the superior role. Patriarchy has designed it so man has the inside track to success. The opportunities for women are usually leftovers, men having kept the choicest for themselves.

Even these lesser opportunities are offered reluctantly because men are addicted to their power over women. Since most men have accepted the pursuit of power as the only meaningful ambition in life, the power over women represents an indispensable (to many, the only) sign of their efficacy. To give it up would brand them as complete failures, in their own eyes as well as in the eyes of other men.

Thus patriarchal men must deny the need to bond with women. From a glandular perspective alone they cannot advocate isolating from women completely. However, they must make every effort in every area to minimize women's significance. Only thereby can they keep women available to fulfill men's needs, even as they keep women isolated from access to power.

Of course patriarchy provides another reward to men. From their superior position they get to service their own needs first.

Some patriarchal men would protest, saying that they always see to the needs of their family ahead of their own. For these men this may be true to a degree. But as patriarchs they still retain ultimate control over their families and the power to prioritize needs. By sharing or surrendering that power they would, in effect, abdicate their positions as patriarchs. This they cannot do without seeing their masculine self-image crumble, and with it, their tenuous feelings of self-worth.

Those men who accept the patriarchal approach fight a never ending inner struggle to subdue their true nature. They feel compelled to fulfill natural human destiny by bonding with women. This generates an enormous amount of internal energy which must be subdued and contained if patriarchy is to be successful.

To feel such a pressing need seems to fly in the face of one's superiority. So men have painstakingly constructed a fragile framework of patriarchal rules that allow them to relate to women while maintaining their superior position. This code is often difficult to live up to because the psyche, with prodding from biological need, recognizes that the rules support detrimental behavior. Nevertheless, men exert the power of conscious will guided by strict adherence to the code to restrain the natural instinct. They become boilers with patriarchal concepts serving as boiler plate trying to hold back tremendous pressure. Many of these boilers blow up.

Some men hate themselves for their "weakness." But it is far more comfortable to direct their resentment toward those who are undermining them from without—women. This is especially easy when they can point to women having guilefully used sexuality against them.

Men find self-image most vulnerable when trying to fulfill their sexual natures. This is because sexual need can only be satisfied completely—physically and psychologically—in a relationship with someone else. Since patriarchy abhors and condemns homosexuality, patriarchal man must look to woman to satisfy his sexual needs. This gives women power that men find extremely unsettling.

Although men have the power to rape, forced sex is not acceptable to the patriarchal man. As well as causing women trauma in an unchivalrous manner, rape amounts to violating another man's property, or potential property—a strict no-no under patriarchy.

In addition to providing a vessel for procreation, patriarchal men need women to fulfill them sexually in a willing, subservient manner that complies with the patriarchal code. This means that women must supply sex for and at men's pleasure without ever using it to make demands. Women are also asked to fortify patriarchal men's self-image by demonstrating enjoyment of the sex act with a dominating male.

Patriarchal men can convince themselves that they can do without women in every other way. But they can't deny that to achieve fulfilling sex and perpetuate themselves through progeny, they need a woman. Indeed, they even lose face in each other's eyes—a miserable humiliation—when they fail in this area.

And so although women remain crucial to the physical and psychological well being of patriarchal men, these men must do their best to downplay or deny it. When women won't cooperate, using sexuality as a tool to exercise power (thus pointing to men's vulnerability in this area), men are offended and outraged.

The way for men to escape victimhood, just as it is for women, is for patriarchy to be dismantled. Women can more easily see this because they have felt patriarchy's boot upon their necks for centuries. But conditioning has ingrained in men the fear that if we surrender dominance we will not only lose our power, but our very manhood and become "feminized." This, of course, is another clever tactic propagated by advocates of patriarchy—to brand attributes commonly seen in women as not only inherently inferior to those commonly seen in men, but also injurious to masculinity.

Sadly, men have not yet come to recognize that abandoning patriarchy is not a sacrifice but rather a purification leading to evolution and eventual inner peace. Male resistance is so strong that seldom if ever do you hear men use the word, "patriarchy." Some men suffer from self-imposed ignorance and don't even know what the term means in the context of gender issues. Some don't acknowledge that patriarchy has existed as a means of consolidating power in the hands of men. And many simply don't care about those subjects that would bring the word into use.

Most of those men who are familiar with the term "patriarchy" and its context in gender issues, take use of the word as an attack, a criticism or an insult. For "patriarchy" implies male domination of women, something men generally don't wish to admit having been a party to.

From those few men who outwardly embrace patriarchy we hear arguments as to its merits, often cleverly reasoned and based upon "scientific proof" or the scientific method. The fortress of patriarchy depends heavily of science and scientific thinking—the religion of the intellect—to defend itself. The same intellectual approach which holds that humankind can control and mold nature has been used to defy women's seeking to establish themselves on an equal plane.

Even many feminists have been so conditioned by the patriarchal worship of science that they follow the example of their male adversaries and run desperately to laboratories seeking evidence, no matter how flimsy, to prove their hypotheses. This "evidence," of course, can be easily contested by other scientific "evidence" dredged up by clever patriarchal men who know how to use science. Further extensive study is usually necessary to unravel the controversy. This allows patriarchal men to maintain the status quo, often indefinitely, since new corroborating "evidence" on one side can usually be refuted by similar "discoveries" from the other.

Science is a wonderful tool. Properly used, it can unravel many of life's mysteries that otherwise defy understanding. Misused, however, science becomes a millstone. Progress is thwarted while those who wait for the scientific method to prove the obvious, stand in the way of change. Physicist Thomas Kuhn has pointed out:

> (Science is) a strenuous and devoted attempt to force nature into the conceptual boxes supplied by professional education.

Too often these "conceptual boxes" prove inadequate or misleading. Consider the Voyager space probe which, on its visits to Jupiter, Saturn and Uranus, collected a great deal of data that flew in the face of heretofore sacrosanct scientific law.

In the past few centuries we have seen scientists argue for years, sometimes even decades, through the mediums of scientific journals and symposiums regarding discoveries and theories. Many of these have eventually had significant impact on daily living after having been "held up" by scientific debate in which the opposing sides sought recognition leading to financial grants and ego gratification. Commonly in our patriarchal society brilliant scientific minds take upon the mentality of ferocious dogs fighting in a pit over raw meat.

Granted, the ultimate reality underlying gender dynamics will someday be explained in depth scientifically. Indeed, science can help us understand gender issues now. But because science cannot validate or invalidate certain points of view does not necessarily detract from their merit. We must live and relate now, not wait for science, in its necessarily plodding fashion, to show us the way. Waiting for science is suspiciously convenient for patriarchal men.

A major argument posed in favor of patriarchy by men of scientific persuasion is that if patriarchy is so detrimental to humankind why did it, not matriarchy or some other form, arise in all parts of the world, even those isolated from each other?

Legitimate question. Yet just because the species survived under patriarchy during primitive times does not mean it was the best system then. And because it rose universally does not make it the best system now. The ecological crises the earth has been made to suffer under the stewardship of the patriarchal system point to patriarchy as ultimately the wrong system for humankind to employ. Until recent decades patriarchy's mismanagement has been hidden by a favorable ratio of population to square mile of environment. Now that men cannot escape the repercussions of mismanaging their environment by moving on to new frontiers, the folly of patriarchal attitudes stares us in the eye.

One can easily recognize, and even justify, the factors that led to the advent of patriarchy. When people suffer from psychological insecurities they reach out and grasp whatever power they can. The more control a person could wield the more secure they must have felt. Competition for power and control likely existed on every level, from competition with the elements to competition between humans. And since physical prowess usually prevailed in these contests, men wielded power over women.

Men who defend patriarchy contend that the system was necessary to protect communities from aggression. But aggression from whom? Other patriarchal communities, of course. Patriarchy breeds competition which encourages aggression. The negative aspects of patriarchy stimulate its growth and spread.

Advocates ask, "what about all the good done by men under patriarchy?" To answer, one must raise another question. Was that "good" instigated by patriarchy or by men capable of performing good under any system, acting in spite of patriarchal mores? Might not that "good" have been increased manifold under a system that didn't foster domination and aggression?

Oft-quoted author of men's literature, Sam Keen, asks, "Should men repent of the Renaissance or only the Crusades?" He thus conveniently ignores the fact that had men not torn down classic civilization through wars of aggression that led to the Dark Ages, there would have been no need for a Renaissance. He also fails to admit that the Renaissance would have been far more intense and constructive had half of humankind—women—been free to contribute to their full capabilities.

In Keen's book, *Fire in the Belly*, he cites a poll which indicates that the role models most admired by men are Jesus and Gandhi. Can we believe this? Look at our society. How many men even try to emulate the attitudes and lifestyle of Jesus or Gandhi? A few at best. Compare that to the masses who embrace the attitudes of men like Ronald Reagan, Douglas McArthur and Winston Churchill.

Where are most men drawn? To churches? Altruistic endeavors? Are they dominated by social conscience? Or do we see the vast majority instead focused on the personal pursuit of power, wealth and status? Do we see them speaking out in advocacy of peace and healing between nations and races, or do we see their attention on guns and military solutions? Do we see them donating their free time to help the downtrodden, or spending it upon aggressive sporting activities that seek symbolic domination? Do you think you would find more men, if they had to choose, in a spiritual place meditating, or watching their favorite sporting event?

This fascination with violence, competition and combat has prevented most men from examining the gender hierarchy and their role in maintaining it. Many refuse to acknowledge that throughout history, throughout the world, men have subjugated women. It is difficult to understand how any man can, in good conscience, argue this. But many do. Many see themselves as victims. They see women as wielding the power, reaping the rewards of being supported while forcing men to live a life of tedious work.

And yet, how much more subjugated can one be than to be held as another's property without the right to choose the course of one's life? Historically it has been very nearly universal for women's property rights to be subordinate to men's. She has been denied choice of a marriage partner. She has been denied access to official decision making power concerning the course of her society. In those societies which practiced voting rights, she was denied them until this past century. In the United States as recently as the 1960s, in several states she was denied the privilege to sit on juries. Until recent times she was denied access to advanced formal education and to biological self-determination. Even today in Western Society she faces attacks on her rights to the latter. In other societies she not only faces biological slavery but, all too frequently, physical mutilation to accent her inferior status.

Feminist Janet Radcliff Richards says it well:

> Beyond question, all social arrangements, institutions and customs which defined the relative position of the sexes were designed to ensure that women should be in the power and service of men. Not only did rules and laws keep women from gaining status and independence, but women were prevented from participating in the lawmaking, or changing process. So until some men were willing to champion their cause, women had no hope of changing their situation.

While many men deny subjugating women, others proudly admit it and speak out strongly in favor of patriarchy. They point to women's apparent frailty and inability to compete with men for power as legitimate reason for men to maintain authority.

Once again I must draw from a feminist, Carrie Chapman Catt, who wrote in 1902:

> The world taught woman nothing skillful and then said her work was valueless. It permitted her no opinions and said she did not know how to think. It forbade her to speak in public, and said the sex had no orators. It denied her the schools, and said the sex had no genius. It robbed her of every vestige of responsibility and then called her weak. It taught her that every pleasure must come as a favor from men, and when to gain it she decked herself in paint and fine feathers, as she had been taught to do, it called her vain.

To return to Ms. Richards:

> The idea that the greatest good a woman can do is get on quietly with her limited work is transparently the result of men's subjugation of women. Why should anyone try to prevent someone's doing as much good as it was in her power to do, except to prevent her getting power in general, keep her in a lesser position and retain exclusive possession of her services? Once the victims have been convinced, however, the oppressors are safe because if more goodness consists in inconspicuously getting on with a confining job, you can account for the position of the subject group by attributing it to virtue.

And finally:

> While some women are ideally suited to be housewives, it is quite wrong to think of the avocation as the most valuable thing which all, or even most, women could do. To hold up home and family as the highest vocation of all is to try to cheat women into doing less than they might and wasting their abilities.

The rigid male attitudes which degraded women under patriarchy made it inevitable that eventually women would revolt. Often the feminist counterattack has been graceless, ruthless, outrageous, unreasonable and irrational. But would men have paid attention otherwise? They hadn't for 6,000+ years. Can those who have seen their gender stigmatized and shackled for all that period be blamed for lashing out and screaming invective? They don't represent all women. And many of their radical strategies may no longer serve women's best interests. But if they have carved out a value system which alienates many traditional women, they have also aided these same women by acting as the vanguard—the shock troops most responsible for breaking down many of the barriers to equality erected by men. For that they deserve respect.

Here I find it necessary to take a closer look at feminism because of the effect it continues to have upon today's streamlined, but still stubbornly resistant, patriarchy. I will not try to undertake a comprehensive study. Thousands of books have been written on this topic by individuals with a closer association to the movement and deeper insight into its diversity and complexity. Meanwhile feminism continues to evolve and feminists continue to try to define and redefine themselves. My purpose here is to examine the influence of feminism upon those who remain standing outside—men and non-feminist women.

One treads on thin ice when they try to compartmentalize feminism for it is a phenomenon with wide ranging views. The most radical feminists see men as the enemy who must be overcome for gender equality to be established. They wish to pull down patriarchy completely; obliterate the system—good and bad; destroy all vestiges of institutions that can be identified with males; even separate the genders to where they have minimum contact. In the process they seek to polarize the genders even further so that as women they can pursue objectives like lesbianism and single motherhood which preclude men from participating.

The more moderate feminist wing wishes to establish equality so that women can compete within the system, leaving it intact except for certain modifications to those institutions that have oppressed women. They wish to see the system provide things such as child care for mothers and equal pay guarantees for all women. They want the movement to address issues of more importance to the common woman and thus gain the interest and ultimately the votes that can make feminist issues triumphant.

Both extremes make solid contributions to the advancement of women. At the same time, both have serious shortcomings which set them at odds with each other and allow patriarchal men to defend anti-women positions otherwise untenable.

I have already spent considerable time making a case for dismantling patriarchy, a course strongly advocated by radical feminism. But when they take the giant leap to advocating separation of the genders they not only alienate most men (including many of those sympathetic to women's advancement), but they alienate an enormous number of women who otherwise might multiply their ranks.

Most women feel comfortable with their heterosexuality and treasure the concept of a family under dual-sexual parenthood. Many of them, in spite of being subject to patriarchal institutions, have had positive experiences relating to men. They don't wish to sacrifice this and instinct tells them they should not be forced to do so in order to pursue women's rights. They would like to take a more active part, but find it distasteful to be classified as a "feminist," which carries with it a media-imposed label of "radical" and "lesbian." Thus they shy away from embracing radical feminist positions. This leaves a vast number of women on the sidelines allowing patriarchal men to hold at bay the relatively few feminist radicals.

Radical feminists tend to castigate these women as if dealing with traitors. As already mentioned, Marilyn French calls them "caryatids"—feminine columns that prop up patriarchy. Indeed, one can see justification in this metaphor. However, many of these so-called "caryatids" might very well swing over to actively support feminist ideology if much of it was not so contrary to basic feminine instincts. I think many of them support feminist meat and potatoes but can't palate the other vegetables. Unfortunately all of it is served to them as a stew.

One can easily see how radical feminists, in response to oppression, came to develop their views. One can justify many of these views, particularly those that promote the rights of women in general. But what one cannot defend is the advocacy of splitting the species into two distinct, isolated genders. The fact that men have accomplished this to a degree under patriarchy does not give license to feminists further poisoning the relationship. The well being of the species demands gender merging, unification and harmony. Most men and women sense this instinctively and are justifiably turned off by radical views promoting gender separation.

In contrast to the radicals, a large segment of feminism seeks access to playing, on equal terms with men, the game established under patriarchy. They wish to be able to compete equally for high level positions in business and government. They want the privilege to be able to enter combat. They want equal access to competitive sports. They wish to relinquish primary responsibility for their children's needs. To secure equal status they are prepared to embrace those same behavioral patterns that they claim have turned men into dominators.

It would seem that by seeking membership in a heretofore exclusive club, one inadvertently grants approval to that club's institutions. A relatively new voice in the feminist movement, Naomi Wolf, disagrees. She advocates what she calls, "Power Feminism"—an assertive effort by women to use all the power that patriarchy gives women to gain even more power within the system and ultimately change it. She contrasts this to what she calls, "Victim Feminism," which she claims has defined necessary changes but has made little effort to address them. Ms. Wolf points out that women do have considerable power under the system, particularly at the ballot box and in their consumer spending.

Ms. Wolf's view seems to have merit. After all, women do make up more than 50% of the population and they possess an enormous dollar clout. However, two major questions arise. First, are women willing to use the power that the system gives them to seek status that would allow them to change the system? And second, would women who gain status be willing to change the system, thereby giving up their hard-won status to include less fortunate women?

Recent electoral results point to a negative answer to the first question. Ms. Wolf, in her 1993 book *Fire With Fire*, took heart from the 1992 elections in which women heavily supported Democrats, giving Clinton the White House and sending several more women to Congress. In this she saw her "Power Feminism" taking effect and expected the trend to build momentum. But in 1994 48% of women voted Republican (the party notoriously slow in its recognition and support of women's issues), allowing a complete Republican takeover of Congress which immediately began pushing a radical right anti-women agenda. In 1996, some women shifted their allegiance back to the Democrats, saving Bill Clinton. But nevertheless, the Republicans maintained control of Congress, albeit somewhat chastised. These results clearly show that a large percentage of women are not even ready to stand up for their rights under patriarchy, much less fight to dismantle it.

The answer to the second question also remains highly doubtful for we're dealing here with basic human nature which has a pretty clear track record. (I'm assuming, of course, that basic human nature is shared by both genders, a view that some feminists would contest in their effort to make women superior to men.) Very few people who participate in a dirty game, including millions of women, do so with the purpose of prevailing so that they can change the rules to make it easier for others to attain the same status. Indeed, the dirty game dictates that in order for some people to have high status others must remain lower. Unless participants are willing to sacrifice the status they have worked so hard for, the game can't change. Granted, historically a handful of individuals have made that sacrifice. But the vast majority have clung to their status at the expense of others.

That in mind, "Power Feminism" promises to do little more than to change the gender mix of the dominators. The disaffected would remain as large a group as ever, but gender would no longer be a determining factor. Some of the heretofore privileged men would be bumped down the ladder. The pecking order would be maintained by using the remaining prejudicial factors, particularly race and intelligence.

By pursuing such a course feminists inadvertently prop up the patriarchal system. A system which through embracing competition nourishes the seeking of superiority and dominance over others. A system to which true equality is an anathema; which is constantly seeking to declare winners and losers; to define dominant and subservient; to honor the highest achievers while ignoring all others. A system which has denigrated and virtually enslaved women.

Feminist Andrea Dworkin made this astute comment some years back:

> Equality within the framework of the male sexual model, however that model is reformed or modified, can only perpetuate the model itself and the injustice and bondage which are its intrinsic consequences.

Elizabeth Debold, Marie Wilson and Idelisse Malave in their book *Mother/Daughter Revolution* add this pertinent observation:

> By mastering the disciplines as they have been constructed out of male experience and desire, women risk losing their perspective as outsiders as they hope to gain the security of being accepted as insiders."

Sadly, the major focus of modern feminism seems to be to seek parity with men. Rather than learning from man's shameful deportment under patriarchy to avoid developing poor attitudes and practicing cruel misbehavior, feminists seek the right to behave like men. This, of course, they should have the right to do. But considering the atrocities perpetrated by patriarchy, women should be very selective regarding which of men's pursuits they wish to embrace. So far they've shown no such propensity. Consider feminism's advocacy of women participating in highly competitive physical sports and in military combat.

A perfect example of this attitude is represented by Rene Denfeld in her recent book, *The New Victorians*. In it she describes two young women:

> Dallas Malloy: "Fierce young female amateur boxer who fought in court for the right of women to fight in the ring." Shannon Faulkner: "The courageous young woman who battled for her right to attend the Citadel, an all-male military school."

Both examples describe women fighting for the equal right to act as inhumanely as men.

And yet, after leveling all this criticism upon it, I must admit that feminism has been a blessing to humankind—both men and women. Yes, men too. This statement may seem odd in that feminism has unleashed such withering attacks against men and our male-dominated society these past decades. But without feminist tenacity, activism and even hyperbole, many men (including myself) and women would remain ignorant of the abuse women have been subjected to. And for men to truly conquer their inner ghosts they must come to grips with their confusion concerning the significance of gender identity. Feminist reason, even when presented as diatribe, keeps reminding men that something very basic is seriously amiss and must be addressed. Failing to do so injures men in addition to devastating women.

Unfortunately, in today's patriarchy most men have responded to the feminist rebellion by trying to hold their ground and not surrender an ounce of their power. Others beat a slow retreat, begrudgingly giving up pieces of ground hoping to assuage women while surrendering as little power as possible. And then there are the counterrevolutionaries. These have launched a vicious counterattack, not only failing to acknowledge men's domination of women but also blaming women for most of men's problems.

Most men resent being blamed for women's problems under patriarchy. They defend themselves by asking, "Why dwell on the past and cast blame?

I do so because men today harbor many of the patriarchal attitudes of their forefathers; because these attitudes have placed this planet in serious ecological jeopardy; because most men practice aggressive, destructive behavior rather than behavior that seeks to enhance their species; because although recently in Western society women have made gains, patriarchal attitudes still restrict female evolution. Throughout the rest of the world these attitudes are blatant, leaving women to lag far behind men and in many places remain little more than chattel. Men retain the primary power in our society and need to exercise it to correct rather than sustain these injustices.

Some men say, "Why blame me? I didn't do it. Other men did." Other men may have set the rules. But every man who, without protest, participates in a system that victimizes women strengthens that system and adds to women's predicament. All of us men, because we have not stood up as advocates of equal status for women, have aided their oppressors.

Until the past few decades men have had little reason or pressure to examine their role in society. Why should they? In spite of various hardships some of them had to endure, they had it far better than women. They had mastery over their household and authority to control their economic destiny. Yes, some of them surrendered power in their household to their wives. But this was voluntary—a choice they made to maintain a relationship they had voluntarily entered into. At the same time some of them found themselves in economic slavery. Again, this was usually because of choices voluntarily made. In contrast, women generally lacked the power for economic self-determination and could not wield power within the household unless the man allowed it.

In those situations where men did surrender power, the vast majority of other men looked down upon and often ridiculed them. "He's got no balls," and "who's wearing the pants in that household?" were common put-downs to men who shared power with women. This implied that it took masculine authority to run a household whether embodied in man or woman. Masculinity was to be dominant; femininity subservient.

Gender harmony cannot occur unless, first, men's views that led to the subjugation of women have been rooted out. This can't happen without completely exposing these views and convincing men to repent of them. Since it is men who have made and still enforce the rules, it is men who must change them. The first step is to stop buying into the system. Men must choose between pursuing wealth and social status or pursuing inner peace. The way our society is structured, only a few can maintain their moral principles and achieve both.

How can women help men reach that state of repentance? The first step is to tone down the hyperbolic rhetoric. Certainly men are deserving of criticism. But if this is to have effect it must be incisive and factual rather than exaggerated. Even the more moderate feminist view espouses claims that men find unreasonable and refutable. Overblown charges only serve as a casus belli for men who have been seeking validation for maintaining their status over women. Any such views, radical or moderate, turn off reasonable men and are used by stubborn men to fortify weak positions.

A good example comes from feminist Marilyn French who, in her scholarly, enlightening book, *Beyond Power*, claims that virtually all men feel contempt for women. She backs up her charge by suggesting to men:

> Imagine how you would feel if someone told you were 'womanly' or asked you to dress and act as a woman for a day. You are a rare creature if you are male and do not react with horror.

Does this argument conclusively prove that men feel contempt for women? Consider: if you saw a cat walking down the street barking and acting like a dog, you would likely either find the creature comical or disgusting. You would certainly not find it normal. That would not necessarily mean that you hate dogs. Rather, that you found it unusual and very possibly objectionable to see this cat acting so out of character.

Patriarchal society, to its detriment, assigns behavioral characteristics to each gender. But just because a man shrinks in horror at the thought of his acting like a woman does not mean that he hates womanly characteristics. To make such a claim only undermines one's credibility.

In Ms. French's case this is unfortunate because she has written an otherwise powerful, pertinent book. By saying, "virtually all men," she antagonizes most men, including those who could be converted into allies. By posing an argument that makes little sense she undermines a portion of her thesis and plays directly into the hands of patriarchal men. She further energizes the determination of, and provides ammunition for, them to defend their positions and keep the genders polarized. She also fails to endear herself to many women whose experiences with men have been mostly positive and do not validate her charges.

I know, it seems unfair that women, in order to free themselves from male oppression, should have to make an impeccable case. But that is the nature of this battle.

It is unlikely that women will soon, if ever, be able to wrest their share of power from a male gender united against them. They can, however, succeed if feminism can enlist the many women who now fear it and potential male allies that await conversion via rational argument.

In order to achieve these two objectives we must clear away the smoke from the hostile rhetoric coming from both sides.

Chapter Four
Feminist Charges Against Men

A woman friend of mine asked me why I even need to address exaggerated feminist charges hurled at men. Why not just dismiss them as not worthy of comment and move on?

My answer is that while the conclusions drawn in making the charges may appear absurd, much of men's behavior toward women justifies deep feminist suspicions. To be fair, much truth lies behind feminist accusations. It helps us understand the roots of gender conflict by examining the charges and what has triggered them. Only by recognizing the dynamics at work can we hope to convince men to cease their mistreatment of women.

Screaming irrational invective at men only hardens them. On the other hand, overlooking their cruelty gives it a stamp of approval. We must tread a middle path, resisting men's misbehavior with rational argument presented forcefully, even passionately, but absent the caustic illogic that taints much feminist argument.

Clearly, women are justified in feeling frustrated and angry. I find it sad that more of them don't experience those feelings in response to their poor treatment. Even so, women must recognize that the way out of their dilemma is through harnessing their emotions and focusing them into laser-like arguments for which male bravado has no defense. Knee-jerk lashing out invites combat, and combat is patriarchal men's thing.

Typically you can take the most rational and intelligent of these men and push them, either physically or figuratively, and you will see their composure and rationality tossed aside. You will see them instantly prepared to respond with raised voice and clenched fist. Any aggressive challenge to their concept of manhood they will meet with irrational aggression. And they're so effective at using this tool that women attempting to employ it against them have little chance of prevailing.

In this chapter I hope to strip the invective from some common feminist charges without invalidating the genuine claims of injustice that lie behind them.

Patriarchal Conspiracy

Feminists hurt their cause when they claim that patriarchy has been enacted and maintained through a male conspiracy that continues to this day. This allows men to scoff and dismiss further discussion since most people recognize that the vast majority of men (certainly in recent times) have not been meeting clandestinely to impose patriarchal institutions. The public would be hard pressed to identify any men involved in such an organized plot. Therefore the conspiracy charge just will not stand up.

Many informal institutions in our society have been accepted for so long that we follow them almost unconsciously. For centuries men have grown up expecting privilege while women have accepted subservience. Like tradition, these views have been passed down from generation to generation without being questioned. Both genders through lifelong conditioning have found a measure of comfort in this relationship. Any attack upon this protocol elicits fierce resistance from men (and many women), not because they are defending a conspiratorial scheme, but because they feel their personal sense of security threatened.

So, when men are accused of being involved in a conspiracy they find the charge easy to laugh off. In the process of getting together with their fellows they may, on occasion, discuss women pushing for rights that interfere with the male agenda, but they don't conspire. They don't feel a need to. Instinctively they recognize that patriarchal conditioning of both genders maintains the anti-female bias within the system by momentum alone. They feel this bias is justified because their reason, molded by their conditioning, tells them they are both physically stronger and more intelligent, making them superior. Feminist charges of conspiracy only fortify men's view of women as being irrational and thus, inferior.

Mysogyny

Perhaps the most prevalent charge hurled at men by radical feminists is that of misogyny. This belief seems to be fundamental to these feminists who frequently raise the issue in their writings and in interviews. The charge makes no sense to most men and is down-right painful to those who are sympathetic to women's plight. The vast majority of men—even those who seek to dominate women—cannot identify within themselves a feeling of hatred toward women.

To most people the word "hate" connotes a conscious, projected dislike. You don't want to be around those you hate. You find their basic essence deplorable. You don't wish them well. Just thinking of them brings up a rush of negative feelings.

Most men don't experience women in this way. And yet men's be-havior points to an attitude toward women that falls far short of benevolent. They treat women as if they do not like them. Even so, the word "hate" does not seem to fit, especially from the male view-point.

It would seem that I am trying to split hairs. After all, what can be the substantive difference between "hate" and "not liking," particu-larly when the latter leads to the mistreatment of women?

Actually there is an important, albeit subtle, difference in this case. Men admire what they perceive as feminine characteristics and traits—in women. Most men seek closeness with this feminine as-pect of women, especially when seeking a mate.

At the same time men fear the influence of femininity. They have come to view it as a threat to masculinity, both by it challenging masculine influence in the outside world, and by it threatening to invade the inner masculine psyche.

For example, by accepting the nurturing impulse in themselves men imply that nurturing is not an exclusively feminine character-istic which denotes weakness. If other female traits were similarly validated, men would refute their age-old premise that males pos-sess distinctly different traits and characteristics from females which demand that men wield power over women. Women would no longer appear that different and could therefore lay claim to shar-ing power. At the same time men could no longer justify delegating "nurturing" tasks which they consider demeaning, to women. Both consequences frighten men.

Most men have come to view femininity as synonymous with weak-ness. This, of course, further denotes an unfitness to rule. These conclusions are both convenient and necessary if men are to main-tain their exalted position.

To see a man portraying feminine traits frightens and angers most men because they see it as a crack in male solidarity. If one man is vulnerable to acting "feminine," then all may be—a terrifying thought. Therefore "feminine" behavior in men must be wrong. And if it's wrong it must be resisted. To make an effective resistance men usually fall back on anger fueled by resentment. But this "hatred" is triggered by the perceived feminine incursion into previously sanctified masculine territory, not by femininity itself as exemplified in women.

Men view the feminine incursion as taking place on a second front as well. Not only are men displaying "feminine" traits, but women have been freeing themselves from the traditional roles men have restricted them to. By displaying aggressiveness, leadership, physical efficacy, etc., women show that men do not possess exclusivity in these areas either. Once again males feel threatened, not by the traits themselves, for these are considered "masculine" traits, but rather because women have burgled men's arsenal. Suddenly women are showing themselves to possess those very traits that men have maintained are crucial to wielding power.

The vast majority of men cling desperately to the concept that masculinity is something exclusive. Even the so-called "New Age Man" hedges by claiming that men have a "feminine side." That term allows him to indulge in sensitive, nurturing, "feminine" behavior while clinging to masculine separateness—his concept of being male exclusive of female. He can claim undiminished fitness for rule by pointing to his "masculine side" as the dominant and most frequently operative side. He still believes in male dominance. Otherwise he would see no reason to define characteristics and traits as masculine and feminine.

But why would any "true male" want to experience anything "feminine" if indeed femininity was an anathema to masculinity? Why do "New Age" men find it appealing to practice "feminine" traits if these threaten to undermine their malehood? Are they suffering from some character flaw or weakness?

They don't seem to think so. They seem to think that expressing the sensitive ("feminine") side of themselves enhances them. And yet they cannot accept this side as being an integrated part of their human maleness. They still cling to the traditional concept of masculinity by claiming that their sensitivity springs from a "feminine" side. This implies that they still possess an untainted "masculine" side which remains as insensitive and aggressive as ever.

Why must nurturing and peacemaking be considered "feminine?" Why shouldn't they be considered "human" traits? Even Sam Keen has said:

> In my own experience I can locate nothing that feels feminine about holding my daughter in my arms, allowing myself to be comforted, weeping for the pain of the world, or exercising my intuition. I am as much a man when I am tender as when I am fierce.

To this point I have been hard on Keen and I will be so again. But the above statement displays uncommon male insight and courage for it stands in contrast to the viewpoint most often stated within the "Men's Movement." If one accepts it they should begin to see that the need to cling to concepts of exclusive masculinity are signs of insecurity. But does this fear of feminine influence really constitute classic "hatred?"

Feminists cite numerous examples which at first sight seem to fortify their argument that men hate women. For example, they point out that typically boys will ridicule other boys who are acting in ways normally attributed to girls. What feminists fail to see is that these boys are ridiculing other boys who they perceive as male distortions. Many boys look down on girls and may even ridicule them. But most don't "hate" what they see as feminine behavior when acted out by girls.

Feminists claim that men through the ages have "hated" women. They point to the seemingly heartless exchange of women between bands and villages in primitive times. While this certainly indicates an insensitivity to the needs of women, it does not prove that men hated them.

In primitive times men recognized that the reproduction level of each community was determined by the number of females. Survival considerations prevailed since too many women could lead to overpopulation while too few might lead to extinction. Granted, men were not exchanged similarly, indicating that women were valued less. At the same time, while one village was ridding itself of "unwanted" surplus women, another was accepting them, indicating that women were valued to a degree. To what degree primitive men appreciated women would be pure speculation at this point. So, to base a claim for misogyny on the behavior of primitive man, who constantly faced circumstances threatening survival, is to fall back on weak evidence.

Yes, even today men undervalue women, misperceive women's talents and fear female efficacy. They don't acknowledge women as equal partners of equal importance to humankind's existence. Facing this, modern women certainly have every right to feel un-loved, disrespected, and thus, outraged. It is easy to see how they could conclude they are victims of male hatred.

And yet based upon my earlier definition of hatred this is not the case. So, if hatred is not behind men's poor treatment of women, what is? What is behind men's fear of femininity and its influence? Why does it make them feel insecure?

The answer is fear of losing power over women. This power, this feeling of being the exalted gender, remains men's basis for feeling secure.

To imply that men "hate" women is an oversimplification that only breeds more confusion and resentment. Remember, most men see themselves as valuing women. Many would die to save or protect those who exemplify what they see as feminine. (When lowering the lifeboats the majority of men have always accepted the rule, "Women and children first!") True, this image usually does not co-incide with the image women have of themselves. Nevertheless, both images have similarities and share many characteristics. This indicates that both genders value feminine traits.

Right or wrong, most men see masculine and feminine roles dis-tinctly divided. I believe that the majority of men have no innate contempt for femininity—in women. Many men treasure, even idol-ize femininity. Even so, they despise the genders acting outside what they conceive of as "normal" roles. That's significantly different than holding women in contempt.

Of course, even if most men do not feel contempt for women, that doesn't relieve the burdens heaped upon women by a patriarchal society. Many men have accepted the twisted view that the true expression of man's love for woman comes through domination. So although they may rationalize that they are loving women by domi-nating them, that doesn't make matters any less painful for the women victims.

Considering the mistreatment suffered by women at the hands of men over the centuries it is easy to see where a large segment of women feel unappreciated and undervalued by men. These perceptions are justified and need to be hammered home to the male population, a large segment of which, in spite of their macho conditioning, find their consciences aroused by rational female argument. But to leap to the charge of misogyny undermines women's credibility in most male eyes. It allows men to turn their backs without their consciences being disturbed. The female cause only further suffers.

The Glass Ceiling

Another issue which erodes feminist credibility is their simplistic claim that women's lack of economic equality is due to men conspiring to keep women subservient. Feminists make it sound as if men who possess power in our economy regularly plot in their private meetings how to keep women from advancing to positions of power in their companies. These same feminists seldom acknowledge the role women play in undermining their own opportunities.

If we're going to get to the bottom of the economic equality issue we must first examine its complexity, particularly in our society. No reasonable, fair-minded person would deny that women have been deprived of the same opportunity as men to pursue economic opportunity. Since the feminist revolution of the 60s things have improved, but after rising from virtual exclusion women still have much ground to make up in the employment marketplace. Is it men's gender-biased anti-woman sentiment that is primarily responsible for women being held back?

Over the past 30+ years, and even today, cases abound where men in power have ignored qualifications and denied women advanced positions in business purely because of gender bias. One might not be far wrong to describe these decisions as conspiratorial. But only the most paranoid feminist believes in the existence of an organized conspiracy to repress women's advancement. Any attempt to paint such an unrealistic picture only allows unscrupulous businessmen the opportunity to escape accountability. Furthermore, attributing all women's advancement difficulties to sexist-based discrimination allows women to escape responsibility for those factors they bring to the equation.

To begin examining this more deeply I must re-emphasize a point

I've made more than once—we live in a physical world. An economy, if it is to be successful, must respond to the demands of that physical world. People must use physical skills, usually in the control of tools and machinery, to harvest crops, make things, deliver products, etc. We like to think we're in the "age of information." But information only enhances our ability to perform the physical. We can do without computers, but not without the physical skills and tools that interact with our environment to extract physical sustenance.

Just as the physical nature of our world and our needs in relationship to it define those things which the economy must provide us, so do physical considerations define efficiency in the economy. Concepts of fairness and morality by themselves won't get the tomatoes harvested. Someone has to go out and pick them. The more people picking, the faster they get picked. The more experienced the picker, the more that get picked per worker-hour. Computers can plan and project and advise, but unless pickers remove the tomatoes from the plants, there will be no tomato harvest.

Quite simply, certain physical realities—particularly the quality of tools and the skill and availability of the labor force—dictate the level of productivity. And naturally, the more productive the economy, the more benefits available to society. Few people would argue against the value of a productive economy.

In pursuit of this our society has embraced the free market system under which, theoretically, those who provide the best products, services and labor are those who gain the greatest reward. This system has gained acceptance from the vast majority of society's members to the point where criticism is widely equated with blasphemy.

Even so, there are those, among them certain radical feminist groups, who do condemn the system. They point to the large number of people who are left behind or completely out. I will not embark on an examination of the various merits of capitalism and socialism. What concerns us here is those women who embrace the free enterprise system yet quarrel with its "discriminatory" policies.

Once again, we must admit that women's claims to widespread discrimination are justified. Restricted access to influential jobs and lower pay for similar work, are only two of the legitimate gripes of women in the labor force. Both of these are well-documented realities in this country. However, both could use further examination.

In the process of seeking to rectify these inequities, women tend to attack male employers as being gender biased. While some employers are indeed guilty of this, others who prefer to employ one gender over the other may not be biased at all. They may be compelled by the dictates of competition as manifested in a free enterprise, profit oriented economy to discriminate.

Take for example the construction business which has traditionally resisted the advancement of females in its physically demanding jobs. Even though laws have been passed to eliminate outright discrimination in hiring, the macho mentality has not completely changed.

Keeping that in mind, imagine the owner of a company in need of salespeople to market his products to construction companies. He may have no gender bias himself and may be willing to hire female salespeople. But if his client base includes many men who still harbor the old macho attitude toward females in construction, his business may suffer no matter how qualified his female salespeople are. (So may the females' income if they are on commission, making it appear for statistical purposes as if they have not been equally paid compared to their male counterparts.) The employer, in order to run his business most profitably, may be forced to employ salesmen exclusively.

Granted, we are still dealing with discrimination here. But the reasons behind the discrimination are more complex than employers simply seeing women as inferior and wanting to withhold opportunity. We're dealing with centuries old conditioning that has polarized the genders and assigned each separate tasks. Many men distrust women's knowledge and dexterity in certain areas and would prefer to buy the associated goods and services from other men. (This also works in reverse in the marketing of products and services predominantly sought by women.) In these cases the consumer, not the employer, initiates the discrimination. The employer goes along in order to maintain his business.

The culprit here is the age-old stereotyping of gender and gender behavior. Attempting to eliminate gender discrimination in employment by pressuring the employers targets the wrong group and blunts the effort.

Yes, many employers still do discriminate and these should be penalized for doing so. But to attack all employers by passing regulations that do not address discriminatory attitudes across the breadth of our society, unjustifiably discriminates against employers and injures our economy. In effect we are placing all the responsibility for discriminatory attitudes on employers. Thus they can make a legitimate case for lack of fairness and on that basis further resist changing discriminatory policies.

In addition to facing job discrimination because of their gender, women claim to face it because of child bearing and rearing responsibilities. This, of course, is true. But once again we must examine the reasons behind this before trying to implement solutions. For women to ignore the negative impact to their companies caused by their taking time off to bear and care for children is disingenuous.

Remember, productivity is determined by both the skill of the workers and their availability. In our modern economy, the tools provided by technology have placed women on nearly an equal skill level with men. (A few jobs still exist where extraordinary physical strength is a requirement.) At the same time, women who have chosen to be working mothers are often less available. Pregnancy, delivery and recovery by themselves usually require leaves of three months or more. Subsequently the needs of the small children will often require periodic short absences.

While in theory the needs of children would also increase fathers' work absenteeism, in reality it is the mother who must sacrifice the most work time for young children. First of all it is the mother who must undergo the delivery process. This includes time off for preparation and recovery. Secondly, many demands of infants can only be met by the mother. (I will discuss this in detail later.)

Modern women have demanded that they be granted child care absences without penalty. They have asked that both government and private industry provide child care facilities. They have also suggested that fathers share in the child rearing responsibilities that demand periodic brief absences.

None of these requests would seem unreasonable. And yet what about the repurcussions to their job responsibilities? Women are asking companies to sacrifice efficiency during their absences. They claim to possess crucial expertise which should allow them equal pay and responsibility to that of men while refusing to address the adversity inflicted upon their companies by extended pregnancy leaves. If they are so easily replaceable then their demands for extra responsibility and equal pay would seem unjustified.

The truth is that they are very valuable to their companies and that their absences are sorely felt. These not only reduce productivity in their own area of responsibility, but also interfere with others whose work depends on theirs.

That in mind, isn't it only reasonable for an employer in a free enterprise economy to hire employees who promise the least absenteeism? Companies cannot function at full efficiency if their employees are frequently taking leaves of absence for parenting.

Which raises the question: what is more important, our economy or raising our children? Most of us would like to believe that choosing between them should not be necessary. But in a free enterprise system where stiff competition weeds out the inefficient, child raising often becomes a detriment to economic success. What is a "job" to the employee is often a crucial position to the employer. The responsibilities of these positions need to be carried out daily with the expertise achieved, in many cases, over years. Often times the employer has no adequate replacement.

So to advocate the free enterprise system and then complain when employers resist providing adequate pregnancy benefits or avoid hiring women likely to become pregnant, is again disingenuous. Quite simply, anyone who asks an employer to provide time off for pregnancy is asking them to donate a portion of their personal profits. Depending on your point of view, that may or may not be reasonable. In either case, it is what it is.

A related issue is the widespread women's demand that employers be forced to provide child care for their employees. In theory, by providing this service the employer gains the benefit of interdicting absenteeism among his employees. He, however, would find it more profitable to employ people who have no child raising responsibilities. This way he wouldn't have to foot the expense of child care.

The bottom line is that we must either radically restructure our society/economy or demand that parents be prepared to sacrifice careers for the privilege of raising children.

Notice I say "parents." Men who wish to become fathers bear equal responsibility toward raising their children. Traditionally fathers have been expected to fulfill this responsibility by working and providing financial security while mothers remained home to raise the children.

The structure of modern industrial society has demanded that at least one member of the family work within the economy to generate income. How then can both men and women be asked to sacrifice careers when choosing to have children? The answer lies in defining the difference between "career" and "job."

The term "career" connotes a primary focus. One usually has spent great effort developing associated skills for the purpose of achieving success in this specialized field. Great time and energy are devoted to pursuing career opportunities and the resulting financial rewards. Career usually takes precedence over wife and family, ostensibly because it provides the means of their support. However, more often than not the career-oriented person values their career more than their family. Thus, career will usually determine where one lives and how much time is available to the family. The picture painted does not portray devoted parenthood.

"Job," on the other hand, connotes an activity engaged in to provide income. While some people do focus on their jobs, by their nature jobs do not necessarily conflict with parenting in our modern society. True, they often make demands of time that deprive children of needed attention. But the family needs income to survive so attending to the needs of one's job is crucial to the well being of the family.

The crucial difference between a "career" and a "job" is where one places priority. A person pursuing a career usually gives that endeavor top priority. A person holding down a job usually will see to the well being of their family first and will often change jobs to aid their family.

So, when I say that aspiring parents must be prepared to sacrifice "careers," I am suggesting that they shift occupational focus. They should be working for the benefit of their families, not for some occupation-focused personal fulfillment. True, some people can continue to pursue "careers" without depriving their families. But this is a sparse minority.

A strong indication that a large percentage of men are not committed to imposing a "glass ceiling" is the treatment of the Equal Rights Amendment. Feminists point to its failure to be ratified as an indication that most men opposed it. However, it passed the male-dominated Congress, was signed by a male president and was ratified by the male-dominated legislatures of 37 states—falling one short of full ratification. Thirty-seven out of fifty (74%) indicates very strong male support of the Amendment. Some states later withdrew their ratification, but this occurred after patriarchally oriented women rose up to exert pressure. So when feminists blame men for the failure of the ERA, they once more lose credibility.

All Men are Rapists at Heart

This is a charge that only the most radical feminists make and yet it has received enough attention and is so inflammatory that it downgrades the image of all layers of feminism. The problem with this charge is that although it is totally inaccurate as stated, it does raise pertinent questions regarding men's sexual behavior toward women.

First of all, within the framework of patriarchal society few men rape. This of course refers to the common, traditional interpretation of rape—physically forcing someone to engage in sexual activity against their will. Feminists would disagree with this definition and submit that any man who coerces his wife or girlfriend either physically or in any other manner into having sex is also a rapist. If we apply this definition (which I agree with) the above charge is less outrageous even if not accurate. For while many committed men do coerce their female partners into having sex, many do not.

The next pertinent question is, are many men rapists at heart but restrain themselves because of fear of legal repercussions? Think about that. What if it was not against the law or any moral/religious code to rape (force sex upon someone)? Would rape significantly increase?

The behavior of armies not tightly constrained both in times past and present indicates that it would—drastically. The recent revelations of sexual harassment in the U.S. military further back this. It seems that when men are given unrestricted power over women, a significant portion of them form strategies on how to force or coerce sex from women.

I'm also convinced that men without official power entertain thoughts of forced or coerced sex. Most women in our society have experienced numerous times where overly aggressive males were only restrained from carrying out sexual acts by the fear of arrest and conviction.

To what extent, then, are men rapists at heart? Many men would never rape under any circumstance. And yet, I suspect, many would. I wouldn't even begin to guess the percentage split. However the vast number of potential rapists gives the feminist charge some credibility. The problem with making the charge is that it's inaccurate as stated and outrages those men who would never rape because they see rape as a dastardly crime. Those very same men are the ones who stand with women in seeking to stamp out this crime. To be lumped with those they abhor is a deep insult and tends to erode their sympathy for this and other women's issues.

(Rape deserves analysis in much greater depth so I have dedicated a later chapter to that topic.)

Men Love War

This charge is not easy to refute considering man's history and the frequency of warlike acts taking place almost daily across the planet. Close examination tells us that few women are responsible for or are involved in this activity. This seems to be a pastime of men. And yet most modern Western men cannot identify inside themselves a love for the carnage of war. The charge therefore comes across as outrageous because of the way it's presented.

No one enjoys suffering hurt or seeing their loved ones suffer. However many of those same people get pleasure from inflicting hurt upon others. The ability to inflict physical hurt upon others provides a feeling of power relished by the insecure. This is sought particularly by men, who have always tried to overcome feelings of inadequacy by exercising physical dominance.

Even in Western culture this is true. However, most Western men do not gain satisfaction from dominating the helpless. Their victims must in some way be perceived as a threat whether it be physical or ideological. (In years past, a "commie" was considered a serious threat no matter how passive.) Only then can they strike out and, if necessary, unleash war.

War is often viewed from two distinctly different perspectives: the unleashing of weaponry and its result. Many who contemplate war do so from one of these perspectives, ignoring the other. One group focuses on destroying one's enemies and glories in its potential to do so. The "bomb them!!" mentality of air warfare advocates particularly personifies this group. Like those who unleash the destruction, the advocates remain at a distance and can ignore the full impact of the resulting carnage. In contrast, the other group envisions only the horrors of war and can see no redeeming value to inflicting them.

Few modern Western men would admit to the world or themselves that they enjoy seeing the death and destruction resulting from war. Charred, dismembered bodies, ruins of buildings, bloodied, crippled soldiers and civilians—all tend to raise compassion in most men. In peace time these are the first images that usually come to mind when thinking of war and thus the vast majority of men think of themselves as hating war.

These men take feminist accusations of men loving war as absurd and hypocritical. After all, aren't feminists seeking the "right" of women to enter combat? And, haven't women been pushing to enroll in military academies across this country? This would indicate that men don't love war any more than women. And thus men can shrug off the charge and assess it as another strike against the credibility of the feminist movement.

But if men don't love war, do they hate it? Remember the other half of the war equation—the unleashing of weaponry.

Can anyone honestly deny that the majority of men in this country enjoy observing weapons unleashed? Or, participating in war games whether they be computer simulated or real life (e.g., the burgeoning paintball fad)? Consider the number of war-oriented violent movies and the war and weaponry oriented TV series documentaries. In these what is mainly showcased is the unleashing of devastating weaponry and the power that lies in the hands of those who wield it. Slow motion, close up, beautifully colored photography presents our weaponry and ability to wage war as if it were an art form. Impact on victims? Not displayed except to illustrate how weaponry deals death to hated enemies deserving of their fate. The long range societal and environmental effect of the destruction? Not discussed.

(This approach brings to mind the movie Terminator II in which Arnold Schwartzenegger, playing a robot who has just been given orders to stop killing men, proceeds to shoot a defenseless one in the leg and announce, "He'll live." This attempt at humor totally overlooked the fate of the victim who, if the situation had been real, would likely have needed extensive surgery, long rehabilitation, and be crippled for the rest of his life. Of course, this was just a movie. The victim disappeared. Many more people were slaughtered and maimed with as little attention paid to their fates. The act of killing was portrayed as inconsequential and yet the Director later claimed that his movie was a statement against violence.)

Consider the wide ranging protest to the assault weapons ban passed recently by Congress. These weapons are weapons of war and have no practical use in a peaceful society. Even those men who claim they wish to own assault weapons as insurance against governmental tyranny must admit that their solution is to wage war against their own government.

With all of this male focus upon war as a practical solution to solving disputes it is easy to see where feminists can make, with some justification, the charge that men love war. However once again, the charge is both simplistic and inflammatory. Men do indeed have a "romance" with war. But the term "love" has a far deeper connotation which can be disputed in this context.

When one "loves," the connotation is that one completely embraces the love object in all of its aspects and nuances. General George Patton loved war. He loved planning it; unleashing it: facing its dangers; seeing the resulting destruction; killing the enemy. He was not appalled by the spilling of blood, at least not in the same way as average citizens. He saw the killing of the enemy as an honorable, rather than regrettable, action. And he saw spilling one's own blood, either in death or through wounds, as a noble sacrifice which one should be eager to endure to experience the glory of combat.

There have been many others of his ilk. In a recent TV documentary, Theodore Roosevelt was revealed as a man who hungered for the experience of war to flesh out his manhood. He purposely resigned as Secretary of the Navy in order to experience combat. Then, as leader of the "Rough Riders," he repeatedly exposed himself unnecessarily to enemy fire. He emerged unscathed to become president, but two decades passed without his thirst for combat diminishing. As a portly, warmongering iconoclast in his late fifties, he unsuccessfully begged President Wilson to assign him a combat command in Europe during the First World War. A short time later his attitude abruptly changed when he lost his favorite son, Clinton, in that war.

We find this attitude more prevalent in other societies and in other generations. Certainly the patriarchal hierarchy in pre-twentieth century Europe was dominated by the willingness to wage war. But it is just as certain that in the half-century since the Second World War men's attitudes toward war have been undergoing a major alteration. The Patton mentality will always exist, but it is not as predominant as it once was. Quite simply, the public has become more aware of the horrors of war and therefore is not as ready swallow the propaganda that has driven men to endure them.

Thus, in their own minds the vast majority of Western men do not see themselves as "loving" war. And yet a vast number of this vast majority enjoy the thought of unleashing the horrors of war upon other societies that oppose us. This is where "romance" becomes the applicable description. For like in many jaded romances where men extract what they need—particularly sex—with no intention of taking responsibility for the consequences, modern Western warmongers can wage war with a minimum of danger to themselves and to the military personnel who serve them. Few enemies stand a chance against our superior aircraft, cruise missiles, and smart bombs. War does not have to be "hell" for the Western soldier. And so many of us entertain it as a viable solution for international problems.

But face us with the prospect of involvement in guerilla warfare and the appeal of war vastly diminishes. For in such circumstances our superiority diminishes significantly and we, or those we send, face significant danger. Suddenly compassion for war victims wells up. Bloodshed becomes less appealing. Many men, in spite of a fascination with unleashing war, can also recognize these gentler feelings in themselves. Athough these feelings may not be dominant, these men feel justified in protesting when accused of "loving" war.

A large percentage of men do experience a romantic attraction to war. But the term "love" has a far deeper connotation which can be disputed in this context. Use of it allows men to escape having to justify the destructive "romance" they have been carrying on for thousands of years. (I will discuss this "romance" in further depth later.)

Men Are Materialistic

This charge is usually accompanied by blaming men for ravaging the environment. It destroys feminist credibility not because it is wrong but because women are just as guilty. Feminists themselves use the fruit of this "decadent" materialism to carry on their fight. Virtually all fly in airplanes, own computers, use sophisticated communication equipment, watch television, drive automobiles, listen to stereos, launder clothes in washing machines, etc. How many live in austere quarters with limited modest possessions? Are they wrong for taking advantage of the fruits of our materialistic culture? Only to the extent that they criticize men.

Are men overly materialistic? I believe so. Are they more materialistic than women? The evidence seems to say no. Go to any shopping mall and determine what percentage of the myriad of items available are female oriented compared to male oriented. Indeed, try to determine what percentage of shoppers are male compared to female. Shopping has long been a stated hobby of a vast majority of women, whereas it has far less appeal to most men. In terms of the environment, I believe that if you searched the nearest dump you would discover as many, if not more, female oriented articles discarded.

This is not to blame or absolve one gender or the other. In Western society materialism has become the passion of the vast majority of both genders. To attribute it exclusively to men unjustifiably lays all the blame upon them and once more hardens their view of feminism and its issues.

Other feminist charges are numerous yet less controversial therefore drawing little attention from men yet fortifying their disdain and drawing cries of "male bashing." A backlash has developed, fueled by male authors whose counter charges are just as outrageous as those they are trying to refute.

Chapter Five
Men's Backlash Against Feminism

In 1991 Susan Faludi authored a book entitled *Backlash* claiming that the Feminist Movement was facing a concerted effort by adversaries to undermine all of its gains. Although many feminists embrace the views in this book, it received a great deal of negative response. Numerous other feminists and, of course, men, condemned it as radical because it tried to label most efforts to resist feminist ideology as conspiratorial. It attacked as traitors to the cause, even heretofore feminist icons like Betty Friedan. By presenting numerous extreme views it leaves itself vulnerable to the usual male counterattacks.

I don't wish to analyze Ms. Faludi's book. She describes what she perceives as a backlash against women's rights which has been unleashed across the entire spectrum of our society. Whether a backlash of such scope exists is arguable. However it is becoming plain that a very callous, insidious backlash is being instigated by male intellectuals who focus on the gender issue. Their purpose appears to be to blunt the painful attacks of feminists and, by counterattacking and portraying men as victims, maintain the status quo in inter-gender relationships.

Because of the incessant criticism they've endured at the hands of feminists, many men are eager to strike back. Some refuse to acknowledge that women have ever been oppressed by men. Those willing to acknowledge women's oppression see it as having occurred primarily prior to the 20th century and therefore not attributable to contemporary men. Both groups see the latter part of the 20th century as a time of women's advancement. Many of each actually view it as a time of gender parity. In their view women have little to complain about, certainly not more than men themselves.

Thus these men find backlash arguments, which sympathize with the frustration men have been enduring under the system, compelling. These arguments are cleverly sculpted to release men from responsibility for the shortcomings of their society. They relieve men of guilt, uplift them, and provide a rallying doctrine. Men tend to feel vindicated and justified in maintaining their current life course. At most, they seek out minor changes which, they hope, will be sufficient to relieve their personal frustrations.

Poet and Men's Movement leader Robert Bly encourages this attitude when he says:

> We know that 19th century men characteristically failed to notice female suffering. In this century men have added another inattention: they failed to notice their own suffering.

Numerous authors and men's group facilitators have been spearheading the backlash movement in the guise of freeing men and helping them find their masculinity. Their positions vary and sometimes even conflict. But you don't hear them arguing with each other. Rather, they focus upon the common enemy—women's views of our traditional patriarchal system.

Currently the backlashers with the largest followings seem to be Robert Bly and Warren Farrell. Both have appeared frequently in and on the national media and through their widespread exposure have inflicted serious damage on men's empathy both to women and women's issues. Bly's work has inspired the Mythopoetic Men's Movement (which I will discuss in the next chapter) while Farrell's *The Myth of Male Power* serves as the current bible of backlash argument. In his book Farrell attempts to refute nearly every criticism leveled against men by feminists.

Backlash leaders claim that by voicing their charges against women they clear the air and foster gender reconciliation. But how can this be so when the result of their charges is to: accent men's problems within the system and downplay women's, absolve themselves and their gender of responsibility for what has transpired, and to blame women for many of the problems suffered by both genders? As we examine some of their outlandish arguments it will become apparent that confrontation and enmity can only be the overriding result.

Men Have Not Dominated Women

The basic premise Farrell-inspired backlashers fall back on is that throughout history neither gender has possessed power over the other. Rather, both sexes have been subservient to the survival needs of the next generation. Each has been forced by circumstances to play roles. Biology has designated women as the creators and nurturers of life, men as protectors and providers. Both are driven by this role division because any other would threaten survival.

At first glance this premise seems sound. In this book even I have defended the need for the genders to play roles. I question, however, the nature of the roles men and women have been forced to play under patriarchy.

Farrell contends that men are powerless because they MUST play the protector/provider role. He maintains that men (as well as women) are forced by biological imperative to sacrifice themselves for their families. In effect, men are powerless in the face of their biology.

I would agree that biology determines roles. But do patriarchal roles conform to biological imperative? Has biology given women inferior decision making powers, necessitating their subjecting themselves to male leadership? Has it made them so helpless to protect and provide for themselves that their survival demands their submission to a male overlord who decides their life course for them? Does it demand that men in their role as protector/provider use the threat of physical force to maintain their authority? I think not. Yet these are the traditional roles assigned to men and women under a system that can only be defined as "patriarchy."

Once given the chance, women have proven that biology has made them equal in intelligence to men. It follows then that patriarchal men have defied biology by seizing the power to make decisions and imposing their role concepts upon women.

At the same time, in those circumstances where men have allowed, women have shown the physical ability to protect and provide for themselves, even when pregnant. Yes, birth and the raising of infants simply works better when both parents play roles. But this does not mean that all women, even those without infant raising responsibilities, must be treated as if helpless and in need of constant protection.

Men have chosen to view women in this fashion. This justifies establishing a hierarchy that conditions women to view themselves as vulnerable to the elements, inferior to men, and lacking in capabilities to provide for themselves. In effect, men have attempted with a great deal of success to mold women into beings that serve the role men have chosen for themselves.

Can anyone honestly believe that a woman who was given the opportunity from birth to achieve her full potential, both physically and psychologically, would not be capable and willing to fulfill virtually all those responsibilities currently assigned to men? Women who escape patriarchal conditioning evolve into powerful human beings not only capable of, but determined to, provide for themselves. An independent woman may voluntarily submit to the nurturing role and allow her mate to provide physical sustenance for her and their children, but she is not biologically limited to this role.

Farrell contends that men are "commanded by the command to protect," and had they not responded to that command the species would be extinct. He implies that, in effect, men have also been conditioned—socialized to save and protect women.

Once again he presents us a half-truth. Yes, men have been conditioned, but by whom? By fathers, of course—fathers committed to the patriarchal view. Fathers who taught boys that males were superior to females. Yes, mothers contributed, but mainly in fortifying the views of fathers. And this only after embracing their own conditioning and accepting their "inferiority."

Doesn't this say then that both genders were conditioned and thereby back up Farrell's assertion that both were powerless?

Hardly. One gender was taught to feel superior; the other inferior. Men were conditioned to expect to wield power; women to accept powerlessness. Both had little power to resist their conditioning, but their conditioning exalted one over the other. If both complain, then one is complaining about being a servant while the other is complaining about being burdened with the responsibilities of a lord. Can we honestly accept that both possess equal power over their lives? Does the lord or the servant have more power to change the system? Which has more incentive to change roles in trying to escape powerlessness? How many men would trade their power for the average woman's?

I find it hard to accept the view that men have been socialized primarily to save and protect women considering all the deplorable destruction occurring during the past centuries, virtually all of it carried out by men. Indeed, if humankind ever faced extinction it was during the Cold War when patriarchal men threatened each other with nuclear annihilation. Somehow men's personal ambitions, exclusive of the "save and protect women" instinct, played a major role in all the war and brinkmanship. Had it not, would men have found it necessary to: prevent women from making their own marriage decisions, keep them uneducated, withhold the right to vote, prevent their earning and/or keeping their own incomes, etc.?

Humankind would have fared poorly and perhaps faced extinction had men completely refused to respond to the "command to protect" when women needed it. But under patriarchy men went to extremes. They used the instinct to protect as an excuse to smother women. Men saw women as lesser beings—property that reflected status. The species suffered because women were prevented from contributing to their full capacity.

Women Have Always Had Significant Decision-Making Power

Backlashers base this claim upon women's ability to use sexuality to manipulate. They neatly overlook that men retain the power and it can only be obtained by women through manipulation. Many women, particularly the sexually unattractive, have little success at this and remain virtually powerless in relation to men. Many men cannot be manipulated and maintain all power over their women. The truth is that because of unequal status assigned to the genders under patriarchy, males are born with power, females without it.

Farrell argues that we have never lived in a patriarchy. He contends that the biological necessity to play roles has divided areas of domination between the genders. In effect, certain areas of society were patriarchal, others matriarchal. In particular, women held power in the home and over children. He even goes so far as to claim that women have excluded men from the birthing process, creating a "women only club."

Women do often attain varied levels of power but this is only because men have allowed it. Until recently the bottom line has always been that men must sign on if women's authority was to carry any weight. Women might try, often very successfully, to manipulate, deceive and trick. But a man "putting his foot down" decided the issue. As one Mexican-American college professor of Hispanic culture told me: "Women ran the household, but man's word was law." This power structure can be traced back through history and was particularly evident in Roman times when it was encoded in Roman law.

Much of the time men have given women power to run the household to keep women occupied and assuage women's feeling of powerlessness. Most men have preferred to focus upon other matters anyway so by giving away the responsibility to manage household affairs they were serving their own interests. Indeed, many men married to provide themselves a housekeeper. In any case, the power over the household was man's to give away and one he could reclaim at any time.

The claim that birthing has been a "female-only club" once again distorts the picture. Traditionally men had been excluded from the birthing process because patriarchal society said a true man should concern himself with other things. Nature had assigned birthing to women therefore men need not know much about it. It was a messy woman thing. To most men, the importance of the birth process was its result—preferably a son to carry on lineage.

Rules of modesty established by male inspired religions and social mores added to women's desire to seek seclusion from men during this special time. Women may have selfishly clung to this privilege because of their lack of power in most other areas. But generally, the more liberated women have become, the more they've favored including their husbands in the birthing miracle.

This same patriarchal role division, which gave exclusive responsibility for the birthing, and primary responsibility for the raising, of children to women, has also given primary custody of children in divorces to mothers. Many men bemoan this fact and resent women because of it. But they have become victims of patriarchal attitudes toward child raising.

Human Survival Required the Killer Male

This Farrell contention is refuted by the discoveries of anthropologists, particularly Richard Leakey, one of the foremost experts on primitive man. During his decades of study, he has come to take issue with the view that "the violence and aggression that we see so much of today is because our ancestors behaved that way." He insists that ethnography doesn't support this.

> Our species has a very long history and for most of our time we have existed on the basis of cooperation and close communication. There is no evidence that this aggression, this division that now separates many of us, is in our genes. It's something that has surely come about recently, perhaps merely in the last ten thousand years.

This in mind, let's further examine the concept of "the killer male." We will assume that "killer male" does not refer to hunters who simply killed for food.

Just whom or what did our "killer male" have to kill in order to protect his family? On occasion he may have found himself and his family stalked by some animal predator. But never have I heard it suggested by anthropologists that mankind was in danger of being hunted into extinction by animals. Indeed, there was a point in human history where weapons were too primitive to provide protection against many larger predators. Against them, men could not protect his family by killing yet humankind survived and multiplied.

The big threat to a "killer male's" family was attack by other "killer males." But if Richard Leakey is correct then "killer males" developed later in human history and were responding to socialization rather than instinct when they killed. Since all were victims of socialization they could just as easily have been socialized to live in peace. Someone at some time chose to embrace the killing of other human beings, rather than cooperation, as a primary survival technique. This necessitated other human beings reacting in kind. Since women were not strong enough to force men to kill we can only surmise that men made the decision.

Many men would like us to believe that women can indeed drive men to kill. They point to women who have convinced lovers to kill husbands. But in that circumstance who is making the final decision to pull the trigger or strike the blow? If a man refuses to do it, how can a woman force him? By threatening to withhold "love" and sex? But who has made the decision to make this man so dependent upon the "love" and sex of this woman? Of course, the man! Even if he is a hostage to his feelings, they are his feelings. It is his perception and response to that perception that makes him a captive. To imply that a man has no power to control these feelings paints a pitiful picture of him. The vast majority of men deserve a better assessment.

How can we then defend the existence of "killer males" as essential in some biological sense to human survival?

Psychologically insecure men frightened over their survival prospects chose to become "killer males," forcing other men to follow this path. Killing became necessary when men chose to make it necessary, not because it was instinctual.

Men often point to women as encouraging the "killer male" by choosing him over the more pacifistic man. But that happened primarily because men have created a system which makes it difficult for women to earn their own way. Once men have initiated bloodletting which women are powerless to stop, women naturally choose those men who can best protect them.

The vast majority of women would rather see their men settle disputes without risking injury and death through fighting. Even in classic "a man had to do what a man had to do" patriarchal movies such as "High Noon" and "The Virginian," the heroines tried to convince the heroes to flee the fight rather than risk death. This would have meant the loss of status for both, but the woman, not the man, was willing to make that sacrifice. Even most patriarchal men recognize that the majority of women would not choose to send their men into harm's way.

War is Instigated by a Primal Fear of Not Surviving Experienced by Both Sexes

This Farrell assertion ignores the many wars fought for ideology and those that were initiated by aggressors seeking to enhance living standards already far above subsistence level. Few wars have been initiated because both sides faced extinction unless the other was destroyed. Naturally, once war began, for whatever cause, survival was at stake for both sides.

Human beings do indeed possess a primal fear of not surviving. But this fear does not instinctually drive us into a war-making mode.

The threat of war generates even more primal fear than does a natural survival threat. (Which generates more fear, the absence of a crop or facing hostile, sword-bearing males intent on cutting your head off?) Therefore it is most often instigated by parties who are not motivated by actual survival considerations, but rather see war as an opportunity for gain. True, the psychologically insecure can be rich yet see their survival threatened by the slightest incursion of those they perceive as potential rivals. But this is an aberrant view of life, not instinctual.

The assertion also ignores that even when survival is threatened by two groups needing the same life resource, humans are offered alternatives to fighting—particularly withdrawal and negotiation. Almost certainly a far higher percentage of women than of men prefer these alternatives when viable. War is primarily a male thing which I will discuss in detail in a later chapter.

Our Society Embraces "Male Killing Sexism"

Farrell needs his "war caused by two-sex fear" theory to condemn what he calls "male killing sexism" in our society. This refers to men being forced to exclusively carry the burden of fighting in wars. If he can establish that women bear equal blame for instigating war then he can portray men as victims of war—those who must die to protect those (women) who have advocated fighting yet refuse to risk their lives.

He tries to make a case that voters send men to war and that women make up more than 50% of the electorate. He conveniently overlooks that currently machine politics dominates candidate selection in this country. Although we do elect a President and legislators, seldom do we have choices which reflect views other than patriarchal ones which accept war as an acceptable policy. (When Edmund Muskie and Pat Schroeder shed tears during the campaigns for the Presidency, they were ridiculed and lost much of their following.) Yes, in theory the voters could change this. But the practical aspects would demand enormous organization and financing, things that grass roots efforts can seldom achieve. In effect because of patriarchal influence which has led to a "good ol' boy" mentality in politics, women have little chance to prevent war through exercise of the vote.

Farrell also fails to point out that only in this last century have women even had the right to vote, yet men throughout history have borne military responsibilities exclusively. So if voters decided in those times that men should exclusively carry the fighting, we should lay responsibility at the feet of males—the only voters.

His pointing toward women as advocates of "male killing sexism" further stands on shaky ground when we consider the traditional vehement resistance by men to women entering the military. Consider the recent action at The Citadel which went to a high court to try to keep the aforementioned Shannon Faulkner from breaking the gender barrier. Subsequently other women have been hounded out of the institution by hazing and physical mistreatment at the hands of other male cadets. Farrell defends hazing as a weeding out of the weak in military circumstances. Even so, if this process prevents most women from participating in combat, we cannot blame them for "male killing sexism."

It is plain that the vast majority of men abhor sending women into combat. This is a traditional patriarchal view which bolsters the male ego. Compassion is one factor. Patriarchal men view women as physically weak and do not like to see the weak subjected to violence. Taken by itself this seems like virtuous motivation, if we ignore that portraying women as weak undermines women overall.

At the same time, to maintain their position of dominance men must prevent women from participating in combat. Women contributing equally to men in combat situations would undermine the patriarchal physical superiority justification for males remaining in control.

War will continue as long as the demonstration of physical superiority is the primary means of settling disputes. This has always been a male rather than female approach. The main reason men, not women, have been forced to endure combat is male physical superiority. The prime physical specimens generally make the best soldiers. (This has been gradually shifting with the advent of technology.) Just for that reason during WWII men with physical infirmities which didn't preclude them from participating in athletics were declared 4-F and rejected as soldiers.

Farrell tries to exonerate the military profession and male members of it by claiming, "The military was a secular form of Jesus. Jesus in uniform." He refers here to Christ giving his life to save humanity.

Although many soldiers do deserve honor for their sacrifices, Farrell's statement is a pitiful attempt to justify men blindly going off to war. Christ fully saw the ramifications of his actions and gave his life to save all of humanity. Soldiers give theirs in an effort to destroy other human beings for a variety of personal as well as national reasons, many of which are not honorable.

Sexist Society Favoring Women Makes Men Expendable

This assertion goes beyond men being sacrificed in war. Backlashers maintain that men have also been "used up and disposed of" by being assigned, virtually exclusively, to performing the "death professions." These include all those professions with high accident rates—fire fighters, garbage men, roofers, etc.

It is true that men who risk death in very necessary professions do not get the recognition or financial remuneration they deserve. But this fault cannot be blamed upon women. We all undervalue these workers. They are victims of society as a whole—a patriarchal society which demands that men occupy these professions to the exclusion of women. Some of these professions do make physical demands which exclude all but a small percentage of women. But men bear some blame here by traditionally discouraging women from reaching their full physical potential.

It is not a fair representation to say that women avoid these "death professions." As women have received more freedom to achieve they have begun applying for dangerous professions like firefighter, police officer and construction worker. Likely more of them would have applied had so many not neglected developing their physical potential after having been conditioned to feel physically feeble in comparison to men. Furthermore, more qualified women would have attained these positions if the vast majority of men in these professions had not protested so vehemently.

Most backlashers would not outwardly claim that a woman's place is in the home, but they excuse traditional patriarchal mores which advocate just that. To do so, then chastise women for not seeking the "death professions" reeks of duplicity.

Without question, generally the lives of men are valued less than the lives of women. As a man, I'm not happy about this. But to a great degree men have brought this upon themselves. By demeaning women's physical prowess; by resisting women's inclusion in the more dangerous professions; by glorifying their own combative, daredevil activities which invite injury and death; men imply that they value their lives less.

Life Expectancy is an Indication of True Power

What backlashers claim here is that survival is humankind's number one consideration. All human beings seek to live as long as possible. Therefore if a wide disparity in life expectancy exists between the genders, the gender that lives longer must have more power. Since statistics prove that over the past few decades women have lived substantially longer than men, women must have more control over their lives.

This argument ignores quality of life. Many factors determine average lifespan. Unquestionably, men experience heavy pressures under our system which lead to life threatening ailments. Those women who live under men's "protection" arguably may or may not experience less. But even if "protected" women are faced with less daily stress, that does not in any way indicate that they wield more power over, or indeed, experience more pleasure in, their lives.

Protectors can protect for selfish purposes—to control the protected and keep them available to serve the protector. Even if the life span of the protected increases they may experience frustration and lack of fulfillment. Widowed women who have been granted those extra years (age 70+) often are without motivation because they have never been allowed to choose their own life course. Many people would choose a shorter life if that would allow them more power to determine their destiny. How many men do you think would be willing to switch their gender in order to increase their life span by seven years? Few, you can be sure. The main reason is the surrender of power and authority the changeover would demand.

Farrell maintains that the average life span of men is shortened compared to women's because more men commit suicide. (Women try more; men succeed more.) It is hard to believe that the number of suicides would statistically alter the average life spans of either gender. Whether or not it is so, he is right in asserting that men's role under a demanding, merciless system causes many male suicides. But if we are to blame the system, we must acknowledge what was responsible for the evolution of the system. The answer: men. Ancient men conceived of it; their descendants advocated, supported, or acquiesced to it. Few men, even today, cry out to drastically change our basic system. And so, it continues to drive many of them to suicide.

Backlashers point out that further adding to men's shortened lifespans is the fact that men, more than women, are victimized by violence. This fact is somehow supposed to make women feel ashamed for complaining that they fear violence from men. All it does is point to the more important fact that most violence is carried out by men, whether it be against men or women. Women certainly do have reason to complain since they are far more often targets than perpetrators of violence. Men, on the other hand, need to accept responsibility as a gender for the epidemic of violence our society experiences.

Men know that violence is primarily a male thing. That's why they offer their services as escort to women. Even so, Farrell attempts to twist this by claiming that men are imposed upon unfairly by being forced to act as unpaid bodyguards to women. I've already mentioned how this claim is unfair because of the obvious reason that men are protecting women from other men, not women. But Farrell finds a way to cast even more blame upon women. He claims that this responsibility to protect women tends to shorten men's lifespans. Men not only face death and injury in this role, but they are flooded with anxiety-induced hormones which over time can lead to killing diseases such as heart disease or stroke.

This is a blatant distortion of the reality of this issue. First of all, few men face death or injury in this role, especially in comparison to the number of women who face death or injury from male attackers. Secondly, male "protectors" only face anxiety in situations when an attacker appears. Women, because of their relatively inferior defense capabilities, justly fear danger a major portion of the time they move about in society. Thus they, far more often than men, become flooded with anxiety-induced hormones triggered by the threat of physical attack. It follows then that women's health is far more endangered by accelerated hormonal activity. This danger is imposed by men conditioned to accept and practice violent behavior.

In addition, women spend more time in the company of their children who are also in need of protection. That protector role further increases anxiety-induced hormones which further enhances a woman's chance of falling victim to a stress induced disease. When dealing with the "protector" role and the need for protection, men have all the best of it.

Women Use Sex to Control Men

This is a biggie for the backlashers. They can dredge up numerous situations to support this charge and, because men feel vulnerable to women in this area, backlashers find a passionately receptive male audience.

I have no intention of trying to refute this charge as it stands. It has always been true, although in recent times more and more women have accepted liberation and rely on other personal characteristics to exert themselves in relationships. I have already discussed at length how women, in being deprived of the right to self-determination, have been forced to use their sexual appeal to influence men. I will not belabor this point here. What is important here is to recognize how exaggerated much of the supporting argument for this charge has become.

One major male complaint is that men are expected to spend money on women to receive sexual attention. Men like to say that the first thing a woman is interested in is the number and buying power of a man's credit cards.

Although gradually changing because of feminism, this is still widely true. But where did this self-indulgent female approach come from? Obviously, from traditional patriarchal society in which women have been kept financially dependent upon men.

Farrell himself admits this dependence when he says that fathers traditionally gave away brides because they (fathers) were giving away the responsibility to protect. Of course he does not address why and from whom it was necessary to protect daughters? Nor, why daughters were physically punished when they demeaned their value to other men (through premarital sex, etc.), or why fathers, to the exclusion of mothers, demanded the right to choose the husband.

Men who cling to the system have no grounds to complain about the custom of men financing courtship. They can legitimately chastise women who have "liberated" themselves and still ask men to bear the financial burden in social encounters. But for men to portray themselves as unfairly victimized by their sexual needs distorts reality.

It has been legitimately argued by women throughout history that men have more power in controlling social contact because men can decide who they wish to pursue while women traditionally have had to wait to be approached. If a man allows himself to be caught in the sexual web spun by a woman he does so voluntarily. For men create their own sexual ideal—the image of femininity that most arouses them. ("She's my type. She's not my type.") All a woman can do is groom and adorn herself in a manner she thinks will draw the type of man she wants, then act out the role. In effect, she's fishing. But it's always the fish who decides which bait is most appealing.

Backlashers argue that women's ability to withhold sex conditions men to focus most of their energy in seeking success just for the purpose of attracting a partner. This helps drive men to frustration and an early grave.

Once more, we can find truth in this claim even though most men pursue success for reasons exclusive of sex. As long as a major percentage of women remain conditioned to the traditional patriarchal view we will have women bartering sex for affluence. At the same time, patriarchy's conditioning men to pursue success leaves men trapped in a quandary of their own making. The only thing many men offer women is success. Naturally, if that is all a man has to offer he will almost certainly attract a partner who's primary interest is attaching herself to a successful male. How could he possibly attract any other type? If a man chooses to marry a woman whose main goal in marriage is security, he has entrapped himself.

Men try to stereotype all women as success oriented. But in reality a large number of women are not the dependent, parasitic type frequently referred to by Farrell. If a man doesn't like the rat race under patriarchy he can drop out of it without losing access to fulfilling relationships. Millions of women exist who are not looking for protection and who respect men who have found their way outside the system. However, if you wave your money and career in the faces of women you will attract those of them who are looking for providers.

One more malicious assertion needs to be addressed here before moving on. Farrell claims that females have an unfair power over males in the sex act. He implies that women regularly deceive their partners into believing that birth control measures have been taken when this is not the case. These women then proceed to entrap their partners with an unwanted pregnancy.

Doubtless this deplorable behavior happens, although whether to the extent claimed by Farrell is arguable. Nevertheless, if men did not leave birth control responsibilities to women, they wouldn't face this risk. Men have always heaped this responsibility upon women and then blamed women when pregnancy occurred. Guys, even if you're not concerned about this responsibility, if you're worried about being entrapped by a woman lying to you about being protected, condoms are easy to use.

Farrell neatly ducks the issue of men shirking birth control responsibilities, claiming that male technology created women's "right to choose" by developing birth control and safe abortion techniques. If this assertion is supposed to convince us that men have had deep empathy for women's birth control concerns, it fails. I suggest that if women had been allowed access to the same scientific/technological education that men had received, birth control technology and abortion techniques would have been perfected decades sooner. Consider: how much effort did the male-dominated scientific community spend upon birth control in comparison to what it spent on discoveries lending themselves to war?

Men's concerns over birth control have centered upon keeping themselves out of trouble rather than in respecting women. Otherwise men would consider birth control primarily their responsibility. Why theirs? Because it's easier for them and more protective of their partner's health. This is one area where men should've led, but few ever have.

Men Participate in Sports to Receive the Approval of Women

Sporting activity consumes so much of our attention in Western Society that I have devoted an entire chapter to it. I must briefly deal with it here because Farrell-led backlashers have used sports to attempt to further prove their previous charge regarding the sexual control women wield over men. In the process they have misrepresented the motivations of men in sports and deceived women, who otherwise have no way to relate to male/male dynamics as displayed in sports.

Recently I had a discussion with a psychotherapist who focused on men's issues. In addition to having his own private practice, he regularly spoke to groups around Southern California.

The subject of our conversation centered upon football, which I had condemned in a published article. He agreed with my views on football but then proceeded to blame women for men's involvement in all sports. He claimed that men participated in order to show off to women; that if women didn't come as spectators or act as cheerleaders, men would lose interest in participating. He cited himself as an example, having participated in football in college seeking the adulation of women.

His personal experience may have been valid, but his general argument was absurd. I suggest that rather than men participating in formal, organized sporting events because of the presence of women, the opposite is far more the case. Women attend games because of the presence of men.

Men seek to play football and other sports to bolster their feeling of manhood. Many use this vehicle to gain scholarships which will either further their education or eventually lead them to financial reward as professional athletes. Can anyone rationally think that these athletes would stop playing if women stopped watching?

Every day millions of American men gather informally at athletic courts and fields of play to compete with each other. At the vast majority of these competitions you will not find a single woman. The men competing are totally involved with each other. Hierarchy, in terms of athletic skills, is very important. For many participants a major reward of these competitions is being able to get away from women. Sports have become gender exclusive cults, particularly on the male side.

Most males play sports because they love sports. Boys fear rejection by boys and a reduced status in the pecking order when they avoid sports. The primary anxiety of adolescent boys lies in their relationship to their same gender peer group, not to females, as Farrell would have us believe.

Boys are driven to sports by a society that demands they measure themselves against each other in this way. They do indeed suffer major anxiety from their need to perform effectively before others. But it is the need to perform as males under the patriarchal system. A portion of this engenders performing for females because one must be successful with females to gain status among males. Yes, the urge to receive sexual attention also plays a part, but this is subordinate to the patriarchal imperatives surrounding sports.

Believe me, if a football player makes a terrible mistake that costs his team a game, his first worry isn't what his girlfriend thinks. He's worried about how his failure affects his teammates, scouts who may be watching, and his image in the eyes of other males. Likely he knows that his girlfriend is the person who cares least about his mistake and will be there to console him when he leaves the field.

In the Process of Seeking Sexual Access to Women Men Act Subservient to Women

Once again, we can find cases where men indeed feel subservient to women. But the Farrell claim that traditional gestures like helping a woman on with her coat shows subservience is way off target. Men do this and practice similar other deferential behavior to show their dominance over women. Men thus portray women as weaker, in need of the care and assistance of men. This is most men's true opinion of women. Yes, men may also show their devotion in this manner. But this devotion is not one of subservience, rather of claiming responsibility for being dominant. It has always been called chivalry—a cornerstone of patriarchy.

For similar reasons many laws have been made which Farrell

claims favor women over men. These have arisen particularly in the areas of rape enforcement, sexual harassment and divorce. The fairness of these laws can be argued. However, the motivation behind their passing can once more be traced to patriarchy. Since men have always seen women as weak, incompetent and inferior, it serves men's patriarchal macho image to make laws tougher on men. Farrell goes so far as to contend that to win women's favor and in subservience to women's honor, men instituted dueling. Once again we see a deceitful attempt to blame women for a barbaric practice which led to the mutilation and death of many men.

The truth is that duelists most often fought over insults to patriarchal concepts of honor. It was their own honor men defended in duels. For a man to fail to issue a challenge when the honor of a woman close to him was insulted, would have branded him a man without honor. If he had just been concerned with her honor he could have struck out immediately and thrashed the individual making the insult without concerning himself with etiquette. By subjecting himself to a duel he risked not only death, but failure to "resurrect" the woman's honor. This risk only made sense if one's own honor was at stake. In any case, the honor of women was honor defined on patriarchal terms. It was only natural in such a rigid patriarchal society that many women used dueling to evaluate male suitors.

Unemployment is to Men the Psychological Equivalent of What Rape is to Women

This assertion by Farrell is so deplorable and inflammatory that although I will be dealing extensively with rape in a later chapter, I must touch on the topic here. Farrell backs up his statement by saying:

> Unemployment deprives men of that which has given many men the respect and love of women: rape violates the body that has given many women the appreciation and love of men. Few men feel they chose unemployment, just as few women feel they chose to be raped.

These views personify patriarchal man's insensitivity to women and/or ignorance of their issues. A woman's body is more to her than just a vehicle which allows women to receive "the apprecia-tion and love of men." It is the domicile of her spirit, the bastion of her identity. While unemployment attacks a man's self-concept, it in no way endangers him physically or drives home a sense of physi-cal helplessness comparable to a rape. Yes, he encounters psycho-logical stress which may lead to physical repercussions. But so does the rape victim—in addition to the physical injuries sustained dur-ing the invasion. He can re-sculpt his self-concept. Rape attacks a woman's very being—her sense of physical security, which lies even deeper than self-concept.

The stability of one's work is often a factor in choosing one's pro-fession. Any man who seeks work knows that he is likely at some point in his life to face involuntary unemployment. That is the na-ture of our free enterprise system, which most men who fear un-employment embrace so tenaciously. Some are affluently success-ful while others face job instability which often leads to destitution.

Granted, involuntary termination is a shock to most of us, espe-cially those who have spent enormous time and energy preparing for a career and have built personal aspirations, particularly a fam-ily, upon career status and compensation. I have experienced it; I know how devastating it can seem. But in most cases it is some-thing we can prepare for, both financially and psychologically. The key word is "can." Too often men ignore the reality of the system and allow themselves to be defined by their work.

Contrast this to a woman experiencing rape. The act is usually sudden and unexpected, leaving the victim no way to prepare. In addition to the bodily invasion, which obliterates their sense of se-curity (perhaps for the rest of their lives), victims are often beaten, and many experience the terror of expecting to be murdered hideously.

An unemployed man always has a legitimate chance to find an-other job or profession that will restore his sense of self-esteem. A rape's scars never completely heal. An unemployed career-oriented man chose the profession that eventually rejected him. What choices are offered to a raped woman?

Farrell's obnoxious charges concerning rape do not stop there. He claims a woman's vagina is no more important than a woman's head so rape should be treated no differently than any other violent crime.

Maybe it shouldn't be treated differently. But it is different than most other crimes. A woman being struck on the head may suffer as much as one being raped. But her head has not been invaded, nor has she been infused with a substance which could cause her a disease of the mind or unwanted pregnancy. The nature of the crime is intrusion and violation of integrity—something that does not exist to the same degree in a typical mugging. Most men just don't get it.

Farrell then proceeds to excuse many rapists by trying to redefine rape. He maintains, as millions of men have before him, that women often say "no" when they mean "yes." He maintains that women can convey a "yes" in many nonverbal ways such as allowing tongues to touch or one's shoulders to be rubbed or one's hand to be caressed. He maintains that many women have fantasies of being sexually overpowered and when signals aren't clear, men often innocently see themselves as performing a service—fulfilling a fantasy by ignoring negative entreaties and forcing a woman into sexual activity. He maintains that because of women's ambiguity, men often have trouble deciphering which "no" means "no."

Many men would like to believe all these things. Whether miscommunication happens as often as Farrell implies is debatable. Nevertheless, a woman who has said "no" to sex then allowed herself to be kissed, her shoulders to be rubbed, and her hand caressed, has not necessarily changed her mind and said "yes." Her behavior may be imprudent, but the man is out of line when he pushes further to sex. The man should disentangle his tongue long enough to ask her permission again. Why is that such a problem? If he does not get a clear verbal "yes," he should back off.

A vast number of rapists justify their actions by claiming they are fulfilling a woman's fantasy. Any man who entertains this excuse obviously has a sex-related problem and is a serious candidate to become a rapist.

Which "no" means "no?" Any "no" means no until you hear a distinct "yes." Men have trouble with this because they don't want to hear a "no." Many are willing to grasp for anything that will give them permission to proceed. But interpretations of body language provide no excuse for ignoring verbal rejection. Even trained psychologists are just guessing when they attempt to read body positions. If a man thinks he has been given a dozen signs indicating that a woman wants sex but her only verbal response has been "no," he must assume she does not wish to proceed. As in a criminal court case, he must receive a unanimous verdict to continue his advances. Is that so hard to understand? It is, only when you don't want to accept it.

Farrell deepens his attack upon women and his defense of rapists by claiming that women who drink and then cry "rape" are unjustly injuring men. He says, "She is as responsible for drinking and declaring rape, as a driver is for drinking and causing an accident."

Neat. This seems to say that once a woman drinks and loses some power of judgment, it's open season upon her sexually. If a woman drinks and is coerced into having sex she ordinarily would reject, does that absolve the man? A man should not necessarily be held responsible for a woman who is sufficiently drunk to alter her judgment sexually. But he is morally responsible for taking advantage, just as a woman should be held morally responsible for manipulating a drunken man into volunteering to give her money. To compare a drunk driver who is entirely responsible for causing an accident to a drunken woman who leads on a man who retains his own powers of judgment and choice, is another insidious attempt to absolve men inclined to rape.

Women and Men Are Equally Likely to Initiate Violence Against the Other Gender

Backlashers begin defense of this charge by claiming that the statistics which say that men kill women twice as often as vice versa are distorted. Specifically, the Department of Justice 1985-88 statistics read: 4986 men killed by women; 10190 women killed by men. Farrell states that these figures are distorted by the fact that not all homicides of men can be properly traced back to women. Such factors as unsolved contract killings, undetected poisonings, women not charged because of gender bias/sex appeal, and plea bargains distort the picture. He has only speculation to back this conclusion but nevertheless implies that if the truth were to come out the stats would come closer to being equal. This, of course, is what he perceives to be the truth—indeed, what must be the truth to back his thesis.

He is right when he emphasizes that we should not seek to justify women killing men any more than vice versa. But before we jump to the conclusion that the statistics are distorted let's analyze them a little more.

Contract killings are just as likely, perhaps more so, to be instigated by men. Undetected poisonings can be just as easily carried out by men. It's doubtful that if the truth were to be discovered either of these two factors would change the statistics. At the same time, it is arguable that the number of women deserving to be charged yet escaping due to gender bias far exceeds the number of women convicted for committing a justifiable homicide.

True figures for these situations can never be obtained. Nevertheless, in his assertion Farrell ignores the fact that many women are continuously abused physically and sexually by violent men. Very few men are subject to this type of attack. Numerous women victims can see no other defense but murder. One would have to comprehend the dynamics of domestic violence to understand why. Perhaps murder is not the right solution, but women are offered few others. Men in abusive situations usually have several other options. The bottom line is that women have more legitimate reasons to commit murder than men, yet don't.

In order for Farrell's assertion to be true, during 1985-88 close to 5,000 male murders that should have been attributed to women either remain undetected or were passed off by the legal system due to gender bias. That's at least as many as were charged. If you can believe this I've got a two-wheeled tricycle I'd like to sell you.

Sexual Harassment Charges Are Largely Sexist Attacks to Undermine Men

Whether it be rape, domestic violence or sexual harassment, we will always find numerous women who try to misuse necessary laws to take advantage of and/or strike out against men. Whatever their motivation, their actions must be condemned. Perhaps the laws need to be modified. But backlashers attack the need for laws to protect women against sexual harassment by downplaying the seriousness of this issue and its full negative impact upon women.

Farrell begins his treatment of the subject with this incredible statement:

> If a woman at work caressed a man on his rear, he'd thank her not sue her. So how can a man understand why sexual harassment is such a big issue for women?

This portrayal of men's attitude is outrageously off base and an insult to men. It breeds misunderstanding and enmity between the genders. It is a pitiful attempt to exonerate men for sexual misbehavior.

Just like women, most men do not like to be fondled except by those women they are seriously attracted to. A man can be happily married and be attracted to a woman at his office without having any intention of seeking sexual contact. Such men are usually shocked and annoyed when they are fondled and certainly would never thank the woman for doing so.

The vast majority of men, particularly patriarchal men, whose self-concept depends upon maintaining control of women, do not like being intimately touched unless they invite it. Just like women, they view this as an intrusion and an insult to their right to privacy. Many of these men would justly feel sexually harassed if they were approached this way. Because of their macho self-image they might laugh it off, but if the behavior persisted most would make attempts to stop it. Few would have to resort to a lawsuit because most men have other tools.

The attempt to excuse sexual misbehavior in the work place includes portraying the telling of dirty jokes as usually an innocent practice which has no connotations of sexual harassment.

Farrell says:

> A dirty joke is often a male boss's unconscious way of getting his staff to not take him so seriously and therefore not be intimidated; his way of creating an atmosphere of easier feedback, of getting his staff to bond.

While this explanation may hold true on occasion, it distorts the motivation for most dirty joke telling. Dirty jokes are most often told by the insecure—both men and women. They have little confidence in being able to impress others with who they really are so they do something outlandish or out of place in an attempt to display "courage" in defying the system. For men, these jokes usually serve as attempts to portray macho bravado, especially to impress and intimidate women. Lacking self-esteem, the teller usually has poor judgment as to propriety and timing.

Another tack used by backlashers to discredit the sexual harassment issue is to claim that widespread sexual harassment charges hurt women by making business executives wary of hiring women and granting them entrance to inner circles of power. (Hmmm, interesting admission considering that backlashers claim that men have no power advantage over women.) This may be true, but are women then supposed to sacrifice their personal integrity and subject themselves to improper sexual advances and sexual intimidation in the workplace in order to make paranoid executives feel secure? That's like holding women's advancement hostage to men's sexual discretion.

Some women do indeed abuse men by making unwarranted sexual harassment charges. But it is far more common for men to sexually harass women. Women need sexual harassment laws to protect them. Male executives must be willing to admit that their fellows are the primary cause of these laws. Then they must demonstrate their leadership in the workplace by outwardly communicating their concern with the sexual harassment issue.

Sexual attraction can occur anywhere. However, people have an obligation to control their sexual impulses at work. Both men and women are guilty of failing to do so. Granted, it is hard to do since all of us are driven by the biological urge to bond with the opposite gender and our jobs occupy a large segment of our time while providing much of our social contact. Unfortunately our job—the means we use to provide for our physical survival—has biological priority over sexual fulfillment (no eat, no sex). It is possible to ethically pursue romance at work. But if one wishes to follow this course they must realize they do so at their own heavy risk.

In summation, the only men who have difficulty understanding "why sexual harassment is a big issue for women" are those who don't want to understand. They want to be able to pursue their self-indulgent, aggressive sexual behavior without restriction. And backlashers defend them.

"Discrimination" Against Women Has Often Benefitted Them

This is another big one for backlashers. They redefine "discrimination," as defined by feminists, to make it appear as if men are actually performing a service. Backlashers claim that since women have their so-called "oppressors" (men) laboring to support them, women cannot be truly "oppressed" after all.

Here, of course, the definitions of the subject words have been neatly twisted. When you claim something as a possession you must work to maintain it. A house or car cannot maintain itself. Nor can a wife, if her husband chooses to keep her from supporting herself or has assigned her in-home work duties crucial to their marriage. In most cases he is working to support a lifestyle that he prefers which includes maintaining a subservient woman at home to give him approval, sex and children.

Backlashers also claim that when marriage was the norm and divorce was rare, discrimination in favor of men at work acted in favor of their wives at home. This is a clever way of rationalizing gender discrimination in the work place. Men need preference in the work place because they must support dependent women, therefore giving men preference works not for the benefit of men but rather for women. It follows that working women should not feel put upon when they are victimized by male preference in the workplace. If they are loyal to their gender they must be prepared to sacrifice so that homemakers can benefit.

Backlashers even go so far as claiming that polygyny served women more than men by giving more women access to men of means. This assertion neatly ignores why women must attach themselves to men of means and have no access to substantial means of their own. The culprit, of course, is patriarchal regulation, which takes from women the option of supporting themselves.

Women's Yearning for Liberation and Male Mid-Life Crisis Are Driven by The Same Need

I won't devote much space here to trying to refute this charge. I've devoted the entire book to that task. All that needs to be said here is that men's mid-life crisis has been brought upon by their failure to take responsibility for their lives and exercise the power available to them to make changes. They have bought into the system while women have been struggling to obtain the power to make changes in the system. As one feminist put it:

Women are fighting for their lives; men for peace of mind.

We've Never Had Patriarchy; Patriarchy Was Inevitable; Women Must Lead Reluctant Men To Patriarchy

These three theories, although irreconcilable, are all propounded by male backlashers in their effort to legitimatize the system we have been functioning under for centuries. Backlashers seem willing to grasp at any concept they can use to defend a system that places power in the hands of men. Some efforts are outright attacks. Others are smoke screens attempting to confuse. Still others are labyrinths of cleverly twisted logic designed to exhaust those trying to refute them. Many of these efforts would conflict if compared with each other. But backlashers don't argue with each other (just as we were willing to accept Stalin as an ally during WWII). They attack women's views, trying to keep women on the defensive and maintain a system that can only be described as a patriarchy.

I refer to a standard Webster's Dictionary definition of patriarchy: "A form of social organization in which the father or the eldest male is recognized as the head of the family or tribe, descent and kinship being traced through the male line."

In trying to debunk the assertion that we live in a patriarchal system, Farrell prefers to use a radical feminist definition: "The universal political structure which privileges men at the expense of women."

I've already discussed at length Farrell's claim that a true patriarchy never existed. Obviously I don't agree with him. I think both definitions of patriarchy have merit and both fit the system we currently live under.

A more direct defense of our patriarchal social system has been spearheaded by Stephen Goldberg. In the 1970s he began writing a series of books personified by the title of one: *The Inevitability of Patriarchy*. Goldberg presents the traditional patriarchal arguments regarding man's superior strength, male hormone stimulated aggression, and patriarchy's universality, among other things, to back his claim that patriarchy has always served the best interests of humankind. I have been addressing these arguments throughout this book so I will not do so here.

In contrast to Farrell and Goldberg, an English sociologist, Geoff Dench, has found an even more convoluted method to defend male domination. He portrays men as irresponsible, in need of being bribed with power to get them to accept their proper role. In a recent book Dench writes:

> The woman who submits to marriage is the one whose sacrifice unleashes the latent altruism in men and integrates the community. The independent woman undermines and challenges this.

He suggests that feminists do womanhood a disservice by advocating that women share equal authority and play the same roles as men. He claims that the typical man naturally tends to shy away from responsibility. Men can see no advantage in sacrificing a life of freedom in order to accept family responsibilities on equal terms with women. A single man can run about and pursue selfish interests, while a mated man must burden himself with providing for wife and children. Men must therefore be coerced into accepting community responsibility and the best way to accomplish this is for women to exalt them and give them power.

This argument has appeal to both genders—men because it advocates their maintaining power over women; women because they see so many modern men shirking responsibility. In a backhanded way, women are praised. It is they who are sensitive to community needs. It is they who are more aware and evolved. And in reality because of this it is they who hold the power. Men need them for sex and ego-stroking.

At the same time, men are demeaned. They are painted as lacking community concern and self-motivation. If they are to play their proper role in the community they must be manipulated by women.

But this can only take place through coercion—not confrontation, for the latter will only drive men away into a world of idleness and trivial diversions.

Women must therefore use their greater wisdom to maneuver men away from their propensity to idleness. They must get men to accept responsibility by placing men in a position of authority, making them the exclusive power within the family. Women can only do this by remaining primarily in the home environment as caretakers and raisers of children. Only then will men view themselves as indispensable in their role is as primary provider. In clinging to the resulting ego gratification men will devote themselves to their families.

If women invade men's realm by seeking careers while asking men to perform domestic duties, they remove that which attracts men to accept responsibility. Single life beckons once again and we find ourselves with a flood of deadbeat fathers and abandoned women and children.

Of course, this means that in order to keep a man dedicated to his family responsibilities, a woman must subordinate her own natural desires and interests to his. Even so, women can take solace in knowing that they are truly in control.

This backlash approach appears to chastise men and disapprove of their attitude and behavior even as it absolves men of responsibility for their actions and places it upon women. Accepting a little guilt is a small price to pay for maintaining men's privileged position under patriarchy. It's like trying to get off by copping a plea.

The backlash charges discussed above represent only a portion of those being unleashed. They come from and appeal to men who are hurting. In typical fashion, these men have responded to age-old conditioning and reacted to pain with anger (in contrast to the conditioned woman who will often cry). But instead of directing their anger toward the source of their pain—the system their gender has created and which they have supported—they attack women for not remaining compliant to the system, thereby increasing men's pain.

Feminism indeed suffers a shortcoming in ignoring or downplaying the pain suffered by men in our social system. But women have been suffering pain of their own—the pain of being enslaved to the wills of men (in my view, a pain far greater than that experienced by men).

If you care about someone and they show unreasonable anger toward you, you hold your ground, but it serves no useful purpose to counterattack with unreasonable anger of your own. However, if their anger is justified you accept it, apologize and seek to rectify what you've done. The secret to a caring relationship is listening and being willing to modify behavior. We, as men, should care about women and listen more. Listening, even to unwarranted charges, without counterattacking, brings the genders closer together.

Backlashers would argue that women aren't listening to us and therefore must not care about us. To a degree this may be true, but that doesn't justify our behaving similarly. A mature, well meaning, psychologically fit human being concerns him/herself with the propriety of their own behavior first.

If at times women go too far in making charges, that is their issue. As men, we should not try to use it to escape ours. Indeed, we should be grateful for their charges. These have pointed to us the way, not only to free women, but to throw off our own shackles. To attack women only distracts men from coming to grips with the forces that truly enslave them—those inherent in the patriarchal system.

Chapter Six
The Men's Movement

Most men use backlash argument to fortify their inertia. However, a small but significant number of them do respond by taking action. Each year thousands of men, seeking to escape a haunting lack of fulfillment, follow the urging of poet Robert Bly and retreat to areas of seclusion with their fellows to seek access to the "Wild Man" inside. Those who participate would lead us to believe that the men's groups which sustain these gatherings constitute a significant "movement." It has been labeled "Mythopoetic," due to its heavy reliance on ritual and storytelling as teaching tools.

As with all "movements," philosophies, theologies, etc., one can find variance in the approach used in individual groups, depending on the personality, personal issues, and personal priorities of the facilitators. However, generally this variance is small. Most group members and facilitators accept the mythopoetic approach and ideals as expressed in the writings of movement leaders such as Bly.

Robert Bly and Iron John

The importance of Bly in this movement cannot be overstated. He conducts his own Mythopoetic gatherings and is often quoted at those held by others. In spite of the fact that his main claim to fame is as a poet and lecturer, he has served as mentor to many trained psychologists and psychoanalysts involved in men's work. Many facilitators see themselves as his disciples.

That in mind, it seems appropriate here to examine the most famous work of Bly, *Iron John*. This book has served as the primary scripture to the Mythopoetic movement. It gives us deep insight into the man who has served as the movement's main architect.

The inspiration behind *Iron John* seems to spring from Bly's stated distaste for what he sees as widespread passivity in modern men. He views this in stark contrast to men of old who were called on to "pierce the dangerous places, carry handfuls of courage to the waterfalls, dust the tails of wild boars." He deplores the degradation of man's hunting instinct, suggesting that parents misstep when they ask their sons to "bypass hunting and go directly to ethics."

And so Bly in his lectures and men-only conferences explores such concepts as male archetypes, the masculine soul, masculine hunting energy, fierceness, and feminized men. He seeks to reawaken men to a birthright he sees as eroding away under the incessant pressure of modern society coupled with inadequate parenthood.

In *Iron John* Bly weaves philosophy around a myth. The ancient story features a wild man who serves as the mentor of a young boy. Ultimately "Wild Man" rescues the boy from meek, purposeless boyhood and turns him into a "fierce," wise young man who through the exercise of real manhood wins a king's daughter and a kingdom as well as his own lost royal birthright. Bly pauses frequently in the telling to draw lengthy parallels to young men growing up in our modern society.

"Wild Man" represents raw masculine energy and instinct, untempered by female influence or cultural conditioning. Bly says that inside each male resides "a large, primitive being covered with hair down to his feet." He further asserts that if a man is to ever self-actualize and find his true masculine identity he must connect with his "Wild Man" and learn to honor its counsel even as he continues his life in this society. That means periodically retreating from our culture to areas of solitude where nature remains preserved and "Wild Man" feels more at home. Eons ago, when man was a hunter/gatherer, he allowed "Wild Man" to run free and guide him. Man was a connected creature, with a healthy relationship to the environment. A boy had a clear road to masculinity and manhood. Men might face physical threats to survival, but not confusion concerning their manhood. So says Bly.

While Bly's assertion that a major portion of a man's true character lies submerged seems astute, he fails to point out that this anomaly is not unique to men. Character suppression in women has probably caused them even deeper wounds, for they have not only become disconnected from themselves, but they have also been forced into subservience to disconnected men.

I cannot quarrel with Bly's verdict that disconnection is the problem. However, his metaphoric description of "Wild Man" portrays man's genuine inner character as based upon aggressiveness and a proclivity to indulge in combat. Bly's "hairy" being (he uses this graphic description for obvious effect, stating, "hair suggests all forms of animal hotbloodedness") does not engender patience and nurturing qualities which are also a crucial part of man's inner psyche. Nor does it acknowledge that intelligence (which one might characterize by hairlessness), rather than brute force, has been humanity's primary survival tool and has allowed us (seemingly against our will) to transcend beasthood.

Bly further emphasizes (to the scorn of many feminists) that many modern men have found easy access to softer qualities and by overly indulging in them have become "feminized." These assertions suggest that softer qualities cannot lie at the deepest levels of masculinity. Bly implies—whether intentional or not—that primitive assertiveness untempered is what forms the basic essence of a true man.

Iron John has drawn considerable flak from feminists. They find Bly's advocacy of men recovering lost "fierceness" by trying to access the "Wild Man" hidden inside, alarming. Bly contends that the fierceness embodied in "Wild Man" need not be destructive and is an essential ingredient of all genuine men. But feminists are highly doubtful and wary, for women throughout the ages have been victims of men going wild.

Their suspicions of Bly would seem warranted because throughout his book he makes statements and paints metaphors which place men and women at odds. He makes it clear that he believes in "masculine and feminine realms." He states in no uncertain terms that he views men and women as opposites. In most of his metaphors, often in a subtle, clever manner, he paints women as detriments to men's growth.

His advocates will quickly point out that he admits that women have been subjugated in the past and are regularly mistreated today by many men. He even outwardly states that he respects the feminist movement. However, except in rare circumstances, his group activities exclude women. It is difficult to see how he can respect feminism—a movement seeking inclusion of women in society's power structure—and at the same time blame women for many of men's ills and exclude them from what he sees as healing activities.

The following statements in *Iron John* further cast doubt on his claim to respecting women and their contribution to humanity:

When women, even women with the best intentions, bring up a boy alone, he may in some way have no male face, or he may have no face at all.

A clean break with the mother is crucial, but it's simply not happening.

Women can change the embryo to a boy, but only men can change a boy to a man.

It's becoming clear to us that manhood doesn't happen by itself; it doesn't happen just because we eat Wheaties. The active intervention of the older men means that older men welcome the younger man into the ancient, mythologized, instinctive male world.

She (mother) dreams: 'My son the doctor.' 'My son the Jungian analyst. 'My son the Wall Street Genius.' But very few mothers dream: 'My son the Wild Man.' (Statement attributed to Michael Meade, endorsed by Bly.)

This last statement implies, of course, that women purposely stand in the way of men finding their true manhood, which Bly calls the "Unity of Personality." In his story he represents this as the "Golden Ball."

The boy's "Golden Ball" has fallen into the hands of "Wild Man," who is imprisoned within the boy's father's castle. "Wild Man" refuses to return the ball unless he is set free. The key to the cage, however, lies beneath the mother's pillow and she will not voluntarily surrender it.

Bly states, "the boy must steal the key." This statement further demonstrates his view that women purposely stand in the way of male psychological growth. He advocates the aggressive defiance of female authority by stating, "Getting the ball back is incompatible with certain kinds of conventional tameness and niceness."

It's hard to see how these statements could come from a man who respects women following their own course and reaching their full natural potential outside the influence of men. Rather they seem to fit in nicely with the view of a man who respects women only if they remain subservient to men. Of course, one can embrace either viewpoint and still lay claim to respecting women. The term "respect" can be loosely interpreted.

Furthermore, Bly seems to stand as an advocate of patriarchy when he states: "Much of the rage that some women direct to the patriarchy stems from a vast disappointment over lack of teaching from their own fathers." Does this mean that a "good father" will teach (condition?) his daughters to see the light and accept patriarchy? For thousands of years men have been accomplishing this very thing. Bly seems to be saying that "good fathers" embrace patriarchy. Patriarchy is the ideal state. And thus, the feminists are, and have been, all wrong.

Bly's attitude toward women resembles that of Ronald Reagan (a man who Bly criticizes) toward the unfortunate. Reagan appeared to experience genuine compassion when making direct contact with people suffering from poverty or illness. But when he was isolated from them in his official capacities as President and Governor he seemed to focus completely on the best interests of his preferred constituency—the elite. He canceled and gutted programs, showing no compassion for the unfortunate and adding to the Misery Index, all the while bemoaning the plight of the poor.

Likewise Bly appears to (at least superficially) recognize and regret women's plight. But by conceptually polarizing the genders and placing men in the leadership role through the exercise of "warrior energy," he fortifies that approach which dooms women to a subservient position without prospect for full self-actualization. He has inspired mythopoetic groups to build a superstructure of "truths" based on myths which prop up a belief system that encourages men to remain separate, combative and dominating.

Consider his following statement:

> The Greeks understood and praised a positive male energy that has accepted authority. They called it Zeus energy, which encompasses intelligence, robust health, compassionate decisiveness, good will, generous leadership. Zeus energy is male authority accepted for the sake of the community." And later: "All the great cultures except ours preserve and have lived with images of this positive male energy.

Where does woman fit into this, except as a subservient partner? Is it any wonder that few mothers dream, "My son the wild man" when in our culture the release of "wild man" has always led to remoteness from, and subjugation of, women?

Is Bly using the term "wild" in the same context as feminists? I'm sure he would say no. He makes the distinction between the instinct for fierceness and the instinct for aggression. He recognizes that destructive wildness is common and would assure us that his "Wild Man" is constructive. But can we accept this?

In presenting his concept of "wild man" Bly idealizes what he calls "warrior energy." Once again he goes on at length explaining how this phenomenon need not include all the implications that surround combat and can be channeled into constructive pursuits. In particular, it serves men well when it fuels actions which resist tyrannical acts and corrects wrongs. We might define this feeling of justified outrage as righteous indignation.

Who can argue with the ideal of a man (or a woman) tapping into a special energy source in the defense of high principles? Even some of the world's greatest peacemakers have seen the need to call upon an inner source of forceful energy generated by righteous indignation. Bly would have us believe that motivation of this type in the pursuit of noble causes validates his concept of "warrior energy." However, certain of his examples raise doubts as to his full comprehension of the ramifications of his own concept.

In particular, he laments the loss of the "warrior spirit" in the modern soldier. He cites an example from medieval times where a knight proclaimed his "love" for the other knights who served with him battle. According to Bly these men had established a loving brotherhood in sharing dangers and laying their lives on the line for shared beliefs. Their coming to know each other intimately in pursuit of this cause elicted shared "love."

Bly contrasts this to modern soldiers fighting in masses, being slaughtered by the hundreds of thousands almost in anonymity. Most have no belief in or understanding of the cause. Usually they have been deceived by their government. And often, if they return home it is to an ungrateful citizenry oblivious to the horrors and sacrifices endured on the battlefield. Bly sees no genuine "warrior energy" here.

It's difficult to find fault with the second half of his argument. But let's further examine the first half.

Does his example of medieval knighthood reflect "warrior energy" in a positive context? The fact that men have bonded and are working closely in pursuit of a common goal carries no virtue unless the goal they are pursuing has virtue.

Bly never examined what these knights were fighting for. (History tells us that most knights fought to advance their selfish ambitions and worshipped fighting because they embraced violence as the tool for settling disputes. Justice was regularly meted out through trial by combat.) "Love" of the type he describes is often shared between gang rapists, outlaw bands and marauding armies. For him to admire it casts suspicion, not necessarily on the concept of "warrior energy," but on the merit of his interpretation. Thus feminists would seem to have a case for doubting his veracity.

Warriorhood has always been used for aggression as well as defense. Bly acknowledges this and says that aggressors have degraded themselves and become "soldiers" rather than "warriors." To him a "warrior" only fights for a greater cause. But ultimately who stands in judgment on the worthiness of a cause?

Bly's "madman soldier" who "rapes, pillages, kills mindlessly, and napalms entire villages," has been a hero to millions who saw him acting to defend "higher principles" (e.g. prevention of the spread of communism).

Hitler saw Jews and races of color as evil. By destroying them he was serving a cause greater than himself. Upward of fifty million ethnic Germans agreed with him to varying degrees.

Bly claims that Oliver North served a "corrupt king" and thus furthered an evil cause. But millions of Americans did not agree.

By Bly's definition, all combatants see themselves as "warriors" rather than "soldiers." Each one of them claims they fight for a "worthy cause" even as they fight each other.

The worship of "warrior energy" is usually based on the view that enemies or evil forces exist that must be combatted. These usually take the form of other men (seldom women, for this has always been a male thing) who seek to inflict harm by direct attack or by infringing upon property and/or values. (Seldom do men any longer have to exert "warrior energy" against forces in the environment— wild animals, etc.—to effect survival.) "Warrior energy" is usually needed to combat these other men who, of course, possess their own quantities of "warrior energy" and are using it to fuel their aggressions.

So what do we have here? The misuse of "warrior energy" promulgates the need for "warrior energy." Distorted malehood (in its misuse of "warrior energy") aggressing upon other males forces the victims to embrace the aggressors' distorted values in order to survive. The importance of "warrior energy" swells far beyond what nature intended. It becomes a focus rather than a tool to be selectively used.

If men were to surrender the need to aggress upon each other, "warrior energy" would vastly diminish in importance. The energy inside would not necessarily diminish, but both men and women could devote it to creative projects. We would then no longer classify it as "warrior energy."

I'm not so sure that in their current collective state of mind that men would like this. They seem to feel less than men when unable to direct this inner energy toward aggressive pursuits. How could they surrender something they view as the main source of their self-esteem?

Bly proudly advocates men's combativeness and admits, "the warrior loves the battlefield." However Bly doesn't seem to see that anyone who loves fighting will embrace it to the exclusion of other methods of resolving disputes. They will seek to pick fights because their self-esteem is based upon prevailing in combat. As long as men love combat how will we ever rid the planet of conflict?

Bly asserts that the willingness to argue and debate is another manifestation of "warrior energy"—one that does not necessarily lead to physical confrontation. I would agree, if these encounters took on the nature of discussions in which the participants were truly seeking solutions to problems. What we most commonly see, however, is ego-centered advocates seeking to foist their opinions on others in order to dominate intellectually. The spirit of idea exchange is too often lacking. These "debates" seldom solve anything. Instead they often heighten tension to where the only solution is to determine who is physically dominant. Even Sam Keen admits: "When politics reaches a point of impotence, the warrior's imagination turns immediately to the use of force."

True, in Western society we seldom see debates end in fisticuffs. But this is most attributable to the enforcement of laws against fighting, not restraint by the participants. All this debating, contesting and arguing fosters a combative spirit and thwarts the growth of harmony.

Does that mean that men (or women) should never fight? Of course it doesn't! The key here is one's attitude toward fighting. One should never enter combat without regret. The "warrior energy" that Bly refers to should only be used as a last resort. The energy tied up in warrior pursuits has a much more constructive use addressing challenges that do not involve fighting with people. To fight others may be occasionally necessary, but it is a pitiful waste of a resource that should be used for creating. It should be viewed as such. Only thus can one who fights claim justification for his acts.

This addiction to combative pursuits brings to mind General Patton. During the height of World War II (a time one would hardly call normal) Patton felt most alive when in the midst of a combat zone. Indeed, the thought of being left out of the fighting drove him to distraction. War—planning for it and waging it—was all he lived for. He acted mercilessly toward the enemy and ruthlessly toward his own men. And in the process he became indispensible to his country because these qualities were needed to subdue the enemy (fueled by their own reservoir of "warrior energy") and Patton possessed them to a higher degree than other American generals. He became America's most successful fighting general and thrived on those challenges which demanded his bringing his "warrior energy" to bear.

But when the war drew to a close, Patton was suddenly without a purpose. He even tried to create one by advocating war with the Russians—a conflict that promised to be even more bloody than the one just concluded. He was a man who possessed a seemingly inexhaustible supply of "warrior energy" and suddenly found no outlet for it. Why? Because all his life he had identified his inner energy source with combat.

In *Iron John* Bly specifically denounces Patton's misuse of "warrior energy." But apparently he doesn't recognize that the breeding of the type of "warrior energy" he describes (devoid of softness and nurturing qualities) naturally leads to mentalities such as Patton's. For a warrior, by definition, is a fighting man who engages in warfare. Even if the definition were to carry connotations of behavior modified by peaceful intent, which it doesn't, the primary defining characteristic of a warrior is his focus upon fighting.

Bly's view dovetails nicely with this for he implies that softer qualities are feminine and men who practice them are feminized. Based on this we can only conclude that his concept of "warrior energy" is devoid of the softer qualities. And lacking them, "warrior energy" can hardly help but breed a Patton mentality.

Warriors—those who identify themselves and their deepest energies with subduing enemies—lose their purpose when conflict ends. Therefore to maintain their sanity they must find enemies to subdue and conflicts to wage. Men like this exist everywhere. And so, throughout his book Bly hints that we live in a world where warriorhood is essential. Upon this he bases his analysis.

Only a fool would try to maintain that our world is not consistently burdened with conflict. But if our goal is to evolve as human beings and to truly create a peaceful world, then we must identify the "warrior spirit" as a distortion, only occasionally necessary when survival is at stake. The hidden wellsprings of energy inside all of us must not be identified as "warrior energy." We may have to occasionally tap that energy to wage war, but that should be done with regret, not with pride. To identify oneself as a warrior is dangerous to one's psyche and proliferates to others who would otherwise become peacemakers.

Bly seeks to further fortify his theory by relating aspects of his myth to gender roles in modern society. He is particularly attentive to the role of the mother, whom he suggests is a detriment to the growth of her son. He sees many women today playing the same role.

What is conveniently overlooked is that the mother in *Iron John* is a product of a patriarchal society. She is not free to self-actuate naturally, according to her true instincts. Rather, she has evolved in a distorted world where "warrior energy" reigns and physical power dictates. Likely, (although Bly has left her character thinly sketched and has not presented her thusly in his story) since her physical power is limited, such a woman would have learned to be cunning and devious so that she could wield a measure of power and control over her life through manipulating men.

One area of power she would cling to is control of her son. And why shouldn't she? She lives in a world where women's physical security depends upon the good will of those men close to them. Her son is an insurance policy against a future without a husband.

Is her attitude proper? Not in an egalitarian society. But men created such a society in which women could not control their own destinies. By doing so they brought on the mutation of women into creatures who had to steal power in order to survive with some measure of self-respect. If in the process, women become a threat to boys, then men made them so.

We can see how the patriarchy establishes its own moral grounds to perpetuate itself. Patriarchal men place women into a subservient position. Seeking security, many of these women control their sons' growth by clinging. This tends to make these sons sympathetic to the plight of females ("feminizes" according to Bly) and therefore not as capable of taking on patriarchal responsibilities which include maintaining power over women. Patriarchal men must therefore wrest their sons away from their wives. In the process they feel justified in maintaining dominance over these weak, misguided women. After all, women, as evidenced by their propensity to smother boys, pose a danger to manhood and must therefore be kept in their place. It's all very neat and "rational." That is, if you subscribe to patriarchy.

But the self-actuated woman, one who is allowed to evolve naturally with access to power outside of bondage, will have a completely different outlook on her sons. She will have no need to "smother" them because her own physical security is not a factor in their raising. She will not face a husband whose goal is to turn the boy into a dominant patriarch. Culture will allow the boy to equally value those aspects of both father and mother that have heretofore been classified as "masculine" and "feminine." She will be happy to see her sons introduced to the "father's world"—a world defined by the biological characteristics which separate male from female.

But first the "father's world" must be a genuine world, not one evolving from a neurotic/psychotic attachment to the "warrior spirit." Also, the "father's world" must not be defined as separate from that of women. It must simply expose all children to the unique view of the world dictated by physical differences possessed by men.

Like so many other men and feminists, Bly presents a bifurcated view of the human species. He embraces the concept of natural pairs of opposites, citing: light and dark, limited and unlimited, the resting and the moving, the one and the many, odd and even, and, of course, male and female.

But all of these "pairs of opposites" are opposite only in the view of the beholder. If indeed "natural opposites" do exist, they are very rare. The concept of "natural opposites" is a way of looking at things which may be common, but not necessarily correct nor even universal. If one were to look more closely they would see that virtually all subject pairs that are viewed as opposites are really contrasts.

For example, take Bly's comparison of dark and light. Dark is the absence of light, but light exists in varying degrees, from the dimmest glow to intense starlight of unlimited brightness. A perceptive person recognizes that light and dark are not opposites at all.

Similarly, this person recognizes that we live in a universe of comparative movement. In effect, nothing is at rest. An object may only appear to be because it is moving at the same rate and in the same direction as the observer.

Arguments based on such perceived "opposites" appeal to the gullible and lazy-minded. Pedagogues conveniently use these subjective, often erroneous, comparisons to prove points which cannot otherwise stand up to sound reasoning.

To Bly and the mythopoets it is important to embrace the concept of "pairs of opposites" in order to keep masculinity and femininity separate. He can thus proceed to validate his gender concepts such as, "ancient, mythologized, instinctive male world."

Bly bemoans the absence of fatherhood in modern society but does not seem to recognize that it may be directly linked to the gender polarization attitudes he advocates. The male perception that men must remain distinctly separate as a gender and develop distinctly different views from those embraced by women tends to discourage men from exhibiting those nurturing qualities necessary to a good father. After all, nurturing is considered a feminine attribute.

Many modern men, because of their fear of being classified as feminine, find nurturing difficult. Too often they run from any responsibility that calls for it. They can even find justification for this in Bly's concepts of gender difference which fortify the age-old perception that independence is a birthright of true manhood. By embracing this view men find easy excuses for allowing physical or emotional distance from their children.

The story of *Iron John* is a medieval myth. Throughout Bly's book he reaches back to other myths and prior times, implying that men were more enlightened in the past; that in other cultures men were more self-actualized. Can we really accept this?

Most other historical civilizations—virtually all of which have been patriarchies—ultimately deteriorated and collapsed. In the process they degraded their women and killed and enslaved millions of people. Those existing cultures from which Bly gleans inspiration are primitive and in stasis, their members living short lifespans of backbreaking labor, stalked by disease and bereft of spiritual growth. Would anyone seriously suggest that we should look to these people as examples?

If we are to solve our plight as a society we must look beyond what has gone before. Other failed cultures can teach us lessons, but none have ever achieved a satisfactory level of civilization. Most have embraced the warrior philosophy and that as much as anything is what destroyed them. We have the capability of evolving beyond that.

Carl Jung and the Mythopoets

The use of myth, archetypes, "natural opposites," gender stereotypes, and the general classification of behavior traits as either masculine and feminine, closely adheres to the theories of Carl Jung. Indeed, a number of the more active facilitators of the Mythopoetic movement are psychologists who consider themselves Jungian. They openly expound his theories to give their work an air of authority.

Jung's views of gender have alienated the vast majority of feminists, many of whom have extensive background in psychological studies. It is no wonder why, since many of his statements reek with sexism. The following two quotes are examples of an attitude that abounds in his work:

> They (women) are so empty that a man is free to impute to them anything he fancies. In addition, they are so unconscious that the unconscious puts out countless invisible feelers, veritable octopus-tentacles, that suck up all the masculine projections; and this pleases men enormously. All that feminine indefiniteness is the longed-for counterpart of male decisiveness and single-mindedness, which can be satisfactorily achieved only if a man can get rid of everything doubtful, ambiguous, vague, and muddled by projecting it upon some charming example of feminine innocence. Because of the woman's characteristic passivity, and the feelings of inferiority which make her continually play the injured innocent, the man finds himself cast

in an attractive role.

> It should be remarked that emptiness is a great feminine secret. It is something absolutely alien to man; the chasm, the unplumbed depths, the yin. The pitifulness of this vacuous nonentity goes to his heart (I speak here as a man), and one is tempted to say that this constitutes the whole "mystery" of women. Such a female is fate itself. A man may say what he likes about it; be for it or against it, or both at once, in the end he falls, absurdly happy, into this pit, or, if he doesn't, he has missed and bungled his only chance of making a man of himself.

Psychologist/feminist Demaris Wehr, who is receptive to other Jungian views, comments:

> Describing women in these terms does nothing to restore their sense of worth, nor does it address the issue of woundedness of women in patriarchy who end up 'empty.' Even though this passage has a romantic overtone, it is damaging to women to be seen and described as 'other.' As a result of the prevalence of such descriptions, women learn to experience themselves in alienated terms.

Of course it also fortifies men's view of themselves as superior. It gives the mythopoets "sound, scientific basis" upon which to base their programs. Jung's determination to construct a psychological reality which views the genders as opposite fits neatly into the mythopoetic approach which conceptually seeks to set the genders apart from each other. It also allows mythopoets to address their issues without having to surrender their perceived gender superiority.

The Mythopoetic Format

Mythopoetic groups who take inspiration from Robert Bly and his colleagues offer certain assets to men who are seeking to find inner peace. They also engender (no pun intended) serious negatives.

By embracing Bly's view, then urging men to form groups that meet exclusive of women to focus entirely on what they perceive as masculine issues, mythopoets deepen the divisions between the genders. By identifying with their gender first, they turn women into adversarial spirits and drive a spiritual wedge between them-selves and females.

This they adamantly deny. They claim that by accessing their hith-erto repressed true masculinity they can forge closer bonds with their mates and their children. But when one considers himself a man first, then a member of the human family, his loyalty will be first to his concept of manhood and second to his family. And if mythopoets did not consider themselves men first, they would not find it necessary to gather themselves in groups away from women in order to "heal." Men's group leader, Aaron Kipnis admits this when he says:

> It's important not to enter the combat ground between the sexes prematurely or naively. If too much attention is given to this sort of work it can be at the expense of men contacting and healing their own pain. First men must find their own mythology, solidarity, alli-ance, brotherhood, and sacred relationship to other men and the earth.

We can see from his statement that Kipnis believes men's affilia-tion to their gender holds primacy over affiliation to the species.

Mythopoets, in general, prefer not to admit that they hold this view. Yet their writings reek of it and they structure the format of their gatherings to fortify gender identification and division. These fol-low a typical pattern although they may vary slightly depending on the theme chosen for each. Kipnis describes the motivation behind this format:

> When you meet with men, then meet with men. Don't have a woman near the meeting space, no matter how much positive regard or re-latedness she shares with you. Men's-lodge space is a private, sacred space. Since the dawn of time men in every culture have met alone and in secret to approach their gods and find their collective magic.

Thus, during their retreats mythopoets seldom, if ever, mention women's issues much less discuss how many of these issues are directly attributable to men. If women are discussed, the subject usually revolves around how they are a detriment to men or how men can maintain their gender identification while relating to them. The fact that women and their issues are crucial to the well being of the human community is not considered. The fact that women live perpetually in physical fear of men is not acknowledged. Mythopoetic men are encouraged to be kind to women, but more in the spirit of showing courtesy to something foreign rather than in acknowledging that women and their specific issues carry equal status to men and theirs.

Kipnis again:

> The transformation we wish to effect is the creation of a balanced partnership between men and women. However, it's important for us to develop ourselves as men without our soul work being defined, directed, or controlled by women. So we need to tread slowly on this path. It's important to hold a strong boundary around our men's meetings and not give them up to do this gender work.

Mythopoets commonly further fortify that consciousness of difference that breeds dissension by dividing their groups into subgroups which they refer to as clans. By their nature these subgroups ask members to identify with characteristics or issues which separate them from the other subgroups. Each subgroup meets in isolation and soon the members begin to feel closer bonds to their subgroup brothers than to the full group. A spirit of competition is aroused. Instead of this being addressed as a detriment—the alienation from, and loss of empathy for, other subgroup members—it is, in effect, condoned by being overlooked.

The overall result is to fortify the age-old destructive male urge to accent differences between men, then isolate from those different. In society this attitude has always resulted in discrimination, attempts to dominate, conflict, and ultimately, war. Thus in this misguided effort to promote bonds of brotherhood mythopoets ultimately promote a spirit of divisiveness. This harmful approach is a major men's issue and should be examined in the group setting with the intent of rooting it out. Instead it receives fortification through justification and is carried back into society.

Another counterproductive Mythopoetic viewpoint is the advocacy of ritual. Mythopoets claim that ritual is a major welding force in the human community and that its absence in modern western culture has left our society adrift. In particular, they bemoan the absence of rites of passage for young men. They link this to the absence of proper fathering and in their effort to redefine manhood during the mythopoetic gatherings, make ritual a focus of the program.

But can ritual transform children into adult human beings? If a boy has not psychologically evolved over several years to place himself on the brink of manhood, can a ritual suddenly make him a man? Can we take an immature 18 year old, cut skin off his penis, or drive hooks through muscles on his chest and hang him from a tree, or send him out with primitive weapons to kill a wild beast, or isolate him from women, and suddenly expect the experience to turn him into a man? Anyone who accepts that theory has a very limited view of what manhood is. Ritual can place a label of manhood on a boy, but it cannot impart the depth of maturity that denotes true manhood.

The negative influence of ritual is not limited to rites of passage. Ritual can provide direction to a directionless society, but anthropologists have found that it is usually blind direction. Societies that depend heavily on ritual have difficulty advancing. Members are forbidden to question who and what went before. They're discouraged from reaching inside to their creative source to improve conditions or correct immoral practices (consider the Nazi youth groups which mesmerized young people into carrying out the atrocities inspired by Hitler). Instead they are conditioned to accept the teachings of the elders. Societies stagnate (or worse), their members remaining stuck at a level determined by past generations. This hardly looks like the type of culture to which we should look for guidance.

Much of Mythopoetic ritual is practiced amidst a serenade of tribal drumming. The expressed intent is to encourage participants to open up to the creative side of themselves and to feel free to express those impulses generated by the pure soul—the inner "wild man." The result, however, is to fortify the aggressive side of men while ignoring a need to express softer, compassionate feelings.

The staccato nature of drumming encourages high energy, frantic, herky-jerky movement more characteristic of violence than nurturing. Drummers would contest this, claiming that certain rhythm patterns actually portray softer feelings. This is arguable, but can anyone honestly maintain that the softest drum rhythm can compete with the soft strains of wind or string instruments in representing soft emotions? Serious composers of program music have for the past two centuries demonstrated to us that this is not the case.

In fact, the Mythopoets seldom if ever perform the softer rhythms.

A gathering of Mythopoetic drummers almost immediately bursts out into high energy rapid staccato drumming. The dancing that accompanies mythopoetic drumming is usually dominated by wild movements that simulate aggression, dominance and frenzy.

If mythopoets were to justify their use of drumming as a method of involving all participants, even the musically inept (after all, anyone can beat on a drum), in their various programs, I would grant them their point. But instead, mythopoets sanctify drumming as a mystical experience exclusive of that received from other musical instruments. They defend their energetic style as representing the human heartbeat in various states of excitement—love, ecstasy, exercise, fast dancing, sex, joy, etc.

What they don't explain is why they nearly always gravitate to agitated drumming. Does not the heart beat slowly, too? Don't men value those activities which take place when the body is satisfied and the soul is at peace. The history of man would indicate not.

The passionate striking of drumskins reminds the observer of man's propensity to strike out physically against others when agitated. It's also a reminder of the millions of men who have marched off to war to the compelling rhythm of the drums. Mythopoetic drumming would seem to be celebrating man's negative history rather than paving the way for a constructive future.

Men's deepest problem has been a psyche overbalanced in favor of aggression. His aggressive side is the easiest for him to access. Mythopoetic groups would learn far more by exposing themselves to gentler forms of music which represent the softer emotions.

Finally, Mythopoetic gatherings encourage tunnel vision. Men attend, focusing on issues of personal concern in their personal lives. A major issue is lament over lost fathers and absent fatherhood. Little, if any, attention is paid to men's overall responsibility for having contributed to the degeneration of society. Men may find themselves to be victims of an insensitive society but they seldom acknowledge that it is men, as a gender, who have controlled society and created the system that now preys upon them. They refuse to see that by buying into this system they perpetuate it and bear responsibility for their own fate.

Feminist Laura Brown says it well:

Women and children are being beaten and raped at home—by men;

air and water are growing more toxic by the moment, thanks to industries owned and run—by men; funding for social programs is being cut to the bone by government dominated—by men. And these guys are getting together to lament that they never knew their fathers?

Absent Fathers

Here we should address the "absent father syndrome" so decried by mythopoets.

We live in a society which fosters, indeed, demands gender duality. The absence of traditional paternal "masculinity" does hinder young males in achieving their own cultural masculine identity and will breed frustration due to cultural pressure. This often leads to adverse reactions—violence, shiftlessness, irresponsibility, etc., especially if the mother acts "feminine" in a traditional sense.

But those cultural pressures exist because we cling to concepts of gender duality. As long as we continue doing so young men will be driven to frustration as they resist the dictates of their true nature.

When we bifurcate the species into two separate genders, assigning rigid roles to each, we stunt the development of both. We encourage male children to focus on those attributes that are considered "masculine" by patriarchal thinking, ignoring those attributes which are just as natural but are considered "feminine." Similarly girls are pressured to develop their "feminine" attributes and ignore the "masculine." In reality, both genders would develop along the same line except for anatomical differences which would not deviate that much if girls were allowed to access their full physical potential.

So, this leaves us with "feminized" girls and "masculized" boys, both lacking a major portion of their natural character. When they reach adulthood they become parents.

Many "masculized" fathers, because they have been encouraged to ignore their nurturing side, find the responsibilities of fatherhood inhibiting and therefore flee. The "feminized" mother, of course has been conditioned to accept nurturing as her role so she will remain and provide even though the assertive aspects of her nature remain undeveloped. Not having been conditioned to develop the half of herself that has been classified as "masculine," she will be unable to provide the role example that will stimulate the growth of that same side in either her male or female children. In effect, children of such abandoned women will become "feminized" by default.

This gives merit to the claim by Mythopoetic men that absent fathers cause the feminization of children. Patriarchy has prevented women from developing the assertive side of themselves thus making them unable, as mothers, to pass this on to their children. Only the patriarchal father can do this. So in clinging to the traditional concepts of "masculinity" and "femininity" Mythopoetic men, in effect, instigate absent fatherhood.

If women had been raised to access all of their potential they would be able to provide to both male and female children those attributes which have been heretofore classified as "masculine." The absence of a father would therefore not harm his children, particularly his male children, nearly as much as it does today. Yes, the family would suffer. But not because of an absence of attributes exclusive to one gender. Rather, only because two dedicated parents can more effectively provide for the family than can one.

I would not argue that violence and criminal behavior in children are more prevalent in families without a father. But absent fathers are not the root cause. Rather, these problems are brought on by the absence of necessary human (i.e. genderless) values in families. Single mothers can, and often do, provide these values and steer their children along a relatively trouble-free path.

The vast majority of people, myself included, acknowledge that a father plays a key role in the family beyond the fertilization process. (The only major dissident point of view comes from those—usually feminists—who choose to be single parents.) The most glaring aspect of failed fatherhood is the failure to provide financial support. Virtually everyone condemns this. I need not describe here the stresses experienced by families who are deprived materially because of an irresponsible father.

Yet even among those fathers who materially provide, a large number fail to project a positive role model for their children to learn from. Some fathers are impatient, cruel or cold. Others simply haven't evolved to a mature level or don't display qualities that enhance their children. These children end up lacking interpersonal skills and carry this deficiency to adulthood where they become parents and initiate the cycle all over again.

A common consensus is that boys suffer from deficient fatherhood far more than girls. Mythopoetic leaders even contend that a boy cannot attain true manhood without the guidance of a positive masculine role model. Many men who believe this spend a great deal of time lamenting relationships with their fathers and seek, by bonding with other males, to recapture a masculine "thing"—something they have been deprived of that identifies them as masculine.

I agree that the presence of a well adjusted, loving, dedicated father raises a family to a higher level than can possibly be reached under the sole guidance of an enlightened, dedicated mother. First, such a man provides additional material security, relieving the burden upon his spouse and allowing more time for both of them to spend with their children.

At the same time he demonstrates by example to his children the benefits of a harmonious relationship between a man and a woman. A boy can see the rewards of bearing responsibility and recognize that adult men can achieve happiness by bonding with women. A girl can see that adult men can be loving and need not be seen as adversaries. Having observed bonded parents, both boy and girl would tend to view the other gender as kin rather than as "them" and "us."

I must emphasize that the presence of a "good" father benefits both male and female children, while a "bad" father has just the opposite effect and is worse than no father at all.

This brings us to the underlying reason why mythopoets so decry absent fathers. They believe that girls are taught to be women by their mothers; boys by their fathers. The biological and accompanying psychological changes that girls undergo during their teens are far more easily explained by adult women. Furthermore, the traditional adult roles girls will be expected to play later in life can be much more effectively demonstrated by women. Fatherless girls will lack some understanding of men but under our traditional system they need only know how to properly behave, and this can be taught them by their mothers.

On the other hand, fatherless boys pose more complicated problems for women. Male biological changes at puberty cannot be addressed with the same depth of understanding by a mother as could be by a father. In addition to sexual changes, the full male biological potential—a boy's ability to fully exploit his uniquely masculine physical strength and agility—is not as easily comprehended by his mother. Perhaps even more significant, a mother has difficulty raising a boy to exhibit in his manhood those traits which exemplify traditional "masculinity."

So, why does single motherhood so offend mythopoets and other patriarchal men? These men cannot envision a woman effectively teaching a boy to be aggressive, competitive and dominating—especially to women. Without a male role model to copy, the boy would have more difficulty grasping what is expected of him under our traditional system—a patriarchy.

The cleverly concealed issue here is that when men say that a woman can't raise a boy to be a true man, they really mean a patriarchal man. Their conclusion is not only basically correct, but it falls neatly in line with mythopoetic views which are patriarchal in nature.

Benefits?

Mythopoetic gatherings bestow enough benefits to convince most participants that the experience has powerful significance. Many men do gain deeper access into themselves. They do get the opportunity to relate to some men as brothers rather than as competitors and learn that it is okay to express deep inner feelings other than anger in front of other men. But most tears are shed for themselves, as victims. Few are shed for the havoc men have wrought upon the planet and society. And by shedding tears even while failing to accept the overall responsibility, these men feel better, returning home still blind to the plight facing the world and especially their women. By relieving pressure the experience allows the participant to ignore those issues that most need addressing.

The bottom line is that the most men who attend these retreats do not wish to totally reexamine themselves and make necessary changes. Many of them are well meaning and embrace a number of decent values. But they still cling to basic gender identity concepts and a value system that sprung from patriarchal roots and sculpted their lives. They seek cosmetic changes that make their own lives easier without them having to surrender their position of privilege. Most of these men value the essence of manhood they have been conditioned by society to accept. They sense something is wrong but they're hoping that a small adjustment, fine tuning, is all they need to restore harmony with themselves and their families.

The ravaging of our planet, the brutal domination of our women, and the slaughter of each other in countless wars, have not taken place because of minor flaws in men's character. A major transformation is called for. Returning from the woods with the ability to feel and cry will have little positive impact if these "awakened" mythopoetic men are not willing to delve far deeper into themselves and alter their behavior on the most basic levels. Sadly, Mythopoetic groups resemble the male social clubs that have existed through the ages to fortify male privilege.

A True Men's Movement

Yet just because the mythopoets are, at best, treading water and avoiding the crucial issues of "masculinity," does not obviate the need for a legitimate men's movement. As long as the two genders remain polarized the only way to bring them together is for men, who have exercised the power which has kept us divided, to gather together to devise a strategy for abdication of power, sharing of responsibility and promotion of gender bonding. This would stand in drastic contrast to the current "men's movement" which has evolved to a great degree as a defensive reaction to feminism.

What would a true men's movement look like?

First, it would take shape from men who are seriously committed to making a major transformation in themselves and their society, not just conquering a few personal issues. Building upon that positive intent, these men would meet and form groups. Ultimately they might copy the Mythopoetic format, holding workshops in an isolated environment where members of several men's groups can meet under a facilitator. However, all of the ensuing activities would be designed with one goal in mind: the dismantling of the concept that issues are best dealt with by relating exclusively to one's own gender. As soon as possible the way would be cleared for women to be included in these workshops so that issues could be explored from a heterogenous perspective.

Why do I advocate men initially gathering together after complaining about Mythopoetic isolationism? Why not include women immediately?

Because at this moment we remain gender polarized. We, as men, have power that women do not. We must first congregate as a gender to acknowledge where we are, then commit ourselves to plotting a major course correction. Our first act must be to agree to abdicate exclusive power. For this act to have authenticity it must be done outside the presence of women. In this way we show them that sincere intent fuels our decision, not any pressure from them.

Throughout history men have separated the two genders conceptually and confined women to certain behavioral patterns specifically designed to enhance the lifestyles most attractive to men. The only way we can now effectively reach out to women is to unconditionally raise them. Not just give women "equal opportunity" to play in the game in which we devise the rules. We must allow them equal say in what the rules shall be. The commitment to do this is the groundwork for any worthy men's group. The initial activities after group formation must be based upon men coming to grips with this issue and surrendering.

Let's specifically hypothesize the format of a constructive men's workshop.

The first act would be an open general discussion in a community gathering with the topic being the state of the world in general. (This is very important—to start from an overview, not from the self-indulgent perspective of a specific group.) Attendees would not only acknowledge all the issues that face the planet by describing them in depth, but would acknowledge how men as a gender have been responsible. They would formally acknowledge their own implication, as individuals (even if they were innocently unaware), in the eons-old plot to dominate their species. They would admit that by accepting the arguments that divide the genders into two distinct wings of humanity, with higher value placed upon one, they have helped maintain patriarchy, fostered domination of women and dehumanized themselves. They would further admit that if men face death in wars, lost fathers, frustrating careers and mid-life crises, they need to first look to themselves as individuals as bearing some responsibility. Finally, they would commit themselves to the extent of their power to breaking the chain.

I'm not suggesting we place men on a guilt trip. I'm not suggesting they commit themselves to resigning their jobs and taking to the streets as demonstrators (although that might be proper for a few). I'm suggesting that men remain constantly aware of these major issues, exercising what power they do have in their own lives to effect changes.

They can cease challenging other men unnecessarily, exploiting their employees, dominating their wives, and conditioning their children to be gender focused. In addition, they may find opportunities to speak out to their aquaintances about gender issues rather than nodding their heads compliantly when other men speak disrespectfully about or to women.

Once the confessions are done and the commitment made, the group needs to immediately begin acting upon its words. Members need to begin cultivating a new attitude toward women by immediately discussing issues important to women. Not issues of men's difficulty relating to women. That will come later. Rather, they need to discuss with the full depth of their understanding the issues that concern women—from a woman's viewpoint. They need to examine what part they have played in bringing upon women's frustration and begin discussing potential solutions.

Once all this has been aired, women would be brought into the proceedings. Respectfully, men would attempt to demonstrate that they understand female issues. They would invite the women to correct any misperceptions. They would openly acknowledge their own complicity in the patriarchal conspiracy to keep women subservient. They would make the same commitment to correct these wrongs that they made among themselves directly to these women. This must be done not only to impact upon the women, but as an exercise in humility for the men.

From that point on the group is no longer a men's group. It transforms into a men's/women's group, with both equally participating as they address both male and female issues together. Issues such as lost fathers and mid-life crises would be discussed in the presence of women, who often are a major factor in the latter. Women's feeling of physical vulnerability in a male dominated world would be another major topic. Men would learn that they can relate with tenderness to other men in front of women and not lose the respect of others for not being a man. Women would learn just as many intimate secrets about the feelings of men. True gender bonding would begin because gender identification would be minimized.

Another major issue would be proper parenting. Instead of simply complaining about absent fatherhood and overbearing motherhood, the group would discuss the proper roles of the genders in raising children.

A time or two it might be advantageous to gather separately as genders to address issues that are peculiar to the individual genders. These issues would usually revolve around biological differences. But upon completing the process everyone would immediately reconvene as a heterogenous community to openly discuss what had transpired. This would increase understanding in the one area in which the genders are truly different (biology) and promote empathy for the specific problems the other gender faces in that area.

Ceremony and ritual would be held to an absolute minimum to promote spontaneity and encourage reliance on inner guidance. Division into subgroups such as clans with identifying appellations that members carry throughout the workshop would be strictly avoided so as to maintain community bonds.

Drumming might be included, but in a wider ranging program that would include other music, in some cases, recorded. The purpose would be to promote accessing the emotions through dance movement and song. Women would be encouraged to focus on drums and percussion since it is they who need to break down barriers to higher energy levels and constructive aggressiveness. Men would be asked to open themselves to other instruments which produce notes that more effectively portray gentler feelings. It is these softer emotions that men have more difficulty expressing. Accenting melody, harmony and timbre in music would elicit graceful movement symbolic of compassionate feelings and aid men to gain access to a side of themselves hitherto mostly hidden.

Once the workshop ends, members would seek to preserve the group spirit and maintain momentum on the issues by meeting at regular intervals formally in future workshops and informally in convenient smaller groups. This format is similar to what men's and women's groups do now. My quarrel is not with the structure, but rather with the content and intent.

Yes, many mixed-gender groups already exist. But few, if any, of these have devoted themselves to gender bonding and the elimination of gender privilege. Rather, they usually seek to teach the genders about each other, but in terms of how to cope with each other under guidelines traditional to patriarchy. They seek to reduce inter-gender animosity even as they maintain age-old gender polarization attitudes. That will never work. We need mixed groups devoted to dismantling patriarchy. Groups whose members recognize that men and women are more identical than they are different and that to accent the differences only undermines our survival prospects as a species.

When reflecting upon Robert Bly's concept of "Wild Man," I am reminded of a worthy comment offered by feminist, Margo Adair.

> Giving up self-control does not mean becoming wild; on the contrary, it means becoming vulnerable, affectionate, relaxed, respectful and trusting.

These are the traits that men have most effectively suppressed. Men may hold their "wildness" in check (as perceived by Bly) because of cultural restraints. But once the restraints are lifted most have little difficulty allowing their wildness to leap forth. That in contrast to the other aforementioned traits which seem locked away in a deep vault which seldom can be accessed under any circumstances. Sadly, these latter traits better serve the species.

I am proposing that the primary objective of a constructive men's movement should be self immolation with the intent of using the energy generated by that cleansing fire to propel a new heterogeneous movement that recognizes no particular privilege for any gender, race or class.

Summary

Without question, men (as well as women) suffer from deep pain inflicted by years of mistreatment at the hands of both parents and society. Often this pain clouds the sufferers' judgment and they inflict pain upon innocent others (particularly women and children) through aggression or neglect. In most cases these men don't mean to cause the harm they do. Their reaction to their own pain tends to blind them.

Many facilitators who deal with men's issues would have us believe that men must access their pain and heal their wounds before their destructive behavior towards others can be effectively modified. This reasoning seems well founded in psychological theory. And yet what about those who are victimized by the writhing of suffering men? Must they patiently continue to endure mistreatment while these men try to work through their "stuff?" Is it not a victim's right to demand that their tormentor stops immediately?

Granted, suffering men face a difficult task in trying to overcome their pain. The personal issues they face are serious ones of complexity. But so are those personal issues faced by their women and children; issues made even more severe by having to deal with self-serving men focusing on themselves.

I recently spoke with a psychologist—the long-time facilitator of a men's group who advocated eventually bringing men's and women's groups together to work out gender issues. He stated, however, that both groups would need at least three years of work on issues exclusive to their own gender before they would be ready to deal directly with the other group.

My question is, do we as men have time (three years, one year, one month, one minute) to spend on self-absorption when our children (particularly our female children) are in their formative years being infused with those very same concepts and painful issues that haunt us today? Can any compassionate man truly say, "Sorry, Wife (or partner, or employee), but I don't have time to address those issues that concern you as a woman (equal opportunity and power under the system) because I'm hurting. You'll just have to do the best you can until I get myself together—maybe in three years of so."

In summary, if indeed the Mythopoets wish to "heal," the first step is to examine and, if necessary, adjust that portion of their behavior that negatively affects others. If indeed their goal is to be beneficial to humankind, they should first commit themselves to lifting their collective foot off the neck of womanhood before retreating into the forest to seek their inner selves.

Another feminist, Rosemary Radford Ruether, aptly sums it up:

> Men must begin by acknowledging their public reality as males in a patriarchal society, and not retreat to a privatized self that avoids accountability for that public world. They must see that the private self is not an autonomous entity, but a dependent appendage of these

social power relations.

I invite the mythopoets to come out. The oppressed in this world—women and children in particular—cannot wait for men to "heal." They need full access to their potential now. Each day that women and children are mistreated increases the depth of their wounds and their own pools of pain. Thus they face even further problems relating to their everyday life and a longer path to recovery should they awaken. Oppressed children tend to grow into oppressive adults, thereby repeating the cycle. Men must address this issue immediately, giving their own "healing" second priority.

Chapter Seven
Men and War

In an earlier chapter I concluded that although most men did not "love" war, they found a certain "romantic attraction" in it. Since acts of war have been carried out almost exclusively by men, and feminists have heavily criticized them because of it, war deserves deeper examination in our attempt to understand gender disharmony.

War and its fear has haunted humankind throughout recorded history. Archaeological findings of buried fortifications indicate its common presence in prehistory as well. Feminists would like us to believe that war-shunning matriarchies once existed, but archaeology has yet to bear this out. Whether it eventually does or doesn't, no one can deny that the past six thousand years have seen war and its threat as the dominant force in international and intertribal politics. And these past six millennia have certainly been an era of male domination.

Men maintain that throughout history one of their primary responsibilities was to protect their communities from outside attack. They use this claim to justify man's combative nature.

But before we heap praise upon man for defending his species, we need to ask: against whom was he providing protection? The answer: other men. No evidence has ever arisen substantiating cases (the Amazon myth notwithstanding) where armies of men were forced to defend their settlements against attacks from armies of women.

As a gender, men don't like to be held responsible for war. When justifying their participation, men tend to split into two camps. One group sees themselves as patriots, drawn into conflict because they are loyal members of society and wish to defend loved ones as well as various societal values. They don't see this motivation as male exclusive because many women "patriots" support the use of the military in this context. Rather, men see combat, although regrettable, as often a necessary exercise that can most effectively be carried out by their gender.

These men view the abhorrence of war experienced by the majority of women as a result of female physical inferiority which prevents women from performing effectively as warriors. Having been prevented from participating and therefore lacking combat experience, women do not fully understand war and cannot render intelligent opinions concerning it.

To these "patriots," soldiering serves as a rite of passage for men. Many of those who served like to discuss their military exploits and, rather than seeking to prevent others from experiencing the horrors of combat, demand that military service be universal. They exult when military measures are taken against perceived adversaries.

Unlike the "patriots," members of a second group of men like to portray themselves as victims of war. They claim they abhor war but they have been forced to serve due to circumstances. Either they served to protect their society from a very real enemy, or their government conscripted them to militarily enforce questionable foreign policies.

The most vocal of this group claim that the act of forcing men to sacrifice their bodies in war is comparable to women being raped. This comparison might hold merit if we compare the physical and emotional damage suffered by the victims in each situation. In fact, the case could be made that male war casualties suffer even more than female rape victims.

However, what does not bear up under scrutiny is the contention that men in the armed forces are just as helpless in determining their fate as women in the clutches of a rapist. Men who have served would have us believe they had no choice.

Are men truly forced to go to war? When women experience rape they usually find themselves suddenly overpowered and helpless to prevent their violation. But are men helpless when their government calls upon them to kill or get killed for some cause? True, refusal often brings about punishment and castigation. But they nevertheless have a choice. They have chosen to kill and face death rather than risk a temporary loss of freedom and resulting loss of social status. They have chosen to buy into the system rather than to seek to change it.

Male self-image under patriarchy has demanded that men carry combat responsibilities all by themselves, so men have had to face death and maiming to maintain their images as men. It's true that most women supported their men in war (what else could they do?). Some women even advocated the decision to go to war. But the main decisions that led us into wars were made by male leaders acting out a masculine dominated philosophy. Just as in economic matters, women had little to say regarding international affairs.

Some would assert that men's love for their families has forced them to sacrifice their bodies in war. For this they deserve compassion and gratitude, not criticism. But for Americans, in how many recent wars did men enter the service because they thought they were defending their loved ones?

When the Japanese attacked Pearl Harbor thousands of American men flocked to military recruitment centers to volunteer. Doubtless, a large percentage of them acted out of fear of imminent invasion and the resulting threat to their loved ones. However, another percentage suffered from pugilistic impulses and a desire for revenge. When we add to these latter the thousands of recruits who waited to be drafted, we can see that by no means all American soldiers in WWII participated primarily because they envisioned a direct threat to their families. Many were responding to what they perceived as a challenge to their manhood, and many others went because they were forced.

And World War II was a special case—certainly for Americans. In no other case since the Civil War has the direct safety of our families and loved ones been so endangered. Certainly not in the Gulf War, Viet Nam, Korea, or even World War I. These wars were fought for ideology costumed by propaganda painting exaggerated threats.

In the most recent conflicts, it is doubtful whether most of the inductees went to war with the conviction that they were protecting their loved ones. The Gulf War was fought with a professional army. Most of those involved had joined prior to take advantage of the benefits derived from military service, whether it was the "security" of a career, or the training and perks derived from a limited term of service. It is doubtful whether many saw Saddam Hussein as a direct threat to their loved ones.

Viet Nam posed a different case. Thousands were drafted into service and sent to fight. Once again, it is doubtful that many of these saw the Vietnamese as a serious threat to their loved ones. Out of fear of social castigation and punishment, they faced death anyway.

The same holds true for Korea.

So if we wish to be honest about our assessment of recent men's motivations for serving in armies, only a small percentage has done so for the purpose of protecting their families. (Unless, of course, we consider staying out of jail for refusing induction an exercise in protecting one's family.) The vast majority has done so in acquiescence, to serve the purposes of an ideology. Some of these may have understood and embraced the ideology with significant passion to justify to themselves their risking death or permanent disabling. But a large portion fought out of pure obedience and fear of repercussion.

Currently a hypocritical distortion of attitudes during the Viet Nam War is being foisted upon us by the self-righteous, pretentious claims of those who demonstrated against it. Many of the youth of that time—especially the men—would like us to believe that they stood by their morals in opposing the war.

The truth is that few people demonstrated moral outrage against the hideous violence being inflicted upon the Vietnamese until President Johnson vastly increased the ground force commitment and with it, the draft. It then became apparent that draftees would be sent to fight and die.

Suddenly the young people's moral concern for the fate of the Vietnamese flared. Until then, it mattered to few that thousands of these "commies" were dying. We saw no major demonstrations on campuses. Draft card burning was unheard of.

During the 50s and early 60s the vast majority of young people didn't care what their government did as long as it didn't interfere with their own individual pursuits. All young men were subject to the draft. They had a choice. Serve your two-year term and be free of obligation, or serve a six-month term and join the reserves for a twelve-year period, during which you were subject to callup should major hostilities break out. No one opposed military service on the grounds they didn't believe that war was a moral solution to problems. No one protested the sacrifice of conscience they were forced to make once they were inducted into the armed services. The attitude of that period was that you had to serve your time. Hopefully there wouldn't be a war while you were doing so.

That in mind, the prospective draftee made his choice of service terms with a finger to the political wind. Most young men didn't like the idea of having two full years carved out of their lives, especially if they were in the midst of pursuing a college education. Six months was more attractive, even if you had to attend a monthly meeting for the next twelve years. However, if war broke out, as a reserve you would be called up immediately. If you had served your two-year hitch you couldn't be called back unless the war turned into a national emergency.

Few draftees liked the military, but their focus was on how to serve their time without getting caught in combat. This acquiescence to the dictates of the Selective Service System during peace time indicated a lack of inner convictions in young men. For the avowed purpose of military training is to dehumanize the recruit by breaking down common moral values and instilling blind obedience to a hierarchy. Only in this way can human beings perform the subhuman acts necessary to prosecute successful war. The recruit undergoes this conditioning whether war is taking place or not. While in the military they can be imprisoned or shot for not displaying blind obedience. To allow oneself to be placed in that situation, then to submit to such conditioning says little for the depth of a person's inner conscience.

Since a paltry few potential draftees displayed concern over the fate of the Vietnamese during the fifties and early 60s, we can hardly commend them for moral integrity. Deep compassion suddenly and suspiciously arose once the finger began pointing at them as a possible combatant.

Warren Farrell and others who try to excuse men obediently going off to war paint a picture of able-bodied men facing few alternatives in wartime. Young men could either enter combat, endure civilian punishment, or flee. Farrell cites a case where an acquaintance of his tried to claim conscientious objector status during the Viet Nam War and was subjected, due to an absence of religious affiliation, to a bewildering government legal onslaught that destroyed his social status. This is supposed to illustrate the absence of self-determining power experienced by the potential draftee.

While the anecdote may have been accurately related, it does not accurately portray the alternatives presented young men by our government; certainly not during the Viet Nam War period, when conscientious objector status was highly sought after. During that time men were afforded a legitimate path to attaining conscientious objector status. But you had to convince your draft board that your conscientious objector views had not suddenly arisen because of the imminent danger of being drafted and sent to fight.

Specifically, the Selective Service Act allowed young men to claim conscientious objector status on more than one basis. In effect the regulations read that a man could be granted that status if he could show that military service conflicted with his religious *or* philosophical beliefs.

Men did gain conscientious objector status by claiming opposition to war on purely philosophical grounds. I know—I did. In spite of admitting that I was an atheist, I received this classification after spending less than an hour in front of my draft board. I did not make my case based on a moral stance against killing, but rather against the dehumanization that occurs in the military. In addition, I made my case prior to the time President Johnson ordered draftees sent into combat. By my doing so I risked prosecution when it seemed likely that I could have served my two years without being exposed to fighting. This helped establish my credibility. It was plain that the two members of my draft board didn't like me and found my views despicable, but they never bothered me afterward. Why? Because they believed me. Nothing in my lifestyle conflicted with the views I presented.

This was the major obstacle for those seeking conscientious objector status. Unless they were members of specific religious sects, they lacked credibility. Most had lived their lives as part of the system, never displaying any aversion to war or the military. Naturally, when the Vietnam War reached such intensity that draftees were sent to fight, those who claimed conscientious objector status without a history of opposing war and killing were suspected of being cowards rather than conscientious objectors.

Although "coward" is a cruel, unreasonable patriarchal term in most circumstances, the truth is that most men who sought conscientious objector status were afraid of being killed or wounded, rather than averse to seeing the Vietnamese slaughtered. Many either held lucrative jobs or were pursuing college degrees in pursuit of future success. Draft boards saw these men as being advocates and beneficiaries of a system ("the American Way"), yet unwilling to defend it from its enemies. It was this hypocritical attitude, apparent in the past indifferent behavior and attitudes of these men, that destroyed their credibility and landed them in court, and in some cases, jail.

For those who displayed a different attitude toward our system the machinery existed to avoid combat. But even when one was granted conscientious objector status he was expected to make sacrifices. Like the draftee, he was required to give two years service to his country. This primarily fell into two categories: non-military service (1-O classification), which entailed a two year stint performing public works; or non-combatant military service (1-A-O) as a nurse, medic, etc. Thus the government did provide the legitimate conscientious objector a path to avoid combat.

Only the most radical feminist would deride men who would join an army to protect their homeland from invasion and their fellow citizens from mass slaughter. Even women joined the service during WWII to prevent that. It would seem that based on the innate imperative of seeking species survival, some circumstances justify fighting and shedding blood. The question seems to be, when is our survival sufficiently threatened to justify resorting to this mass violence? Thus the subject turns to ideology, for that is what most wars are fought over.

Shouldn't a man (or woman) be willing to physically fight for ideals? Could we possibly maintain our freedom without being willing to fight?

It would seem not, as long as people try to force their ideals upon others. But at the same time we need to examine who it is who is aggressing, both physically and ideologically. Since societies are male dominated and the frequent wars seem to be instigated by male attitudes toward solving disagreements, it would seem fair to lay the responsibility at the feet of men.

Men's advocates would have us believe that women have significant power and control the motivations of men. They insist that men go to war to protect (and serve the best interests of) their women. But who is it that determines when nations go to war? Who controls the governments who make these decisions? Except for a handful of women sprinkled about in various governments of the world—these suspiciously man-like in problem solving approach—vast majority of politicians and rulers are men. The approach to international relations is decidedly masculine.

Men's advocates seem to be saying that most average men are

pulled into these whirlpools of violence by forces beyond their control. And yet at what point does the individual man take responsibility for his destiny? If he does not embrace the ideology that is sucking him into the conflict how can he justify facing the guns? How can he justify to himself dying or being maimed fighting for something he doesn't believe in? Perhaps worse, how can he justify killing others? Did he take every opportunity to persuade (by voting if nothing else) his government to take a different path? If he believes in finding a peaceful solution to a conflict how can he kill?

During World War I in battle after battle thousands upon thousands of men were slaughtered by machine guns and artillery, most often with no tactical gain. Seldom did more than a few yards of ground change hands. Yet time after time waves of men would respond to whistle and trumpet and charge out of their trenches to hurl themselves against barb wire entanglements and then be cut down. In some of these battles an amount of men that would fill a baseball stadium were killed or maimed—in one day! These were flesh and blood human beings—potentially talented, creative, nurturing beings who were certainly loved and probably needed economically by family members.

Why did these men—British, French, German, Russian and American, among others—respond to the call time after time and challenge the guns in these suicidal efforts? Between each battle those lucky ones who emerged unscathed spent the intervening hours or days living, eating and sleeping in mud, stalked by disease and haunted by the terror of sudden death or maiming. They watched firsthand as close friends and comrades were riddled with bullets, gassed, or blown apart. Under this incessant pressure nerves shattered. And yet very few of these men said, "No! It is time to call a halt!" Why?

Advocates of patriarchy suggest that women had as much to do with the appalling duration of that war as did men. They point to those women who sold war bonds or who encouraged recruitment or who stood at the train stations and docks urging men on to victory.

Granted, a number of women did participate in these activities. But women of those times were members of a subjugated gender, conditioned to accept the dictates of patriarchy. Many were brainwashed to believe that war and military duty were necessary in a patriarchal society. Only a handful visited the front. The vast majority were inundated by war-mongering propaganda which made them see their role as trying to boost morale, thereby increasing the chances of victory and shortening the war. No count of the millions of women who remained at home in silent protest, sickened by the number of dead and maimed but helpless within a patriarchal society to effect a change, was ever attempted.

No, it wasn't the urging of women that drove the vast majority of men to sacrifice themselves either in the trenches of the first World War or on any other field of battle. Most men fought because of their perceived obligation to society. Often they had been indoctrinated to believe that the personal needs of their families would be best served by their giving their lives to preserve the ideals and ambitions of the society they lived in. But even most of those who did not believe in the cause went to war anyway and many of those ended up just as dead as those who did believe. The need to belong to one's society, to be accepted and approved of, overrode the colossal physical danger one would face in combat. Even the parade of corpses and limbless veterans returning home could not override the fear most men held of being jailed or called a coward.

Today a large percentage of men still fear losing social status even more than losing life and limb. That reflects how deeply they are invested in our system—one that advocates male dominance. It also shows how tenaciously they are willing to defend that system, whether it be against a foreign enemy or against their own women seeking civil rights.

Would war have been less prevalent or even absent, as feminists maintain, if women had ruled? That's not an easy question to answer. Certainly women have always suffered from the same tendency to insecurity as men. But whether they would have resorted to war to establish a sense of security is not so certain. For in primitive warfare oriented societies women did not fare well. Anthropologist Marvin Harris says:

> In primitive societies warfare leads to high rates of direct and indirect female infanticide." (Naturally those who will become the warriors will be valued more highly.) And: "When men and women are equally competent to perform vital military and production tasks, then women's status rises to parity. But if there are vital aspects of production or warfare that men carry out more effectively than women, then women's status will be lower.

This, of course relates to societies even today. So it would seem unlikely that women would ever prefer war over other means as a solution to political problems. Yes, 76% of American women approved of the Gulf War. But that isn't a fair example of women's attitudes toward war. Most women approved of that war because of the blatant aggression against, and mistreatment of, Kuwait along with the inhumane behavior of Sadam Hussein. If we assessed the percentage of women approving of the Vietnam War or Grenada we would likely see a vastly different split.

However that does not mean to say that women lack a reservoir of aggressiveness that would rival men's if they had equal opportunities to express it. Women may appear to suffer such a lack, but their aggressive potential lies repressed under male domination. To act aggressively with those physically stronger is counterproductive, potentially self-destructive behavior.

We see female leaders instigating war under patriarchy, but they could hardly act differently and maintain their leadership role in the system. In a matriarchy or gender-neutral system the use of physical force would not likely be exalted or employed as indiscriminately. Otherwise women would not likely reach dominance or parity, for when one gender is physically stronger, the other must use means other than physical to maintain equality or a position of authority. Matriarchs would likely seek to find solutions to arguments by other than physical means. Otherwise men would soon recognize the importance of a resource they possessed in superior quantity and, employing it, wrest away control.

Feminists would like us to believe that women would shun war because of some innate higher standard of morality. I don't believe this. I believe that women have embraced higher moral standards because they have been downtrodden and better comprehend the problems and feelings of human beings who have been dominated by force. I also believe that women do have a higher respect for the fragility and preciousness of human life due to their being the vessel of creation and initial provider of nurturing for the human young. This, however, is learned and could be so done by men if they were not so engrossed in pursuing power over others.

Men and women have equal potential as nurturers and aggressors. But in the power struggle between them, one technique works more effectively for one, and the other for the other. End the struggle and we have two genders with equal proclivity in both areas. In that scenario I would like to think that both genders would strongly favor their nurturing instinct.

But as it is now, men continue to rule as they have for thousands of years. And in doing so they have tended to employ physical force to solve political disagreements. Often this has resulted in warfare.

Is humankind doomed genetically to wage war against its fellows? Many anthropologists, particularly the aforementioned Richard Leakey, don't think so. Agreeing with him, although from a slightly different perspective, Marvin Harris concludes:

> It is because of ecological and demographic advantages, not genetic imperative, that warfare has been recurrently selected for during the evolution of band-and-village peoples.

In both opinions genetic impulses do not explain man's propensity for war. It follows then that some distortion of our character—likely psychological insecurities and resulting prejudices—drove us to conquer rather than share with others of our kind.

No big mystery obscures the underlying causes of war. We live as physical beings in a physical environment. Survival is our ingrained imperative. We have often had to exert physical force against environmental forces and other species in order to survive. It is one small step further to justify exerting this same force against our own kind when we perceive them as life-threatening competitors.

The very thing that sets us apart from potential animal competitors—our intelligence—has also led to warfare. During paleolithic times when the population of humans was small the "ecological and demographic" advantages that Marvin Harris spoke of would not have been the major factors they became later. The foraging and hunting ranges of hunting/gathering people, if they overlapped with those of other bands, probably became issues of conflict only infrequently. In those times plant and animal life tended to be abundant enough to where survival would not be threatened by overhunting or overharvesting.

In cases where the territorial survival interests of two separate bands did conflict, combat may have ensued. But drawn out warfare, which would have resulted in at least some of the breadwinners of each band being either incapacitated or killed, would have proven to be counterproductive. It would have been far more sensible for the band which had shown itself to be less powerful in an initial trial of strength, to have removed itself to new territory.

In a territory abundant in food several separate bands of humans could have coexisted. If they recognized that enough food existed for all, survival interests would not have instigated conflict. The fact that conflict did become so prevalent is an indication that humans perceived others of their kind as threats. In some cases this might have been real. But in many, the threats would have been imagined, forged by feelings of insecurity which were not justified by real conditions.

Let's envision a territory which supports a herd of antelope. This in turn supplies meat to two separate bands of hunter/gatherers. Under normal conditions both bands may be able to take all the carcasses they can use without destroying the herd. But insecurity nevertheless raises the fear of each band that the other is a threat to the supply. The fear may not be totally unfounded. A drought or pestilence could decimate the herd. But instead of seeking cooperation with the other band to offset such a potential emergency, human insecurity tends to drive the two bands to confrontation.

Fear for survival is normal among all animals. Even large hunting cats display a level of anxiety after killing prey. They will either attack and chase away scavengers who threaten to steal the catch or they may drag the catch to a secure place. The force motivating them may not seem like fear, but it is indeed that, albeit on a very low level. The anxiety will soon dissipate once they have consumed enough meat to satisfy their needs. At that point they will move off, leaving what remains of the carcass to other animals. Both scavengers and potential prey recognize that the big cats are only dangerous when hungry. Once the hunger is sated, the lion's concern for survival disappears. With its stomach full, it doesn't spend time pondering how to save the leftovers or where the next meal will come from.

Humans, however, possess an intelligence level which allows them to foresee possible difficult times ahead even when they are experiencing a time of plenty. Whereas a lion will not remember a time when prey was scarce and he went hungry for a long period, such an experience weighs heavily on human memory. Unlike lions, humans will change behavior patterns because of it.

This ability to mentally assimilate experiences and adapt in response has been a major fact in our ascendancy as creatures. However, this same ability has often been taken to extreme, threatening self-destruction as a species. For it is this over concern for survival which has led to war.

As a species we have learned that in the best interests of survival we need to plan for both current and future needs. If possible, we should accumulate resources that will see us through future times, even if they are not needed now. We recognize that although our environment may not be threatened now by outside forces, the time may come when such a threat may arise so now is the time to prepare for it. Our intellect is a perfect tool for accomplishing this. It has the ability to contrive most proficient strategies. However, when driven by fear, these strategies can reach extreme proportions.

What may be a very reasonable and prudent desire to build up a surplus of survival resources for use in a future period, can become a mania to accumulate. How much in the way of resources must we store away or seek to control before we feel secure?

Currently the richest man in America is said to possess eighteen billion dollars. Think of it. That's 18,000 million dollars! For what does he need all this money? Even if in satisfying his basic needs, he is a gourmet, wears the most expensive clothing and lives in the world's most elaborate palace, he could not consume but a tiny percentage of his wealth. As far as we know, no major portion of his wealth has been diverted to charitable enterprises. (To this guy even a hundred million dollars would be pocket change.) The vast majority of his assets appear to be held for his own benefit. Why?

Some would suggest that he has the right to bathe himself in luxuries and employ a company of servants to lavish attention upon him. But even that would consume only another tiny percentage of his fortune. And why would he need to experience such luxury? I suggest that beneath all other motivations lies a fear for survival. Luxury distracts him from this fear.

To those who know this individual—perhaps to the man himself—the possibility of his suffering from survival anxiety probably seems absurd. However, how would he feel and react if he was suddenly threatened with losing his fortune and reduced to a common millionaire?

This, of course, is an extreme case. But the vast majority of us are driven by this same need. Indeed, society itself drives us to pursue this need, attempting to instill in us fears for our future. The medical and insurance professions are the most guilty. The former paints the human body as a machine that is virtually helpless to defend itself without medical aid against numerous hostile forces in a dangerous world. The latter paints life as a tenuous experience constantly threatened by impending disaster.

When adding this induced fear to that already haunting each of us, survival becomes a mania. Some of us outwardly pursue security, becoming workaholics and/or misers. Others, to varying degrees, try to push down this fear by distracting ourselves with "interests" or opiates. But nevertheless the fear remains a driving force and an interpersonal dynamic.

In assessing our own survival prospects reasoning tells us that other human beings may need to consume that which could be a source of insurance for us against a future of privation. We may not need these resources for the foreseeable future. We cannot even be sure we will ever need them or that other abundant resources will not become available. But our intellect, which has been put to work devising the most effective approach to surviving, nevertheless sees these others as a threat.

If a field of grain will feed two families for a year, it will feed one family for two years. Remove one family and the other's survival prospects are enhanced. Recognizing this, the intellect immediately faces a quandary imposed by two separate emotional impulses—the fear for personal survival and compassion for other human beings. Historically, survival fears have predominated.

Pure intellect recognizes that producing survival resources takes more effort than finding them already produced for you. If they have been produced by nature and lay unclaimed then good fortune allows you to take possession. But if they are possessed by others then you are faced with the decision of either seizing or doing without them. If you are stronger then it may be easier to seize them than to produce them yourself.

The intellect also recognizes that a finite natural resource lasts longer with fewer drawing upon it. It therefore behooves your survival interests to keep others away from this resource. The intellect further recognizes that chasing others away is not the most effective way of controlling a resource because these others may return when you are not aware or when they have gained strength. A much more effective approach is to dominate and control, or even kill them.

The aforementioned principles lead us to conflict on a personal level and societies to war. Upon them we've built an elaborate superstructure of ideologies, temporal and religious, which redefine morals to allow humans to see each other as enemies.

We find this necessary for even as we entertain thoughts of war we find ourselves haunted by compassionate emotions which tell us it is not in our best interests to harm other human beings. Instead of seeking a balance between these two opposing emotions, most societies have embraced ideologies which attempt to dehumanize those who oppose us. Only if we define other humans as less than human can we justify our attacking and killing them. In historical times men have taken this approach to the extreme. Individual insecure minds have run wild concocting schemes to promote personal ambitions that ensure physical security. Typically this engenders the pursuit of wealth, for greed is but a symptom of fear. Whether this fear is that of having to someday face physical destitution, or that of facing a life without purpose, it is nonetheless a symptom of deep insecurity.

This same insecurity manifests itself on a political level with the same goal pursued by different means. Countries or societies seek wealth—the means to improve their standard of living (survival)—by threatening or waging war.

Warfare is the ultimate expression of competition. Those who advocate competition assert that it drives people to higher levels of performance. In theory this can be true, as long as competitors are governed by some rules of fairness. But those who regularly compete know that they can be much more successful if they can find some way to circumvent the rules. If your opponent is following the rules but you do not, he/she is far less likely to win.

In a foot race why concentrate upon running at full speed if instead you have an opportunity to incapacitate your opponent without being observed? Victory has thus been assured, even if you only jog to the finish line. The late 19th century American "Robber Barons" epitomized this abuse of competition. Warfare, of course, exploits this unscrupulous philosophy to the extreme. This brings to mind a quote from the Greek historian, Thucydides, who said: "Right is only in question among equals in power; the strong do what they can and the weak suffer what they must."

If, as Richard Leakey maintains, ancient humans were cooperative and that only recently has humankind turned upon itself, then maybe we have hope. Absent a genetic imperative, humankind must have consciously drawn conclusions and made decisions that set its members at odds. This would have occurred gradually, over lengthy periods of time, one generation teaching the next to hate. But if the young could so effectively be taught to tap into their survival fears and behave with hostility toward fellow men, couldn't they as easily learn to access the compassionate side of themselves and see humanity as a gigantic family?

To do so, certain concepts, particularly those which separate the genders would have to be discarded. For stratification by gender is the most basic human division, and any division eventually leads to conflict.

Chapter Eight
Sports

It has been said, particularly by feminists, that sports serve as training exercises for war. While this may be an exaggeration in a literal sense, the statement nevertheless has merit. Individual sports encourage aggression, insensitivity to the feelings of opponents, and the pursuit of domination. Team sports, as they are coached and played today, further these negative pursuits by encouraging the subordination of personal feelings and ambitions to those of the group as a whole. Thus, those who participate heavily in team sports are more prepared to practice the blind obedience necessary to carry out the team oriented aggression demanded in military operations.

Yes, sports can also teach a participant the valuable lesson of being able to perform as a team member. But when, in addition, team members are taught that winning is everything and that the fate of the opponent is inconsequential, sports become a negative influence. Teamwork is constructive only when it is used to perform constructive acts.

Many of those who participate in sports would have us believe that they abhor war. On a subjective conscious level this may be true, if they've failed to make the above connection between sports and war. But can this claim be genuine in the overall picture?

The vast majority of athletes certainly are not averse to using an aggressive approach to seeking domination over those they view as enemies. They certainly take no issue with undergoing strenuous physical training and mental conditioning. And, they certainly do not detest inflicting physical punishment on opponents (consider football, boxing, hockey, rugby, etc.). What they seem to dislike is that the risks of death and maiming are far more prevalent in warfare.

The Geneva Convention aside, no rules govern war. In sports one always faces the prospect of serious injury. But only in the rarest of cases does death occur. In warfare, however, not only is death common, but injuries are often of the most hideous variety. A large percentage of participants suffer loss of limbs and serious permanent impairment of important body functions. While an athlete can train his/her body into a high state of resistance to athletic injury, no amount of preparedness or training can prepare a soldier's body to resist bullets and bombs. So while athletes find establishing physical domination over others as natural, few have the stomach to face a high risk of being maimed or killed. Thus, for most it is the personal risk that repels, not a moral abhorrence of war. Those who truly abhor war, abhor inflicting pain and physical harm upon others. And the very act of participating in highly competitive sports indicates a strong need to exalt oneself at the expense of others.

Globally a vast weight of opinion accepts that sports serve a useful purpose in providing exercise while allowing the release of negative emotions in a non-destructive manner. Many maintain that sports provide a peaceful outlet for aggression, reducing the internal pressure that drives people to settle disputes through violence off the playing field.

In some cases this may be true. But more often the very essence of sporting activities heightens the propensity for conflict by placing human beings in competition with each other. If participants use these events to release negative emotions, inevitably they will make their opponents targets of negative feelings.

Often participants carry this approach back into society. The practice of seeing others as competitors, and thereby at least to some degree, adversaries, encourages dumping one's emotional garbage upon them. In addition, the sporting experience conditions participants to equate success with high levels of aggression. (And make no mistake—in all sports the most successful teams and individuals are nearly always the most aggressive.) They find it difficult to pursue success in the normal world without employing the same aggressive tactics and attitudes they have utilized on the field of play. Indeed, much of our communication in business and politics is abundantly sprinkled with sports terminology and metaphor.

We have heard said that during times of international tension sports have served to bring nations closer. For example, during the Cold War various sports teams from the U.S. competed against those from the Soviet Union. Sports advocates believe that the threat of nuclear war was significantly reduced by a bridge of sportsmanship built during those competitions.

Perhaps sports did perform a positive function in that circumstance.

But sports do not always act as a positive force in international affairs. Consider the 1936 Olympic Games in which a black athlete outraged Adolph Hitler by disproving the Nazi theory of Aryan athletic superiority. That competition certainly did not improve international relations. If anything, it may have strengthened Hitler's hatred and racial bias. Similarly, many regular participants in sports hate losing and either despise those they've defeated or resent those who've defeated them.

If we examine sports as they are practiced today we seldom see a spirit of benevolence driving them. Although we often hear advocates claiming that sports provide exercise, entertainment and positive learning experiences for the young, we most often see practiced aggressive, insensitive behavior. Most of those who get paid for coaching (as well as numerous volunteers) drive their players mercilessly. Players drive themselves similarly, striving to satisfy an insistent hunger for victory. We frequently hear the quote, "America loves winners."

Perhaps the most telling gesture in athletics today is that of players or their fans waving hands in the air with index fingers pointed skyward. "We're number one!" they yell, indicating the true motivation behind their participation. This quest for superiority, for domination, maintains a stranglehold on sports today.

Many sports advocates will point to the millions of people who participate informally every day, ostensibly to receive beneficial exercise and relieve stress. Certainly many of these participants do gain these benefits. At the same time, however, many have based their entire self-esteem concept upon successful athletic performance in these "informal" activities. Consequently many recreational contests turn into "hard-fought," anger-driven struggles which mirror the temperament of athletes who participate in organized sports. Thus recreational sports lose their innocence.

Of course, it is only natural to feel self-worth and confidence in the efficacy of one's body when you can master a physical skill. And this naturally bolsters self-esteem. But to base a major portion of your self-esteem on the outcome of an athletic performance in which you measure yourself against others indicates low self-opinion which needs continuous bolstering. To those thus involved the negative aspects of recreational sports significantly outweigh the many potential benefits, making these activities a detriment.

A major reason recreational sports embrace significant detrimental aspects is that many participants receive inspiration from organized sports on a college and professional level. Adults and children get swept up in trying to emulate their heroes and heroines who expend every last ounce of energy seeking to dominate their opponents.

The millions upon millions of people who fanatically follow these ritualized games generate billions of dollars for investors. Athletes earn salaries hundreds of times larger than the average worker. We allow our colleges and high schools to be used as training grounds for the professional teams, granting large financial allowances to poorly educated athletes who have little interest in education and no intention of finishing it. Thereby we prevent hundreds of serious students from gaining access to higher education, demeaning the educational process. We debate about the inequities between men and women in the awarding of athletic scholarships. We generally avoid debating whether ANY person should be given a scholarship to receive higher education purely because of abilities that have nothing to do with their potential for academic success.

We know what benefits the athletes receive. But what value does organized sports provide to society as a whole? Each year millions of people spend hundreds of hours of valuable time intently watching football players expressing dominance by crashing into and pummeling each other; basketball players running about trying to throw a ball through a ring; baseball players trying to strike a small sphere with a club. We've reached a point in our society where we don't even question the utility of these events. We call them entertainment.

But why must we get our entertainment from watching senseless, infantile activities, particularly when they're engaged in by adults? Think about it. They're silly! I know first hand because I was an avid participant, official and spectator for many years.

These events seem to have utility only because we've ritualized them. They give followers a feeling of belonging which has been lacking due to a failure of the parent/child bonding process. They also provide an opportunity to experience dominance vicariously. People who have been "losers" in everyday life can become "winners" by attaching their allegiance to a winning team. Sadly this effect can only be narcotic and temporary lasting from victory to victory. A team's defeat strips followers of their anesthesia and leaves them alone with their true inner feelings—vulnerability and low self-esteem. That's why emotional involvement runs so deeply and why the word "fan"—short for "fanatic"—so aptly describes the many who worship sports.

A sad offshoot of this proliferation of sports is women's demand to participate in events of their own. They bemoan the prevalence of sexism in male sports. This takes two forms. Men have tended to try to keep women from participating. At the same time within male sports the participants have been encouraged to view women as inferior, subject to ridicule and domination. Often violence toward women and/or rape has resulted.

We have recently seen the publication of books effectively revealing the prevalence of sexism in male sports. These books serve a valuable purpose. But most suggest that a road to eliminating sexism in sports is to give more women opportunity to participate. This is supposed to, in some fashion, convince males of the value of women.

I totally disagree with this concept. Females entering patriarchally designed sports turn into patriarchal caricatures of the women they should be. Women start acting aggressive and physically violent toward each other. They even begin moving about with the typical male jock macho swagger. This may allow patriarchal men to accept these females, but only because these women are glorifying patriarchy. ("You're trying to be like us. That means you approve of us. You'll never quite reach our level, and therefore will always remain inferior to us. But you're good little girls for trying and thereby legitimatizing what we are.")

Instead of degrading themselves thusly, women should abhor organized sports and seek to wean men away. Society as a whole needs to lure males from competitive sports, not encourage women to become like them. We must not seek inclusion for those members of our society (women and children) who have been thus far protected through exclusion. They have been the fortunate, not the unfortunate.

Most men see nothing negative in their worship of sports. In addition to using it as a self-esteem injection, it allows them to build a sense of camaraderie not easily accessed in other pursuits. Since the patriarchal male image forbids men from sharing feelings with each other, sports gives them an outlet to do so symbolically. Sharing with another the thrill of victory by one's favorite team is the closest many men come to expressing love to another man. At the same time sports fit nicely into the patriarchal system as a honing device for competitive, aggressive instincts.

Athletes often pray before going out on the field and seeking to dominate each other through actions that can easily inflict injury. In Western society they often pray to Christ—perhaps the ultimate symbol of healing and peacemaking—for the privilege of violently prevailing over another group.

Do men see the hypocracy in this? Did football fans see the hypocracy when during a recent important NFL game the New York Jets huddled in prayer in the center of the field as temporarily paralyzed, life threatened Detroit Lions linebacker Reggie Brown was lifted into an ambulance a few feet away. The Jets may have been praying sincerely, but did that stop them from continuing the game with the same level of violence that nearly killed Brown? After watching a human being nearly killed in front of their eyes how many of the millions of people watching were turned off by the ensuing violence not only in that game but in the games that followed?

Few, at best. And those who do recognize the level of violence and the hypocracy played out in scenes such as those are often unwilling to change their own habits. After pointing out the violent nature of football and its negative impact on our society to several friends, I had a number acknowledge my point. But then all of them agreed with one who said, "I still enjoy it too much to give up watching it."

Marc Fasteau, in his book, *The Male Machine*, makes a pertinent observation:

> [male preoccupation with sport] has a darker side: the use of athletic competition as a model for behavior and problem-solving in other areas of life. Competition is the central dynamic of organized athletics. Its other benefits (and costs), unlike those of activities which produce a tangible product rather than abstract "victories," are personal to the athlete and sometimes hard to measure. So it has been easy to make athletic competition into a superficially rational paradigm of total, unqualified pursuit of victory. And because the subtler, personal rewards and pleasures of sports are played down, in fact often destroyed by this approach, the pursuit becomes a never ending one; one's sense of achievement depends entirely on winning.

Absolute team loyalty, unquestioning obedience to authority, respectful fear and hatred of the opposition, disregard of individual injury and suffering—all justified in the name of victory—these are the axioms of the sports system. As a consequence, it attracts, as its permanent managers, men with these values.

Many children find their only role models among adult athletes and therefore seek to emulate them. Parents eagerly cooperate by providing activities to children hardly out of the toddler stage. Many of these children can barely handle the equipment involved with playing these games yet they find themselves draped in a uniform and thrust into competitions complete with officials, determined coaches, and frenzied fans. T-ball, Little League, Pop Warner football, Biddy basketball—all expose children to the stress of measuring themselves against others both through team success and individual statistics (yes, statistics, even at that age). This at a time when their little developing brains should be left as stress-free as possible to evolve at nature's predesigned pace.

A common argument we hear today in favor of youth sports is their use as a vehicle to keep children out of trouble, particularly, away from gangs. Indeed, sports have been useful to many children in this context. But to be so they need not be organized and should not be ritualized. For even those times when sports serve as a useful distraction, they are exposing children to the negative aspects described above.

Further complicating matters, when sports are glorified many underprivileged children tend to focus on sports—to the detriment of education and other responsibilities—entertaining the hope that someday they can become a professional. When this dream fades they find themselves facing despair as an adult. We depend far too much on sports to divert children from destructive activities. We must provide other incentives.

In order for sports to serve a useful purpose a spirit of sportsmanship must exist in the participants. One Webster's Dictionary definition states: a sportsman is "a person who can take loss or defeat without complaint, or victory without gloating, and who treats his opponents with fairness, generosity, courtesy, etc." Based on this definition we can conclude that a large percentage, if not the majority, of participants in sports lack sportsmanship. This is certainly the case in organized sports on the collegiate and professional levels where winning overrides all other considerations.

One might try to make the case that sports on other levels—particularly sports played for recreation—engender much higher levels of sportsmanship. This may be true, although the intensity level of many participants often leads to hard feelings and physical confrontations. At the same time, most of those who participate in sports on any level follow organized sports. Indeed, many of those who can no longer participate, or who have never participated, see themselves as fans of various organized sporting activities. What does this say for their level of sportsmanship? Can a person truly embrace sportsmanship when they avidly follow and support organized sports which degrade the spirit of sportsmanship?

Some fans go to sporting events because they enjoy the mechanics of the game. They will find enjoyment no matter what the outcome. They will favor one team over another because of greater familiarity or perhaps because they like a certain style of play. They would prefer that their team wins, but losing does not detract from their interest in the game.

In contrast we find fans who totally focus on winning. They view a loss by the their team as a personal affront. They become angry with team management when the team consistently fails. To these fans sportsmanship takes a back seat. We can see how large their number by noting the fluctuating attendance figures experienced by professional teams. In most cities, teams which endure a period of losing seasons after winning consistently, experience a corresponding vast attendance dropoff. A transition back to winning, reverses this glaring trend.

These fans use sports to bolster their sagging self-esteem. They have come to subconsciously accept self-worth as based upon being able to dominate physically. Many of them either lack the physical capabilities to express themselves in this way, or lack the outlet. In either case, by identifying with a team of athletes who can act vicariously for them these fans have a chance to grasp a feeling of self-worth that has hitherto been beyond their reach.

Those who value sports without sportsmanship are driven by the same impulses that drive men to war. However, sports participants can express self-indulgent aggression and seek domination without taking life or facing the threat of having one's life taken. Thus they can deny the similarities between athletic competition and war.

But if we shed our blinders and look closer, the parallels are obvious.

Football provides the most glaring example. It is fast becoming the most popular sport in America, even as it remains the classic example of sports reduced to its ugliest. It is the sport that most closely personifies warfare in that the object is to dominate territory. By examining it closely we can see how it lacks sportsmanship and glorifies the worst side of humanity.

Football coaches see themselves, and are seen by fans, as generals of an army. Their training sessions are run like Marine Corps boot camps. They have staffs of subordinate officers (assistant coaches) and send out reconnaissance patrols (scouts). The game demands that the players become highly specialized, neglecting the development of well rounded physical abilities. Indeed, widely ranging physical types are needed to carry out the varied tasks. Therefore some players have gargantuan strength but can't run well; some can run like cheetahs but can't catch or throw the ball; and some can't do anything but kick. In addition, players must become blindly obedient to strategy as passed down through a hierarchy—coaches, quarterback, defensive captain, etc.

To play successful football one must act violently. The game was designed as a test of physical brute strength—one side trying to force themselves through or past the other. The team that can exert the most brute force usually wins. Numerous regulations govern, but the most basic—that which gives this activity a distinct character—dictates that movement of the ball can only be stopped by the person in possession of it being put down on the ground by someone from the opposing group.

Since the rules place little restriction upon how roughly the person with the ball can be handled, it is to the advantage of the opposing group to collide with and drive the carrier into the ground with as much force as possible. This may dislodge the ball, causing change of possession, while inflicting serious punishment on the carrier's body, reducing his efficiency as the contest continues.

During the action a great number of equally violent collisions occur between other participants as well. If the ball carrier's comrades can hinder by bowling over, tripping up, falling upon, etc., several of the opposing participants, the ball will advance further. Again, the more violent this contact, the more effective, since the more viciously an opponent is felled, the less likely he is to quickly get up and resume the chase. In the heat of conflict it is of little concern whether someone is injured. Thus, many injuries occur. Every game several players limp or are carried off the field. (The NFL Physicians Society has reported that from 1980-88 16,200 injuries occurred. This amounted to three per team per week! Another estimate has it that during a seven year period of NFL competition a player will absorb over 100,000 full-speed blows!)

To withstand this punishment intense psycho-physiological conditioning is required. One must somehow remain prepared during each and every moment of participation to endure violent blows, often sudden and unseen. To operate in this alien mode puts an abnormal strain on the body, unnecessarily mobilizing its survival instincts over protracted periods of time. At the same time, participants must insensitize themselves to the damage they might cause to other men's bodies—indeed that they might injure someone for life.

Great care is taken to induce this insensitivity before each contest. Often players are discouraged from having sex the night before so that their sensitive, loving side does not surface and interfere with psychological game preparation. During pre-game meetings players are conditioned to shunt aside normal reason and seek an infusion of adrenalin. But adrenalin will not flow unless a person is frightened or angry. Since fear hinders the pursuit of victory, they do everything they can to make themselves angry. The easiest way to become angry with someone is to dislike them. The greater the dislike, the more intense the anger—the greater the flow of adrenalin. Pure hatred is the ideal state. In that state the hormone flows freely and the player can perform superhuman feats of violence while remaining insensitive to the damage he inflicts upon others.

The physical demands of football dictate that participants undergo strenuous conditioning programs designed to add strength and weight. What often results is a misshapen hulk, sometimes exceeding 300 pounds, that looks more like a two-legged pachyderm than a man. Whether caused by the long term effects of ballooning their bodies or the numerous injuries (a recent survey reports that 78% of retired professional football players suffer physical disabilities), the average life expectancy of those who have played a significant amount of professional football is about 56 years.

The distorted attitudes of the participants are evident from the moment they leave their dressing rooms. Many yell at the tops of their lungs and throw fists in the air, signs that an infusion of adrenalin has already generated energy difficult to control. Many will hold their index fingers high and wave them about as sign that they claim superiority not only over the opposing group, but over any other group that might challenge them. This quest for dominance overrides concern for sportsmanship.

During the contest team members hug each other with jubilation whenever they inflict bone crushing setbacks to the opposition. Many will taunt and threaten the opposition, often instigating shoving matches and fistfights. When players carry the ball across the line that indicates their team is to be awarded points, they often erupt into an emotional frenzy, holding the ball up to the crowd seeking adulation, then slamming it down on the ground as hard as they can in disdain for those who failed to stop them. In normal life this juvenile, narcissistic conduct would be punished or severely chastised. In football it is smiled upon.

After the contest, the participants will express regrets over the serious injuries that result. Most will shake hands with the opponents they tried to savage and have you believe that all is forgiven. But can we really turn our emotions on and off like this? And what message are we sending to the young spectator in the process? Is this pseudo-reconciliation supposed to justify all the brutality that has transpired?

We are told that all this degrading behavior occurs "in fun." Really? Look at the fanatical quest for "rankings" and the recruiting scandals. The livelihoods of the men who manage the teams, the "coaches," depend on being successful. How can they be expected to instill in their players a sense of sportsmanship and to encourage them to have fun? They can't and they don't. Too much money circulates in football. If they are to survive in their profession they must "coach" their charges to ferociously attack others.

Does football build character, as many of its advocates claim? Perhaps. But what kind of character? What kind of person are we molding who is taught to be insensitive to inflicting physical pain upon others? What is beneficial about encouraging someone to build artificial levels of hatred and anger so that he can more effectively attack his fellows?

Today, children are lured into participating before they reach age 10. What kind of training are young people receiving when they are indoctrinated into going out and doing, in a ceremonial setting before crowds of adoring followers, what they would be thrown in jail for doing in everyday life—namely, committing violent physical attacks upon others?

Even boxing does not have as many negative aspects as football. In boxing the two contestants are evenly matched in weight. They are not assailed by unexpected, savage blows from behind and below the belt. And, they are not mentally conditioned into a frenzy to where they lose control emotionally. Many agree that boxing should be banned. Football is worse.

Football advocates defend the violent nature of their "sport" with the same old claim that if participants cannot express their anger and aggression on the playing field they will do so in society. Can we really accept that someone who is insensitive to breaking another person's bones in the heat of a "game" will, because of this exercise, be better prepared to deal with stressful situations out in the world in a civilized manner?

Football does not teach anyone to manage anger and aggressive instincts. Instead it encourages men to feed off these negative impulses to physically dominate others. It teaches that anger is desirable and that a constructive way to release it is to "hit" others. We see the results in homes across America. A recent study of domestic violence has revealed that football players have earned near top rankings as wife and child abusers.

If we are truly a society that abhors violence then we should not glorify sports that thrive on it. We should not teach our youngsters techniques for inflicting it. We should never try to desensitize them to inflicting pain upon others. We should never condition them to become pawns in mass hysteria. And we should never, under any circumstance, advocate hatred.

While football is probably the most detrimental team sport, the other major team sports also possess significant destructive aspects. The basic difference is that these other sports were not designed to showcase brute force and to award those who most effectively practiced violence. Rather, they were designed to relegate bodily contact between opponents to a decidedly subordinate role. In each sport participants can score and prevent scoring without making any contact. Due to the intense animation and intermingling of the players, contact cannot help but occur from time to time. But this is not the object of the game. Indeed, all but "incidental contact" was discouraged in the original rules.

Even in hockey, where it is legal to purposely collide with other players (body checking), many rules strictly control the nature of the contact allowed. It is the twisted interpretation of these rules which has given hockey its violent nature. Many players have, throughout its history, played successful hockey without resorting to the violent tactics we have come to identify with the sport. In fact, for decades the NHL has given a special award each season, the Lady Byng Trophy, to the player who has exhibited the most gentlemanly conduct on the ice. (Naturally it bears the name of a woman.)

Tragically, the vast majority of spectators do not attend hockey games or other team sports hoping to observe behavior that would win players sportsmanship awards. Rather, it is far more often a fascination with violence that draws spectators to these sports. This has enticed the sports hierarchy to instruct officials to bend the original rules and allow acts of brutality.

In baseball, umpires look the other way when players who have already been declared "out," slide into other players and risk injuring them just to disrupt further play. Other players, particularly the catcher, will block the base path illegally without possession of the ball instigating violent collisions. These situations have become known as "part of the game" in spite of the fact that numerous players are injured because of them.

In basketball, although the rules say that contact is to be penalized, the biggest players are allowed to push each other around in seeking position near the basket. Organizers of the sport say that they are catering to the fans who would not like to see the game stopped frequently to penalize fouls. In fact there has been a movement in the NBA to eliminate the 6-foul disqualification rule. This would keep many fans' favorite thugs in the game even after they'd used up their allotment of fouls.

Those who advocate this change conveniently overlook the purpose of the disqualification rule. It was written to discourage fouling and preserve the nature of the game as finesse oriented. When we bend that rule we change the nature of the game in favor of the more violent player. Those in charge of the sport purposely ignore the fact that if more fouls are called and more players disqualified, players will be discouraged from committing fouls. Eventually players will learn to play with more finesse. Fewer fouls will be committed, necessitating fewer game stoppages to penalize fouls. Those players who cannot compete with finesse will have to find some other sport in which to exercise their violent natures.

Hockey is even more glaring in its flagrant disregard for sportsmanlike behavior by allowing fistfights without major penalty. The hockey hierarchy would like us to believe that the high-speed action and bone crushing collisions naturally breeds anger and that the sport cannot be played without players releasing through fisticuffs. This, of course, is absurd. The players act without restraint because the penalty for fighting is minor—a few minutes off the ice. If, as in other sports, fighting was penalized with a game ejection and possible suspension, fighting would virtually stop. But the hockey hierarchy knows that many fans are drawn to the game because they like to watch violence—particularly fighting. So fistfighting receives a small tap on the wrist, making it an affordable technique for a player to use to intimidate others.

As a former basketball referee and baseball umpire, I recognize that in organized competition players play by the rules only to the extent they are enforced. Many coaches encourage players to "get away with" what they can. If the official lets you violate the rules, or you can violate them without being caught, go ahead and do so. Once officials are assigned to enforce the rules, players cast aside any responsibility to adhere to them except to the extent they fear penalty. In effect, morality based on inner conscience is scrapped and behavior is totally controlled by fear of disciplinary action or reprisal by opposing players.

This attitude spills over into society and encourages a lack of respect for the law in general. Organized sports regularly provide fortification for showing disrespect for the law. They send the message that, just as on the playing field, one should obey the law out of fear of being caught and punished rather than out of respect for the law as protection of the rights of everyone. Getting what YOU want is the overriding consideration. People tend to allow the rule enforcers (law enforcement personnel) to establish the boundaries of conduct. As long as they think they can escape punishment, people attempt to bend, stretch and violate the laws and rules in everyday activities to gain advantage. The attitude has become so common-place it is considered generally acceptable, embraced by adults and learned by children. Organized sports fortify it.

Years ago, I was working out at a local gym in preparation for fulfilling my official's responsibilities during the coming basketball season. There a friendly game was being played between players of no great skill. They had no official but this caused them no prob-lem. In spite of playing hard they exercised good sportsmanship by calling their own fouls and generally resolving most disputes with a minimum of arguing.

During a break in the action I asked them if they would like me to officiate, since I was looking to sharpen my skills. They agreed. Subsequently, within moments the game turned ugly. They began questioning my calls and arguing with each other. Their sense of conscience seemed to disappear as they tried to take advantage of every situation.

In the 1996 American League baseball championship series, an incident occurred that illustrates the virtually absolute absence of sportsmanship in sports, especially professional sports. Late in the first game with New York behind by a run a New York player hit a ball that appeared to have a chance to clear the outfield wall for a home run that would have tied the game. The Baltimore outfielder stood near the wall with glove hand raised as if preparing to catch the ball. Then suddenly as the ball descended a twelve-year-old male spectator reached out over the wall from above into the play-ing area and deflected the ball away from the player, into the stands. The umpire, who had been running across the field trying to see if the ball would be caught, did not see the boy deflect the ball and ruled that it had entered the stands without interference, making it a home run.

Immediately after, numerous television replays showed what had actually happened. Had the umpire had the same view as the cam-eras he likely would have declared the batter out due to fan inter-ference. But baseball rules did not allow the umpire's decision to be reversed. His decision tied the score of the game, allowing New York to eventually win.

Subsequently the boy was treated by the media as a celebrity, if not a full fledged hero. His picture made the front page of the Los Angeles Times. He was featured as a guest on numerous network TV shows. Everyone recognized that what he had done was a violation of those rules which govern the behavior of spectators at baseball games. The rules dictated that he should have been ejected from the stadium. But since the game had taken place in New York, the home management looked the other way and the boy was not penalized. The media chuckled about the incident.

In effect, the Baltimore team had been cheated out of a fair opportunity to win that game. But organized sports has come to embrace cheating as acceptable. This has come to be expected by both participants and spectators. Sports officials, using their power to penalize, have become the only defenders of sportsmanship during a contest.

I found the entire incident described above deplorable, not only because it reflected the deep lack of integrity that infects organized sports, but because it presented an opportunity that was ignored. Those people in the high echelons of organized sports who give lip service to the positive role sports can play in the lives of young boys, instead of personifying integrity in this instance, advocated cheating. An enormous opportunity to set a new standard for sports integrity was missed because of the blind pursuit of personal ambition.

Imagine the impact on sports morality in general if George Steinbrenner, the chief executive officer of the New York Yankees, had demanded that the protests of the Baltimore team be upheld. Imagine if he would have said, "In good conscience I cannot accept this victory because I know it was not achieved within the bounds of properly applied rules. I demand that my batter be declared out and the game replayed from the point of infraction. I don't care whether this costs my team a victory or not, winning under these circumstances is not acceptable. If I cannot win fairly I do not care to win."

Had that happened, Mr. Steinbrenner would have been idolized (rather than ridiculed, as he has so often been) by the majority of Americans. Many of the others—those who view winning as the overridingly important aspect of sports (One idolized football coach once said, "Winning isn't everything; it's the only thing.")—would have thought him a fool but would have looked foolish themselves had they criticized him publicly. He would have set a standard against which unsportsmanlike behavior would have been forever measured. Every parent would have been able to point to his gesture as an example of the proper attitude their children should maintain in sports.

But Mr. Steinbrenner looked the other way, as did the rest of the Major League Baseball hierarchy and the majority of baseball fans. He is no more to blame than they. He is simply a small part of the ruthless, immoral philosophy that dominates organized sports.

Organized sports provide a glaring demonstration of the religious pursuit of dominance that grips our society. In virtually every pursuit we seek to establish a pecking order. Most obviously we see it in government and the business world where strict hierarchy and corporate structure prevail. Arguably, efficiency demands such a protocol. But our culture seems to demand that we go further.

In every profession, every pursuit, every walk of life, we attempt to classify individuals as superior and inferior. This goes beyond assigning authority during a specific endeavor so that the effort can be focused. Rather this is an attempt to somehow immortalize ourselves by using performance to claim personal superiority over others.

In sports everyone is seeking more than just championships. They are seeking to be declared "the greatest," or "number one." In movies all principals seek the Oscar. In TV it's the Emmy. In music it's the Grammy. In education we seek superiority through grade point average.

Everywhere we turn: "Who is best?"

Does a sports championship prove that someone is "best?" What does "best" imply? Everyone who has been involved in athletics knows that the teams with the "best" athletes (theoretically the most talented) do not always win the championship. Teams may play at a level higher than everyone else all season long only to suffer misfortune or a substandard performance in the championship game and lose to a less talented team. Does this mean that they must feel inferior to the team that defeated them? Why must either team feel superior to the other?

Many people view winning as the measure of success and that it is only natural to pursue success in anything one does. The latter may be true, but why must we measure success against the performance of others? Why do we choose activities that set participants against each other in order to measure success? Even in team sports where individuals on the same team work together, they are pitted against another team. Even then, team members often measure their performance against each other, sometimes by comparing statistics and sometimes choosing a "Most Valuable Player" from among them.

The need to prevail in either war, business or sports, springs from the same need: the need to see oneself as separate from others, compare oneself to these others, and, hopefully, to establish superiority. Sports participants and their fans are clutching for outside approval to help them forget a daunting sense of insecurity, both regarding their abilities and their mortality. In society's mindset, a championship affixes success in a historical context. Those who doubt their efficacy as beings can always look back in time of failure to those successes they've achieved. Success, of course, is always measured by the degree of superiority society bestows upon an effort. A society-sanctioned championship is the ultimate ego-builder in the eye of the athlete.

An NBA, NFL or NHL championship ring should tell the winners that they performed at a high level for a certain period of time and should be proud of their effort. It makes one team more successful than others for a "season," during which it won the most games and/or a championship game. It establishes nothing beyond. The effort to give more significance to the feat is driven by this maniacal cultural necessity to classify everyone as superior or inferior to everyone else. This is the true purpose of all sporting competitions— to establish a context in which one can establish superiority to gratify ego.

The same holds true in the arts. Nearly all of them have been degraded by the questing after honors bestowed by the subjective opinions of others—often expressed at specially held competitions. We see art competitions, piano competitions, dance competitions, movie festivals. On the professional level we see awarded Oscars, Emmys, Grammys, Tonys and others.

To use the appellations "best" or "greatest" in artistic formats is even more absurd than in the sports context because we have nothing but subjective standards from which to judge performances. Many stirring movies were made and acting performances given without Oscars being awarded. Many inspirational songs were written and performed without winning Grammies. Why should these be considered inferior in some manner to those which won awards?

True, society has been conditioned to pay more attention to award winners and this allows those who win awards to earn greater financial reward. But awards were not created to foster financial gain. Rather, they were established to feed the desire for ego gratification. Financial rewards resulted when it became apparent that the vast numbers of people were using sports heroes to bolster their own egos and were willing to pay for the service. We can see evidence of this in the millions of trophies that are awarded in insignificant competitions. For most recipients, these will not lead to financial reward. Yet they are treasured nonetheless—symbols of one's mastery over others.

All of this fits so nicely into the patriarchal structure we have lived with for many centuries. Yet this is not necessarily a male thing. Recently we have seen women pursuing athletic glory as seriously as men. Both men and women have been conditioned to accept competition between human beings as a valid driving force. However, the conditioning emanates from a male dominated society which glorifies physical strength. In a patriarchy women can only manifest their assertive side in pursuits validated by men. Thus women with high levels of aggression gravitate to sports.

If sports embrace so many negatives, can they play a constructive role in our society? On an adult level they can only act in a positive manner if we eliminate their highly competitive side and use them purely for exercise. The same holds true for juvenile sports although certain aspects of them can be used as constructive teaching tools. Team oriented sporting activities can teach one valid society-enhancing technique—cooperation. But one need not compete against others to learn this. Nor must one practice blind obedience to team leaders and team goals.

Rather than to seek to establish superiority over another team, the objective could just as easily be to compete against one's own prior performance. Imagine a basketball team meeting each day to measure their improvement in shooting baskets. Or a track team training hard together with no meet facing them, encouraging each other to run faster or jump higher without having to measure themselves against others.

Once we acknowledge the value in this, however, we would soon see that the sporting activities we engage in now are too banal to deserve much of our attention. Why would we want to focus so much energy on the possession and movement of a game object—ball, puck, baton, etc.—when we could employ the same energy in addressing many of society's physical problems. One can receive a great deal of exercise from dealing with environmental problems like planting vegetation and restoring habitat.

Am I dreaming? Probably. Sports are too interwoven through our society to be cast aside without a realization triggered by something akin to divine intervention. We therefore should try to make the most of those positive elements that sports feature. For indeed, even when we're swept up into their negative aspects, sports do offer us positive learning opportunities.

Perhaps the most profound lesson I learned from my participation in team sports is the necessity of bonding with teammates in order to achieve success. I also came to see the negative effect of losing team focus and pursuing individual achievements that did not further team objectives.

In a team sport each individual brings unique skills to his/her team. As a game continues each participant will find themselves called upon at various times to exercise their particular skills for the benefit of the team. The skills of certain players will be more important at certain points in the game and of lesser importance at others. From game to game the demand for the various skills fluctuates depending on the strengths of the opponents and how each game progresses. But all skills are required for the team to be successful overall. Otherwise these skills would not have been sought out to include on the team.

Well adjusted team players appreciate the skills of all of their teammates as well as their own. Players find no value in separating themselves into subgroups which exalt their particular skills. They establish no hierarchy which honors certain skill groups over others. These things would interfere with team execution and would destroy morale. Instead they are quite willing to allow various players to play leading roles as the need demands.

This is the lesson of team sports, a pastime that dominates the attention of millions of men. And yet a vast majority of these men either don't understand the important principle just described, or they can't relate it to gender issues. Men seeking to dominate women are comparable to pitchers seeking to dominate position players on a baseball team. Not only would it be unfair and ridiculous, it would be counterproductive.

At the same time, women who are seeking equality by trying to assume roles more suited to men have also missed the point. They can be likened to baseball shortstops who demand the right to pitch even though they lack pitching skills. If allowed to do so they would undermine the team.

Team sports teach us that teams are best served by players assuming the roles best suited to their individual skills. Role playing in no way distracts players from identifying first and foremost with their team. And, each individual role is honored equally among all.

Successful gender dynamics demands the same approach. Perhaps those who have no exposure to team sports can be excused for not recognizing this. But sports enthusiasts should be able to make this association. After all, announcers, commentators and writers incessantly preach to them the importance of teamwork.

If participants can indeed learn these lessons through sports even as they gain valuable exercise, doesn't athletic competition validate itself? In my opinion—no! One can learn lessons and receive benefits from the most destructive acts. War encourages teamwork, promotes scientific discovery, advances technology, and reduces population pressures. Indeed, one past presidential advisor recently advocated us promoting war in Bosnia to allow the pressures of hatred to be relieved naturally. Of course, in wars thousands, sometimes even millions, die, not to mention all the material destruction and environmental devastation. Is this a price worth paying for the lessons we learn from war?

Likewise in sports. The lessons of teamwork we learn from sport are more than counterbalanced by the aggression and hostility we generate towards others. In sport we set human beings against each other. In the end some win and some lose. The winners are often glorified while the losers, by inference, feel humiliation. (Did you ever see the team that lost the World Series or Super Bowl invited to the White House? What message does that send?)

Teamwork can be more properly learned from working in teams to address real issues of concern to humanity. In this way, we turn our instinct for competition (which is nothing more than a concern for survival) against outside forces that would undermine us as a species. In this effort we may not always succeed, but we create nothing but winners by establishing bonds between genders and races.

Chapter Nine
Rape and Domestic Violence

What do men think of rape? On the surface it would seem that all but a handful see it as dastardly and unconscionable. And yet keeping in mind Warren Farrell's numerous excuses for men who commit rape, we can see that men's view of rape varies across a wide spectrum.

A few psychotics and self-proclaimed misogynists actually believe that rape is man's privilege. To them, women are here to serve men. Since men need sex and the species needs to reproduce, men should feel free at any time to force any woman to submit.

Next we find another small group who do not justify rape but who periodically fly into a psychotic rage directed against women and attack them as a result. Most of these men recognize that they have wronged their victim. This was their intention. By doing so they achieved revenge.

A much larger group of men sees rape as regrettable but at times justified due to women's behavior. They see women as temptresses withholding sex to gain advantage. They see women as behaving in a sexually provocative manner and thereby asking for "it." They see women as repressed, really wanting sex but being unable to overcome their inhibitions. These men usually don't see rape as an invasion of a woman's body and violation of her female psyche. In fact, in many cases they see themselves as having performed a favor for her. To them, intercourse is a simple physical exercise. Once completed, as long as the woman's body was not damaged, what has she lost?

In stark contrast stands the group of men who completely align themselves with women on the rape issue. They see no justification under any circumstance for a man to force himself upon a woman sexually. They recognize the extreme psychological trauma a woman faces when overpowered in a forced sex act. They can visualize her fear of disease and unwanted pregnancy. They can comprehend the devastating attack on her self-esteem. They can perceive the anxiety she will face from now on, both in dealing with men and in recognizing that in a world dominated by men she does not have complete control over her life.

I've left for last the largest group of all. These are the men who detest rape, but from a male viewpoint which furthers their own purposes and fails to acknowledge the viewpoint of women. These men see rape as detestable because it is unmanly and defiles a woman's value in the eyes of men. They see the perpetrator as a coward and a loser who lacks the sex appeal to attract a woman and "score" solely on his masculine merits. Since these men look upon women as property or potential property of either themselves or other men, they see rape as a form of vandalism. To them, the "poor" woman has lost something important in a rape—some of her value to men.

This viewpoint has prevailed throughout recorded history. It is the viewpoint of patriarchy.

Some feminists have labeled all men throughout history as rapists for having justified and, at times (especially wartime), advocated rape. While this charge has some merit, it does not paint an accurate picture. Many men detested rape for the reasons mentioned above. The original Roman kingdom fell because of a single rape—that of Lucretia. The abduction of Helen triggered the Trojan War. The Bible and other scriptures, most authored by men, condemn rape. True, these instances reflect men's attitudes toward property—women's status in those times. Nevertheless, it shows that men for the most part did not view rape as a moral act. Even in war the raping of women captives was viewed as a negative act—humiliation of the enemy by degrading his personal property. Today some men oppose including a woman in combat situations for fear of her being captured and raped.

Once again, I'm not trying to justify men's behavior but rather place it in accurate perspective so that modern men cannot escape their distorted views of rape by pointing to outrageous charges by feminists. I'm aware of no society that has advocated rape, except perhaps by their armies during wars. Throughout history the vast majority of civilized men deplored rape and thus cannot be classified as rapists. And yet many of these men by their patriarchal view of women as property cultivated attitudes that ultimately fostered rape by others.

As we can see from Farrell's charges, today men commonly claim that by using sexuality to hold men hostage, women instigate resentment and violent reactions from men. While this may be so, we have also seen how the patriarchal system has not allowed women other means to exercise control over their lives.

In times past, women's only power resource was sexuality—their ability to attract a mate who possessed a measure of real power. In fact, in those times (this holds true for many women today) much of a woman's self esteem was derived from body image and sex appeal as gleaned from the number and "quality" of her suitors. She couldn't attract most men by displaying aggressiveness, competitiveness, etc. She had to portray a patriarchal image of vulnerability and sexual appeal. At the same time she had to withhold her sexual favors, maintaining her "purity" until she found a man willing to purchase it with a lifelong commitment of support.

Even today most women must cloak their very natural urge to explore their sexuality in the image of sexuality that entices men. Thus men have shaped female behavior, particularly when it comes to sex. If men were attracted to women who were behaving according to their natural instincts—i.e., in a manner contrary to that dictated by patriarchal attitudes—temptresses wouldn't exist.

Sadly, old patriarchal attitudes still thrive. We see them in the many men who maintain that the frequency of rape is exaggerated by women. Many of these claim that women often ask to be raped by the signals they send out. They further claim that the definition of rape is too wide. (Remember Farrell: women often mean "yes" when they say "no.")

Is the frequency of rape overstated? Even if Farrell is right that 60% of rape charges are false, does that diminish the seriousness of the other 40%? And what about those thousands of cases that go unreported because of victims' fears of serving as a witness and experiencing withering attacks on the witness stand? Consider the following statistics and keep in mind that experts estimate that only one in eight rapes is reported.

The FBI Uniform Crime Report stated that 102,560 rapes or attempted rapes occurred in 1990. The Bureau of Justice estimated that 130,000 women were rape victims in 1990. The Harris Poll estimated 380,000 rapes or sexual assaults in 1993. The National Victims Center reported 683,000 forcible rapes in 1990. And the Justice Department recently estimated that 8% of all American women will be victims of rape or attempted rape in their lifetimes. (Other estimates go as high as 1 of 3.)

Those men who view these numbers as lacking significance ought to consider what it would feel like to become a victim. I don't mean being maneuvered into having sex with an aggressive female partner. Rather, being forced to submit to sexual activity with someone they loathe (male or female) who might kill them in the act or forever change their lives by leaving them seriously injured, pregnant, or infected with a terminal disease. Indeed, these men need to consider what it is like to live with the fear that this could happen anytime they leave secured premises. As one woman put it, "The possibility of being raped alters the meaning and feel of the night...and it is night half the time." The figures above would indicate that this fear is justified. Men have little to fear in this context because virtually all rapists are men and the vast majority of the victims are women.

Many, men and women, would have us believe that rape is not a sexual act but rather one of violence toward women. The perpetrator seeks to release anger by dominating and humilating his victim.

In those many cases where this appears to be true, sexuality is still involved. If this was not the case then why rape? It would be much easier to simply beat a woman and invade her body in ways other than sexual. But sex means something to the rapist. Perhaps to him its meaning is aberrant compared to that of normal men. Nevertheless, something about the act of raping arouses him sexually. Otherwise he could never sustain an erection during the act. Granted, with these rapists sex and violence are tightly linked. Many of them fear and hate women and can only achieve orgasm through violence.

Of course, some anger rapists do, without being sexually aroused, force victims to commit acts of sodomy. But forced intercourse, the most common act of rape, cannot take place unless the act has sexual meaning to the rapist.

I recently had four separate lengthy discussions, one each with four detectives from different divisions of the Los Angeles Police Department. All had been investigating rape and domestic violence cases for several years. Three were female; one was male. All expressed strikingly similar views on the motivation for and circumstances surrounding rape.

All agreed that sexual motivation played a significant role in most of the rapes they had investigated. At the same time, while it was their view that anger also played a part in many rapes, all found that a much more common motivation seemed to be the need to exercise control. The interrogation of many rapists revealed that most found themselves lacking a feeling of control when trying to experience sex with a willing partner. Forcing someone gave them this feeling and vastly heightened their sexual excitement. If violence was necessary to establish control, then it would be utilized. But for most rapists the motivation was not to employ violence and to inflict harm, but to exercise control. The difference may seem subtle, but it is significant.

Contrary to the stated view of most feminists and many psychologists, it seems apparent that many other rapists are indeed motivated by sexual impulses exclusive of anger. Many of these view sex from a self-indulgent perspective. They experience the act almost completely subjectively, focused on their own pleasure with only the vaguest perception of the desires of their partner. They can even convince themselves that their partner is enjoying the act when all outward reactions point to the contrary. This can take place because they are immersed in their own subjective experience. They experience sex in a juvenile manner.

Granted, the sex rapist is just as twisted psychologically and guilty of criminal behavior as is the anger rapist. But it is important to recognize the different motivations. The sex rapist is spawned in a culture which tends to depersonalize sex.

A vast number, perhaps even a majority, of people experience sex almost completely subjectively. Taking their own pleasure holds priority. They prefer their partner to enjoy the act for they find this ego enhancing. But nevertheless, they primarily satisfy their sexual needs through experiencing their own physical sensations. It is this attitude, this approach, when carried to the extreme, that can turn a person into a sex rapist.

Both men and women are increasingly encouraged to explore their sexuality in a manner which ignores commitment, responsibility and bonding. Subjective sex is being normalized. In the face of this modern perspective, many men have found themselves for various reasons deprived of sex in a world that flaunts it and encourages them to seek it out. Like drug addicts, who steal when they can find no other means to obtain drugs, some men must "steal" sex or go without.

Yes, those with means could seek out prostitutes. But sex with a prostitute has an impersonal quality different from sex with a woman who you find attractive. While the physical kicks might by satisfying, psychologically the client is always faced with the reality of copulating with a well-used partner performing purely for money. He finds it difficult to grade his sexual performance for he cannot trust the response he receives as genuine. Thus he is deprived of a major psychological reward in sex.

Raping a non-professional, however, affords numerous psychological thrills depending on the particular fetish of the rapist. Certainly in most cases, no matter how adverse, he can trust the response of the victim as genuine. And there is always the chance (remote in our eyes, but not necessarily in his) that his victim will respond positively. For him numerous possibilities for psycho-sexual satisfaction exist with a non-professional.

If feminists hope to diminish the incidents of rape they must stop ignoring its sexual aspects. Otherwise we may find some way to deal with "anger rapists" only to find ourselves left with a bevy of untreated "sex rapists."

Consider the following situation which closely resembles a case currently under investigation by one LAPD detective:

A man goes to a bar seeking contact with women he hopes will ultimately lead to sex. It is reasonable to assume that women who patronize this bar have similar motivation. He meets a woman who sexually arouses him at first sight. They share drinks, conversation, and dancing, all of which heightens his sexual arousal. Through his perception of her body language and other gestures he has every right to believe they have made a "connection," even though she has not verified this verbally. They leave the bar together and outside they begin "making out." This sends his hormones raging. Everything seems to indicate that she has been following the same course. Then suddenly she says, "stop!" At this point the man, who experiences sex subjectively, is focused upon "getting off." He rationalizes away her protest and proceeds to force sex upon her.

Can anyone honestly label this man as an anger rapist? Can they claim that he raped this woman because he hated her and wanted to defile her body? Nonsense. This man was swept up in a sexual fantasy. This type of situation occurs all the time. It is just as de-plorable as anger rape, but it is not anger rape. It is sexual rape perpetrated by men suffering from aberrant, self-indulgent views of sex.

Feminists point to pornography as a main culprit in cultivating the violent attitudes toward sexuality that lead to rape. Indeed, their effort to eradicate pornography is based on their premise that most, if not all, porn glorifies violence against women.

This is not even close to being the truth. The bulk of widely circu-lated pornography, be it publication or film, portrays women as highly assertive sexual beings who love the action and as often as not control men in their sexual encounters. One could actually make the case for much of pornography painting women in a light favor-able to non-gay feminists since it portrays them as independent, non-repressed, free thinking persons.

True, a significant amount of bondage pornography exists, and this is certainly violence focused. But it is a less prevalent segment of pornography. Banning it may or may not interdict the rapist ten-dencies of those deviates it appeals to. In any case, by attacking pornography as violent exclusively, feminists can only make a le-gitimate attack on the bondage genre. Their attacks fail to address the negative view of women put forth by the vast remainder of porn. And so the porno industry proceeds merrily on, using feminist il-logic to easily brush off feminist protest.

Feminists would make a much stronger argument against porn if they would acknowledge that sex plays a major part in many rapes. Pornography portrays women as having such a strong appetite for sex that it often overcomes discretion. She enjoys sex with anyone, anyplace, anytime. The message to many men is that when forcing a reluctant woman he is simply overcoming her self-defeating in-hibitions and giving her the pleasure she secretly craves. This is far more prevalent in porn and more dangerous to women than the sadistic line of porn. Sadistic porn appeals to the already aberrated, while "normal" porn instills false images of women in men who may then be tempted to rape.

The reason why most feminists cling to the view that rape is an-ger motivated is because they wish to avoid placing any responsi-bility upon their gender. If they were to acknowledge that men's sexual fantasies trigger many instances of rape, feminists would have to examine the nature and breadth of the sexual signals emitted by women. This they find threatening to the uninhibited lifestyle they advocate.

Which leads us to the phenomenon referred to as acquaintance rape. Men claim that recent oversensitivity to the rape issue has placed them in the position of being easily falsely accused. They say they face a dilemma. Since they have always been expected to be the initiator in male/female relationships, they are confused as to how far they can go. To them, women's signals are not always clear.

This problem is very real. Men do indeed face a confusing situation. A major part of it can be blamed upon our patriarchal heritage.

First of all men have been conditioned to be the aggressors; women to be coy. It has always been unmanly for a man to allow a woman to overtly assert herself and thus control the relationship. Predominantly, women have acquiesced to conditioning, repressed their feelings and played their role as subordinate partner. If patriarchy had not demanded that men and women play these roles and allowed them to experience and express their true feelings, the confusion that leads to and surrounds the acquaintance rape issue would not exist.

The biggest problem with trying to draw constructive conclusions on this issue is that both opposing viewpoints have merit and major flaws. The feminist view would, upon first examination, seem unassailable. No matter what has led up to an encounter, when a woman says "no" that should veto any further advance. She may have initiated a romantic interlude. She may have sent signals that she had an interest in sex. She may even have allowed foreplay. But even then she has the right (just as does he) to terminate the encounter at any point. This may make her a "bitch," "whore," "tease" or "temptress," but that gives no right to any man to invade her body against her wishes. Any man who does so has committed rape. She may have acted irresponsibly and led him to the brink, but he is nevertheless responsible if he forces her the final step.

Many men like to portray our gender as lusty with a sex drive difficult to control once sexual momentum has been built. These are usually men whose main goal in sex is self-gratification. They tend to use the female body as a masturbation accessory. Otherwise a "no" or other expression of unwillingness would quickly dash sexual impulses in an encounter. Rape would not only become unthinkable but physically impossible. In sensitive men who care about women, a "no" drains blood from the penis.

Many men would argue this. I suggest that it is some fantasy that is keeping their penis erect after a woman rejects their advance and that she is purely a prop with whom they hope to fulfill their fantasy. If this woman says "no," it means nothing because the man is relating to his fantasy and in it his lover is saying "yes, yes, yes!"

Men must bear full responsibility for such fantasizing. A woman should not have to tread cautiously to keep from setting off his fantasy or to play along with it once it has arisen. She has a right to be herself with any man no matter how tempting she may appear to him, and she has no obligation to submit to him once he is attracted. This also applies within a marriage. Men have no right in any circumstance to force women into any form of sexual activity.

Having said this, I must now point my finger at women for bearing some responsibility on the issue of acquaintance rape.

Many women are not innocent of bringing on the monstrous consequences that result.

Feminists stand on solid ground when they classify the vast majority of men as patriarchal, dominating, confused, unfeeling and prone to violence. (It is because I generally agree with this description that I am writing this book.) Yet they never seem to question why women gravitate toward making acquaintance with men who ultimately rape them.

By definition, acquaintance rape takes place when the perpetrator convinces the victim to voluntarily accompany them to a place of seclusion where the forced act can take place. The victim would have us believe that her attacker gave her no indication during all the time she knew him that he had designs upon her sexually and a propensity to act them out. In some cases this may well be the case. But the question still arises—how aware was the victim?

About now I can hear feminists screaming. And I grant them this point. No matter how unaware the victim, a man who forces a woman under any circumstance is a criminal who deserves full punishment. Nothing justifies his behavior.

At the same time we must look at the practical. How can we stop acquaintance rape? If feminists believe that the vast majority of men are patriarchal, dominating, confused, unfeeling and prone to violence, what can we say about those women who befriend and date them?

Am I suggesting that women place the vast majority of men off limits for even dating? I'm suggesting that women remain aware of what type of men they're dealing with. If it is indeed a mating and dating jungle out there then women must be prepared to protect themselves while on the safari. Smart safariists don't allow dangerous wild animals to get too close. They don't approach strange animals without knowing whether those animals are prone to attack. And, they don't wander off unarmed into areas where beasts can suddenly turn upon them. Yes, this puts regrettable, inconvenient restrictions upon women. But that is the nature of negotiating a jungle safely.

I realize that the majority of women do not share the feminist viewpoint which looks upon the vast majority of men as being dominated by these animal propensities. I've made this the operative viewpoint here because feminists have made the loudest outcry against acquaintance rape. For them to denounce the rapist without rebuking the victim for her lack of discretion is not only disingenuous, but it also adds nothing to the search for a practical solution.

If women are to make inroads into solving the acquaintance rape problem they must begin to realize that the feminist view of men is largely correct. That doesn't make the vast majority of men potential rapists. But it does mean that when a women regularly seeks the companionship of men, with most she will eventually be exposing herself to serious character flaws that may include the propensity to violence and aberrant sexual attitudes. Most of these men will have these traits neatly camouflaged. Indeed, they will likely have perfected approach techniques designed to charm the unwary. This has been going on for ages and yet it still works. Why? Because women (and men) have not trained their perception to evaluate potential partners.

The attitudes of men, whether healthy or degenerate, are usually discernable if one takes a little time to observe them. For example, dominating men are likely to try to dominate sexually. Men who attempt to deceive and manipulate others will likely use the same techniques upon the woman they date. To an objective observer, these traits are usually glaring. Yet women keep the company of such men. They allow themselves, after a minimum amount of contact, to be charmed into going off privately with these individuals. These women have the power to prevent any mistreatment at the outset by keeping their distance. Instead, gullibility lowers their defenses allowing them to be maneuvered into a position where they can be harmed.

The key factor defining acquaintance rape is prior familiarity between the rapist and victim. Victims claim that they have known their attackers for various periods of time and had no inclination that sex was on the minds of these people. Some of the attackers were considered long time friends. I question how well they knew these individuals before accepting them as "friends" and relating to them in private. To repeat, most men send distinct signals as to their inner attitudes if one is willing to be patient and tune in. Unfortunately many victims of abuse, whether it be psychological, physical, or rape, chose to ignore the signals and roll the dice. Those women who have acted prudently and still been raped by "friends" deserve our complete sympathy.

The area of the acquaintance rape issue where women often bear some responsibility is that which can be specifically referred to as "date rape." If a woman accepts a man's offer for a "date" she is entering the sexual arena whether she intended to do so or not. If she intends to emerge unscathed she had better choose her companions carefully with a mind as to the sexual dynamics involved. Sadly, however, women's choices are often very poor. I say that because I constantly see women falling under the spell of obviously insecure men with an unhealthy hunger for female contact which reeks of something beyond the need for normal companionship.

Many women say that they accepted the offer of a "date" just to have fun. They forget or never realized that unless the participants specifically declare the contrary beforehand, an interest in sex (eventually) is implied when offering or accepting any "date." That is the definition of a "date." Two people of the opposite sex get together to learn about each other with the possibility of deepening the relationship. The term "date" does not apply to two friends of the opposite sex getting together expressly to attend some event or function out of mutual interest.

Sex is even further implied by the custom of men paying for dates.

If a woman accepts a date under those circumstances she is implying that she is willing to play the "dating" game, which many men
see as ultimately leading to sex. These men expect to receive something from their expenditure.

Here I will incur the wrath of feminists by describing a stark reality which they deplore. Men's conditioning dictates that he view the
way a woman carries herself and dresses as reflecting her attitude
toward sexuality. A sexy walk says she is searching for sexual contact. Revealing dress says that she is open to sexual overtures and
will participate more freely than her conservatively dressed sisters.

Most feminists deny that a style of dress must necessarily send out
sexual signals. They maintain that a woman should be allowed to
dress as revealingly as she likes without men drawing assumptions
regarding her attitudes toward sexuality. Perhaps they are right.
Unfortunately this flies in the face of the realities of the fashion
world.

In our society the vast majority of people accept fashion as a statement of who they are. "That is (or isn't) me," is a statement often
heard when they shop for clothing. Few people choose their clothing oblivious to how they will appear to others. Almost everyone
makes a statement with their style of dress. Therefore if a woman
chooses to wear clothing that accents her sexual appeal she will be
commonly viewed as being open to sexual contact.

She may not really feel that way. She may be purely responding to
conditioning or emulating other females without any thought of sex.
Nevertheless, the majority of men will perceive her as being interested in sex. They have been conditioned by elders and peer groups
to evaluate women thusly. This may be erroneous and does not justify unwanted sexual advances, but it is reality. And actually, more
often than not these men find their assessment accurate. They often "score" with women who bear themselves this way. This fortifies men's view so that they view all women who appear thusly as
having the same sexual attitudes. If women are to avoid rape they
must be conscious of what they project, intentionally or not.

Many men and women have difficulty choosing worthy partners
because in addition to other superfluous things, they are attracted
to how another person treats them rather than the qualities that
the other displays. But one's treatment of another can be contrived
style and not originate from inner essence. Few people take the

time to discover the essence of others before granting access to personal space. If they find the advances appealing, they allow an emotional attachment to form without looking to see if the person's substance matches their overtures. When reality sets in, both genders suffer emotional trauma. Sadly, women may also face physical penalties for their lack of discretion.

If I seem to be harder in this section on victims than on rapists, I don't mean to be. I'm simply trying to protect women from the many degenerate men who commit rape. We need to rid our lagoon of as many of these sharks as we can. But we'll never remove them all. Unfortunately that's the nature of an insecure humanity. So, since women must swim, they must keep a lookout. And, for heaven's sake, they must not enter the water with an open wound and then thrash about, drawing further attention.

As men, we can discourage other men from attacking women. We can even intercede when we see it happening. But we can do nothing when a woman blindly chooses to go off privately with one of these disturbed individuals and places herself in a position to be attacked. We can do little when a woman ignores obvious serious faults in a man and enters a permanent relationship in which the faults eventually flare into the open and culminate in violence.

Domestic Violence

In one of their latest efforts to avoid the implications of their holding power over women, men have begun claiming that they too are victims of domestic violence. They cite statistics to illustrate how prevalent female violence against men has become. The figures seem to say that males are nearly as often victims as women.

We certainly can't ignore the statistics, even if they are fragmented and relatively non-specific. Obviously women do attack men physically and the number of cases is sufficiently large to demand attention. But what I find outrageous is men's attempt to place female violence against men on the same plane as male violence against women. In doing so men are obviously trying to escape responsibility as a gender for the brutalizing of women.

Recent FBI statistics tell us that 1.8 Million women are beaten by men every year; 2-4 thousand women die every year from abuse; 30% of all women killed are slain by their partners. When we examine these numbers and compare them to those which point to women victimizing men we can see a vast discrepancy. Even if it were true that women attacked men as often as vice versa (something that is still highly doubtful), the seriousness of these attacks cannot compare to that revealed in the above figures. Thousands of men do not die each year from spousal abuse. Nor can a percentage of male victims of homicide anywhere near 30% be attributed to women.

The experience of the aforementioned LAPD detectives, who must investigate several of these cases every shift, had a small variance. One stated that approximately 30% of domestic violence calls involve charges of women attacking men. This is, of course, a considerable number even if the ratio is less than 2-1. However, she has also found it extremely rare for men to suffer serious injuries in these cases. The overwhelming majority of serious injuries suffered in domestic violence situations have been inflicted by men.

Another detective at first estimated that less than five percent of domestic violence calls involve women physically attacking men. She then hedged by admitting she could not remember ever having investigated a case where a man suffered serious injuries.

The male detective generally agreed with this assessment, although he admitted having seen a few serious injuries caused by women wielding weapons—knives, screwdrivers and hammer. He viewed this as women resorting to weapons in order to offset their male companion's strength advantage.

By far the most prevalent domestic charges filed by men against women entails verbal abuse. These calls are common and reports are taken. However, in most cases arrests are not made because no physical violence has taken place.

Undeniably, verbal abuse can be very cruel and those who inflict it, whether male or female, need to be stopped. But verbal abuse does not threaten life and limb. Nor does it justify physical retaliation.

No justification can be cited for men or women employing violence against each other except to defend themselves from physical attack. This means that women have no right to strike any man with hand, fist or object in any other circumstance. This does happen, and it may happen frequently. It is an aspect of domestic violence that should not be ignored. Men need to be counseled on how to deal with violent partners.

But at the same time it is atrocious to attempt to cover over the age old plight that women have faced when living with violent men. Although we can see certain similar aspects between the violence inflicted by men and women, one vastly different factor separates them. In the vast majority of cases, women are physically helpless to resist their attacker while men facing similar circumstances have far superior abilities to physically defend themselves.

In most cases men have a significant advantage in physical strength, giving them potential control over both situations. As one male victim of female violence put it, "I could put her in the hospital, but I just take it." Indeed, our third LAPD detective estimates that 30% of female domestic violence victims require medical attention.

Few women can defend themselves, much less "put him in the hospital," if attacked by a violent partner. Unless they arm themselves, an escalation that could ultimately land them in jail or morgue, they are virtually helpless. The punch, slap or kick from most women does not carry the destructive force of similar blows from men. Most men have learned over their lifetime how to strike effective blows while most women have never been in situations which demand physical fighting. In most cases the less robust physiques of women are far more vulnerable to heavier male blows than are the physiques of men to the lighter blows of women. Quite simply, female blows generally cause men annoying pain, superficial injuries and general embarrassment. Male blows often inflict excruciating pain and serious injury, necessitating hospitalization. While men can often prevent their injuries by exerting their superior physical strength, women have no such recourse.

The experience of the LAPD detectives verifies this every day. Very rarely do they encounter adult male domestic violence victims who need hospitalization or even medical treatment. Most suffer superficial scratches or cuts. Women victims, however, are regularly carted off in ambulances after having suffered massive contusions, broken bones and other internal injuries, some of them permanently impairing.

A sad aside to this is one detective's description of a freguent scene at a police station in a predominantly Hispanic neighborhood. More often than not after a man has been booked for domestic violence, within a matter of hours the female victim arrives, often wearing bandages, sling, or cast, to plead with the police to drop charges. Had not someone else called the police, the attack would have gone unreported. The Hispanic family tends to view these things more tolerantly, therefore countless acts of vicious domestic violence remain hidden behind closed doors further laundering the statistics in favor of men.

In those domestic violence situations where weapons are employed the male strength advantage is narrowed by varying degrees. Even so, unless a gun is employed, males still fare better in these situations than women. Picture a woman armed with a knife attacking a man, and then the opposite. Which victim will most likely have a better chance of defending themselves?

The qualitative difference between women attacking men and vice versa is the degree of control. Both genders have violent tendencies that they need to address. Both physically abuse the other, although whether to the same extent is highly doubtful. But to imply that the use of violence by one gender against the other has the same implications in both situations is another attempt by men to cover over their abuse of women. To admit to it would be admission of an abuse of their power over women, a power men don't wish to acknowledge for fear of having to give it up.

Chapter Ten
Sex & Relationships

The stubborn effort to maintain gender duality and assign exclusive traits, roles and potentials to each, cannot help but distort mating relationships and the sex that results. Humans evolved driven by a natural imperative to bond with mates and create a harmonious environment which enhances the growth of children. Even if we choose not to raise children, the bonding imperative remains.

Instead, however, men and women within relationships tend to see each other as distinctly different and, consequently, rivals. It has become accepted that conflict to varying degrees will haunt all mating relationships. This conclusion sculpts the opinion of even those professional "experts" who regularly dispense advice on the topic.

Author John Gray in a famous bestseller states, "Men are from Mars, Women are from Venus." This of course implies distinctly different characters for men and women and the book proceeds to prescribe numerous solutions to the conflicts imposed by this alleged intrinsic difference.

Sam Keen states, "Marriage is designed for two people to fall out of love and into reality." He concludes that romantic love is based upon fantasy and then proceeds to advise men how to avoid the pitfalls that accompany "falling in love."

Robert Bly advises men to free their "Wild Man" and thereby divest themselves of the bonds imposed by women.

These authors may come from different backgrounds and appeal to different advocacies, but they share a common role—that of battlefield medic.

A battlefield medic has the function of trying to keep wounded alive by performing emergency measures with minimal medical resources. Ideally the victim will then be rapidly transported from the battlefield to a dressing station and ultimately to a hospital where a full range of medical attention can be given. However, if the medic attempts to patch up traumatized victims and then convince them that they can return to battle in spite of their wounds, he/she has done them a disservice.

This metaphor can be applied to many contemporary psychologists and other counselors.

John Gray qualifies as a relationships medic when he classifies numerous behavior practices as gender exclusive, then declares that the genders are so diverse in their views and approaches to life that they may as well be from different planets. For when we look more closely at Gray's generalities we can see that many members of each gender possess characteristics he attributes exclusively to one planet or the other. But he does not address men who respond to the world in a decidedly Venusian manner, nor women with a majority of traits that, according to him, should only belong to Men from Mars.

Once again, his advice will offer some relief for those who fit his model. Others will find themselves more confused. In any case, his advice amounts to emergency medical attention, not treatment that leads directly to a permanent cure.

Sam Keen's observation about romance and marriage comes from his own experience. Self-admittedly, he has been unable to sustain romance in his marriages. I'm sure he has seen numerous other examples of romantic failure. To him, of course, that means that romance can't be sustained by any married couple. And so he advises all men to devalue romance and build their relationships on other factors. No further examination of the powerful, virtually universal impulse we call "romance" is advocated. Nor does Keen suggest that men look into the personal inadequacies behind their allowing romance to bloom and then failing to sustain it. Instead of recommending deeper introspection on the topic, Keen suggests that men follow his suggestion and view romance as an affliction to overcome. Keen's views are those of another medic.

The approach of most medics seems to indicate that they believe that natural gender differences exist and these will always breed conflict. They see combat in relationships as inescapable. Their goal is to reduce our pain by patching us up and then sketching out a plan which will lead us through the relationship mine field with our suffering a minimum of wounds. Few suggest we can escape being wounded. And virtually none suggest that the war could be ended. Rather, they counsel us on how to survive in the conflict even as we try to extract some measure of enjoyment from it.

Is that our lot then—to fight, to sustain wounds and to be patched up so we can return to the front lines, perhaps with better equipment, to continue the fight? Isn't it about time we begin to question the war? Shouldn't that be part of our healing process?

Throughout this book I have been dealing with the conflict between the genders. I have been trying to make the point that the genders are not all that different and that gender enmity exists because one gender has exaggerated the differences in order to maintain dominance. Here, however, in the area of male/female personal relationships, the genuine differences legitimately come into play. If no legitimate difference existed, men and women would not be driven to seek completion with each other.

Relationship differences can be classified in two types: conflicting and complementary. Obviously, nature designed human gender differences as the latter. We can see the evidence of this simply by examining human physical characteristics. The species could not continue without the two genders coming together sexually and it could not endure as successfully without their physical cooperation.

If then, physical cooperation between genders has been crucial to our surviving, would nature have designed us with conflicting psychological differences? That hardly seems likely, for these would interfere with our coming together in complementary fashion to satisfy our overall physical needs. Thus, it seems certain that gender conflict has resulted from socialization and those professionals who address it as natural undermine the best interests of humanity.

Before I go on I must acknowledge that the subject of inter-gender relationships is very complex, traversing many sociological and psychological levels. Each person who has relationship problems (certainly most of us) has a unique perspective and must travel a unique path to dealing with his/her related personal issues. Many of them can be traced back into childhood—birth trauma, neglect, sexual abuse, and many other causes. Other individuals have spent far more time studying these topics and I will leave analysis of specifics to them.

I do believe, however, that in order to understand gender conflict it is important to explore some basic relationship dynamics. Before we can proceed to solving on a feeling level our deep-seated psychological issues relating to gender, we must first identify and acknowledge on an intellectual level the socially ingrained behavior patterns that inhibit our healing. Only through the exercise of reason can we intelligently choose what course of recovery to follow and whom we will trust to counsel us in the deeper psychological pursuit of constructive, lasting changes.

Personal inter-gender relationship conflict has been greatly intensified by the patriarchal view, which vastly distorts gender roles. The genders try to relate to each other even as they maintain a separateness that protects a distinct gender identity. But since bonding and separateness are antithetical, relationships which seek to achieve both cannot help but breed conflict.

Problems in inter-gender relationships usually grow out of a distorted approach to relationships in general. We therefore must examine how we, especially those of us in Western civilization, relate to people in general.

Throughout our society most of us regularly show disrespect for others. (The most glaring example of this is big city driving, during which other people, hidden in their vehicles, seem to lose identity and most rules of decency seem to be suspended.) Thankfully only a small minority of us are so self-indulgent that we consciously mistreat others without remorse.

However, many of the rest of us who do feel badly when we misbehave, seek to escape responsibility and the need to modify our behavior. We try to deceive ourselves and convince those victimized that our behavior is acceptable. To assuage ourselves we entertain all forms of exotic rationalizations and to placate others we commonly employ hugs, handshakes, expressions of politeness and hollow verbal apologies. Anything to get others to accept us without our having to change our behavior.

People who indulge themselves in disregard to others (and most of us do) cannot help but carry this attitude, even if to a lesser degree, into their most intimate relationships, thus poisoning them. No relationship can proceed constructively when parties are focused on satisfying their own needs and are using their partner primarily to achieve that end.

Many in our society endure this mistreatment because they need companionship. They embrace a philosophy advocated primarily by the religiously oriented and New Agers. Its main theme is: do not judge. Accept people "for what they are." Overlook inconsiderate behavior. Indeed, avoid demeaning yourself by judging other people's behavior as inconsiderate.

When we compare this viewpoint to another large segment in our society which advocates a more vindictive approach—avenge oneself, punish those who misbehave without considering their motivation—the religious/New Age philosophy seems to have merit. A vast majority of people subscribe to one of these two divergent approaches, leaving our society stuck between two extremes when trying to deal with those who misbehave. We tend to either judge them as "evil" and seek to exact some form of retribution (if only castigation or our disdain) or we accept them in spite of what they do to harm others. Both of these approaches undermine human relationships in general, on one side breeding enmity and on the other a permissiveness that encourages the strong to feed on the weak.

Numerous philosophers and theologians have pointed out the morally destructive consequences of judging and being revenge motivated. But few have discussed how the acceptance or rationalization of misbehavior also reflects moral laxity.

Why should we accept others "for what they are" even when their behavior is inconsiderate and detrimental to others? What happens when we reward with approval those who misbehave? Almost certainly they will continue to misbehave and victimize others. Why would one alter behavior which they find personally pleasurable if in addition to satisfying their self-indulgent impulse they continue to receive approval from others?

People seldom behave inconsiderately because they wish to cause others displeasure. Rather, in seeking self-satisfaction they have not even considered the effect of their actions upon others. Even so, most of those acting inconsiderately care, to varying degrees, how others think of them and would be willing to modify their behavior if they thought it displeased others. However, when they receive outside approval for indulging in behavior they find personally pleasurable, they find their behavior extra rewarding and are more likely to repeat it. Thus a case can be made to declare people who display approval for the misbehaving as acting immorally.

Many would have us believe that the act of demonstrating approval (love?) for others does not necessarily imply that we approve of their behavior. True, but unfortunately most people take it that way.

Where then does that leave us? If we are not to judge or not to approve, how are we to deal with those who misbehave? A major factor that must come into consideration is the perpetrator's motivation. Most people experience attacks of suppressed pain that can be traced back to childhood. In desperate attempts to escape this pain many people indulge in behavior that hurts others. Even the most heinous killer is usually a product of terrible mistreatment. We have a duty to recognize that and evaluate people on that basis.

That does not mean, however, that we should approve of them while they continue their transgressions. Rather, we must consider those being victimized and give them priority.

Everyone has the right to live without being victimized by the pain of others. Each of us has the obligation to deal with our pain without affecting others in the process. This, after all, is what caused our mistreatment in the past. Parents in pain mistreat children who eventually respond in kind with their own children. The chain must be broken and this means taking an outward stand against misbehavior.

I do not propose that we focus much of our attention on evaluating the behavior of others for the purpose of conveying our judgment. Too many of us have already carried that approach to extremes. However, when we are mistreated or see others close to us mistreated we owe it to ourselves to be honest about our feelings, at least to ourselves, and preferably to the perpetrator as well. To fail to do so demeans ourselves and is detrimental to the misbehaving person as well, who may have no idea what he/she is doing. Maybe withdrawal of approval will not induce the misbehaving person to stop. But at least the victim is no longer held captive by the need to give approval and can act to prevent themselves from being victimized. This is only reasonable, responsible and fair.

Finally, perhaps we should not judge—that is, condemn others based on stereotyping or rash evaluations of behavior. But it is vital to discriminate. By discriminate I mean determining what behavior is acceptable and showing disapproval for those who practice otherwise.

If we are going to live in a harmonious society we owe it to ourselves to define what we aspire to be as humans, that is, what values we wish to embrace. Such a society cannot survive if basic values conflict. Those who subscribe to the concepts of "taking turns" or "first come, first served" will be in constant conflict with those who believe in "pecking order." Those who respect property rights will be under constant attack from those who don't. Racists will wage a never ending war with non-racists. We have attempted to embrace all views, no matter how conflicting, and have found ourselves with a disharmonious society on the verge of meltdown.

Am I suggesting that one set of values be arbitrarily established and that everyone be forced to accept it? No. No one can be forced to accept values they don't believe in. This country was founded on resisting just this sort of totalitarian approach. But when we embrace everyone, no matter how severely their values may conflict with our own, and then try to accept each set of values as equally valid, we have nothing but conflict.

We must have a common set of values and must work to establish it by encouraging deep introspection into one's own values, research into the nature and origin of the values of others, and compassionate, peaceful discussion. Once our community values are established we must not embrace people who reject or violate them. Acceptance, or even toleration, fortifies the destructive behavior and undermines the value system in general.

Today we see a relentless, desperate quest for "freedom" from the restraints placed upon us by society. We resent government for passing laws. We resent philosophers and theologians for advocating moralities. We resent any authority that enforces regulations. People feel restricted and are eager to burst free at the first opportunity. This may mean getting drunk and "letting it all hang out" at a party, or carousing in a destructive manner to celebrate some sporting event, or exploring danger and wild physical sensation in recreation. Throughout modern pop music you hear the call for "freedom." People want to be able to throw themselves about without restraint, yell and scream, do whatever impulse leads them to do. They feel horribly restrained. But what is restraining them?

What we are most often seeing is an absence of values that take into consideration the rights of others. These people, contrary to what most of them declare, do not "love" or even respect others. They see other people as existing to serve them.

Those who truly care about others do not feel restrained by rules and regulations which exist (as most of them do) to protect the rights of everyone. They don't resent traffic lights as encumbrances to their free movement, but rather respect them as important devices which enhance the safe, free movement of everyone. They don't resent outdoor recreation regulations as restrictive but rather honor them as safeguards to allow everyone to enjoy, while protecting, the environment. They don't resent rules in general because they recognize that a heavily populated society like ours needs rules to function fairly and harmoniously. To resent rules indicates a deep disrespect for the rights of others.

Which brings us back to the specific issue of inter-gender relationships. How can anyone with a strong propensity for self-indulgence (as described above), possibly participate in any relationship which does not promote his/her self-oriented goals? Optimum heterosexual (or even homosexual) relationships demand the ability to subordinate one's own personal agenda to that of the pair bond.

Inter-gender relationships in particular demand that participants sacrifice their "freedom" of self-indulgence for responsibility to others—namely spouse and children. To the well adjusted, such responsibility is not an imposition, but rather an imperative that brings pleasure and satisfaction as well as a sense of completion.

The biggest absurdity of the gender conflict is the attempt by vast numbers of both genders to emphasize gender duality and authenticate gender polarization, even as they seek to find partners of the other sex for companionship, sexual gratification and procreation. Yes, a number of people do limit themselves to same gender companionship. And, a small percentage of humanity seeks to find sexual gratification within their own gender. But, in spite of the advent of artificial insemination—which could only be practiced in an advanced scientific society—virtually no one would deny that the species would have ceased to exist without the mating of the sexes. Men and women were designed to relate and mate. Everything about their physical and psychological makeup verifies this.

Two men or two women could be isolated together and survive nicely. They could easily provide each other the necessary companionship. They might even develop a gratifying sexual relationship. But at the end of their natural lifespans they will have failed to continue the species.

No bi-sexual species would rationally advocate same sex bonding exclusively for this would ultimately lead to species self-immolation. The natural propensity for all bi-sexual species, including humanity, is heterosexual bonding. Survival dictates, and nature provides those instincts which best serve our survival prospects.

Same gender bonding can be rewarding but it cannot by itself fully satisfy the need for interpersonal relationship. For the heterosexual, this need can only be fulfilled in a heterosexual relationship. (I do not consider the homosexual excluded from this rule. However, I will discuss this later in relationship to homosexuality to keep from complicating the issue here.) Same-gender bonding acts in subordination to heterosexual bonding, providing but a small measure of satisfaction compared to the heterosexual bond.

Many heterosexual men do gather together to pursue common interests they see as exclusively male. At the same time the heterosexual male pursuit of same-gender bonding often stems from a need to seek solace from other men because of being unable to fulfill the need for heterosexual companionship. This holds true even for married men, most of whom have not properly bonded with their wives and thus are not receiving the quality of love and attention meant to be provided by a healthy heterosexual relationship. Indeed, among the most common topics of groups of unmated men is commiseration about past mates and strategizing on how to seek out heterosexual contact. Even jocks, once their manhood has been established on the field of play and they've exhausted the sports topic in the ensuing bout of beer drinking, often turn to the discussion of women.

Contrarily, men and women in well-adjusted heterosexual pairbonds can easily find fulfillment without establishing close adjunct relationships with members of the same gender. They may choose to do so to enrich the pursuit of certain common interests, but these same-gender relationships are superficial compared to the heterosexual bond and the rewards received from it.

Optimum heterosexual pair bonds cannot exist among people who embrace gender polarization as advocated under patriarchy. (I emphasize the description, "optimum" because many polarized relationships endure for long periods of time with their members seemingly satisfied.) When two genders that are starving to fulfill the psycho/physical need to bond with each other are forced to operate under the restraints of a hierarchical power structure failure is virtually assured. The structure by its very nature frustrates and prevents the trust and closeness necessary to establish a fulfilling bond.

Nevertheless, no matter how painful, both genders are driven by internal imperatives to pursue the heterosexual bond. Under the patriarchal system both have distorted their behavior and concocted elaborate etiquettes in order to establish and maintain relationships. Members of both genders constantly face the quandary: how can I remain close yet maintain a separate identity relating to gender? For men: how can I maintain independence and a dominant image even while surrendering to my needs? For women: how do I seek fulfillment of my needs while attending to his in a manner which does not threaten his concept of manhood?

Traditionally, women have always faced a more difficult, compelling road to relationships. Under the patriarchal system they have always been viewed and used as sex objects by men. In order to make a place for themselves and establish some measure of security women have had to decorate their bodies and sculpt their behavior to attract men. They have had to make themselves sexually attractive and submit to sexual domination. They have had to largely leave definition of their sexual and sensual parameters to men.

Further complicating their quest to please men, women have always experienced a haunting sense of urgency. A woman's body only produces some 400 eggs during her lifetime. Her "biological clock" looms as a major consideration if she has any aspirations for motherhood. At the same time, patriarchal society measures much of a woman's value by her physical attractiveness—most often youthful attractiveness. So, for women who wish to attract a lifelong mate the "clock" is ticking here as well .

Feminists have taken the lead in rebelling against this form of male domination, but in the process many have attacked the very idea of a woman making herself look attractive. This view has some justification in the argument against patriarchy, but it flies in the face of natural human sexuality. After all, sexual attraction relies to a great extent upon viewing another person as physically appealing. Few women would want to mate with men they saw as physically unappealing. The issue then becomes: what is physically appealing, and is this justified? I'll leave that topic for some other forum.

Ironically, patriarchal men tend to join feminists in criticizing women for spending a great deal of time and energy trying to look beautiful. This male attitude is largely hypocritical because most men enjoy looking. In the process, however, they feel threatened. They conclude that women are laying a beauty trap for them that goes beyond just attracting them as mates. They see women as using the beauty factor to achieve status that has always been held exclusively by men.

While this is so to a great degree, men have established the female sensual agenda. In order to achieve security most women have had to attach themselves to a man. At the same time women have their own sensual/sexual nature and most of them, being heterosexual, need to explore it in the company of men. And since the most important criterion for most men in seeking a mate has always been appearance, women have always spent a great deal of time on appearance. Men are primarily to blame for placing women in the position of having to create a superficial identity based on looks.

As women have become more economically independent they have allowed male appearance to play a much larger role in partner selection. When women gained the opportunity to pursue success on their own terms men found themselves resentfully disoriented by having to measure up to new female standards in order to attract feminine attention. It has become much more common for women to ogle men and for men to pay more attention to their own looks when seeking a partner.

Should men resent this change of female focus? No more than women should resent their being viewed as sex objects. Few people like to be evaluated solely on their looks. And yet both men and women should recognize that the appreciation of physical beauty is a pleasure of living. We should not exalt it above all other human attributes, but neither should we seek to demean it. It is what it is. Just as most of us prefer to view majestic mountains and rugged coastlines rather than flat, barren land, we justifiably appreciate attractive human physical presence. Camille Paglia, oft-quoted author on gender issues, says it well:

> We should not have to apologize for reveling in beauty. Beauty is an eternal human value. It was not a trick invented by nasty men in a room someplace on Madison Avenue.

Still, feminists do have a gripe, for millions of women still spend hours upon hours shopping and primping, succumbing to the pressure of being physically judged by men. Unfortunately, women who are more sexually attractive usually have more opportunity in our patriarchal society. Feminist Janet Radcliff Richards makes an excellent related point when she says:

> It is because women who pleased men sensually received more rewards than her sisters that feminists are so angry and hostile to sensuality now. To go on being outraged allows men's traditional power over women to shape women's views of and attitudes toward sensuality.

In our society most couples co-habitate and reach for permanence only to be unable to attain lasting harmony. A majority of those who make permanent commitments end up forced by disharmony to break their vows. Members of both of these groups tend to sour on the concept of maintaining permanent relationships. Most of those who study relationships and counsel the participants seem to accept it as natural that the excitement of early attraction wears off. Their advice seems to focus upon sustaining relationships in spite of the loss of chemistry.

Must relationships lose, within a matter of months or a few years, the positive emotional intensity that originally drew the parties together? I believe this happens, not because of some natural boredom that sets in, but rather because the relationships never grew from strong roots.

The seeds of relationships germinate easily, energized by the need to give and receive love. Everyone experiences this need because it is normal—a natural offshoot of the bonding imperative. (Many people who have either failed in previous relationships or have observed others failing, try to convince themselves that giving and receiving love is not a factor in their lives and that they prefer to live unattached to others. Virtually all are victims of self-deception. They too are driven to bond. But they are willing to face a life without total fulfillment rather than face the risk of experiencing the pain that results from relationship disharmony.) However, the intensity of the drive often overpowers reason, propelling us into situations that turn destructive over time. Usually psychological factors, such as a childhood devoid of parental love, are responsible. These often create such a hunger that desperation clouds judgment and partners are chosen for superficial reasons, without carefully considering those areas in which compatibility is essential if the relationship is to last.

Nevertheless, no matter how distorted the drive may become, the need to give and receive love is legitimate. We can never feel completely fulfilled without satisfying it. The problem is that we can't satisfy it by attaching ourselves to just anyone of the other gender.

You can't give fulfilling love to someone you don't admire. (I'm speaking here of a subjective love of positive feelings in response to positive attributes in the other person, not some form of objective, spiritual love which can embrace anyone whose heart is beating.) Nor can you receive fulfilling love from someone who does not admire you. Only the exchange of genuine love can create the physical and psychological chemistry necessary for a relationship to endure.

What commonly happens, however, is that our need for love becomes so strong that we cannot wait to find a partner suited to us in a real sense. We tend to form an image of what our ideal partner would be like, then seek out someone who possesses some resemblance. In our need for fulfillment we employ our imagination like a crowbar and attempt to leverage this person into the pattern of our image. Often this means ignoring certain negative traits or cloaking our love object in traits they don't possess. This is necessary, otherwise we could not experience the internal chemical reaction needed to maintain the attraction.

Often our need to receive love is so strong that we eagerly fall under the spell of another's approval, grasping and embracing it as if it were genuine love. In response we experience elation and an outpouring of our own "love," which we shower upon this other person. Sadly, what we are "loving" is his/her "love," not who he/she is and represent. This person may indeed possess attributes that make him/her worthy of our love, but we do not make the effort to look for them. Nor have we examined this other's "love" to see if it is in response to something real in us. We are simply feeding off the exchange of approval. So subsequently, if his/her "love" wanes or is withdrawn, we respond in kind. Since the relationship has been based on nothing but imagination, it faces a major crisis.

Ultimately, of course, all imagery that surrounds a relationship dissolves. Most often we are left with a partner who has little resemblance to our ideal and thus cannot fulfill our need. (I am reminded of Sam Keen's comment about falling out of love into reality.) Even then, especially if children are involved, it might be best to try to continue the relationship. Still, it is important to recognize that relationships which are ultimately devoid of mutual admiration and patched up by toleration are not the optimum we can expect. Many of us reach that state because we have completely surrendered to our pressing hunger for love, ignored reason, and made poor choices that at the outset had little chance for success.

Granted, it is difficult to balance reason and emotion when faced with such a compelling drive. But it must be done if we are to achieve fulfilling relationships. The first step is recognizing the factors that must be present if we are to have any degree of success.

The vast majority of opinion, particularly that of professionals, seems to embrace the view that searching for the ideal in a relationship is unrealistic and breeds nothing but eventual frustration. I see this as true when we seek perfection in a partner. But true pleasure in a relationship comes from close association with someone who meets your expectations. The higher your expectations, the more frustration you will experience when they are not met; and the more pleasure you will experience when they are. If you have no expectations (including practical ones like finding a homemaker, means of support or sexual outlet) you would not likely be motivated to seek out a relationship.

The problem in seeking our "ideal" lies in our lacking self-awareness. Our lack of self-knowledge tends to steer us into glorifying attributes in others that do not serve our best interests. Our mistake therefore lies not in seeking the "ideal," but rather in the "ideal" our imagination has sculpted.

If we are to forge a fulfilling permanent relationship, four ingredients are essential: mutual visibility, common values, similar view of life, and physical attraction. (I call the first three: the 3 V's.) In order to conceptualize our "ideal" we must recognize how these ingredients relate to us personally and what characteristics must exist in a potential partner to make a successful relationship feasible.

By visibility I refer to the feeling that you are being seen by your partner very much like you see yourself. Some of our uniquely personal traits we value highly. Others less highly. Others not at all. If we value our intelligence highly while being indifferent to our appearance, we do not feel visible to a person who praises our physical appearance but totally overlooks our intellect. A good common example of the invisibility principle is the brilliant woman who is proud of her intelligence and wishes to have it acknowledged only to draw dull-witted men attracted to her large breasts. In the presence of such men she feels invisible and unfulfilled.

In addition to common visibility, two partners must also possess common values. These allow them to react to crucial life situations with similar intent and to agree on common responses, providing a major reward of pair-bonding—the sharing of life experiences and the helping of each other through crises.

Similarly, two partners must share a common view of life. Here I speak of goals and life objectives. I need not describe the friction that occurs when two partners have different agenda and priorities. Even if they "respect" each other's interests, their relationship lacks intimacy when they cannot share the same pursuits, or do so with unequal intensity.

The final essential ingredient, of course, is physical attraction. Without it two people lack the glandular chemistry that promotes mating and would find no more reason to bond than they would with a person of the same gender. However, we must not overlook that physical attraction is a subjective phenomenon which is greatly affected by the first three ingredients. Often one who is not a total turnoff physically exhibits such attractive qualities in other areas that a physical appearance that would ordinarily be classified as plain suddenly appears alluring.

Satisfaction of the natural sexual impulse is much more easily accomplished between those who have bonded on a psycho/spiritual level. It provides the closest form of physical togetherness, cementing a relationship even closer together.

A fifth ingredient, which I do not consider essential but which commonly develops between those who share the previous four, is the satisfaction of the nurturing impulse, usually by raising children. Many people have twisted reasons for having and raising kids, but nevertheless this natural impulse provides a powerful opportunity for parents to gain even more fulfillment from the bond between them.

Contrary to the expressed views of my friend, Barbara De Angelis,

I don't believe that through extended effort you can "make love work." True love simply works. Yes, even when strong love cements the relationship partners must expend a certain amount of effort to resolve numerous superficial differences. However, these differences must only be superficial or complementary. Otherwise the term "love" cannot apply. You cannot genuinely love someone when you dislike a major part of their character.

Barbara disagrees with this. She contends that she herself has loved people she didn't like. I believe she and I are defining "love" differently. Yes, you can have strong positive feelings toward those you otherwise don't like. Perhaps they possess positive attributes in contrast to those you dislike. But if you feel strongly enough to dislike a person, how could you love them? (I have never been able to understand how a woman could "love" a man who regularly beats her.) "Love" in this context connotes an overall acceptance of this person and a desire to bond with them permanently. Anyone who would seek a permanent bond with someone who possesses major character differences would be displaying self-destructive or masochistic tendencies. They would be allowing their emotions to respond to a fantasy.

By superficial differences, I refer to any issues not an integral part of the crucial first four relationship ingredients. One cannot experience genuine "love" of sufficient depth to sustain a permanent relationship with someone unless all four of those ingredients are present. Once they are, all other issues shrink to minor significance. They may need occasional addressing, but never will they pose a major threat to harmony or to the bonds that hold the relationship together.

Yes, one can still "love" another who does not possess all four ingredients. But not to the degree necessary to forge a fulfilling permanent relationship. For many, this is difficult to comprehend because all of us experience our emotions as a powerful force. To most of us, experiencing "love" tends to blind us to all but those characteristics which attract us.

Indeed, most committed relationships have grown out of far less than the four ingredients I refer to. We see the results in the high percentage of breakups. And thus we tend to view "love" and the impulsive behavior it generates as forces beyond our control that ultimately lead us into difficulty. This, of course, is where major confusion arises. How can anything feel so wonderful yet be so often detrimental?

Here I refer to "love" in the context of romance. Most analysts seem to agree with Sam Keen, viewing romance as a passing phase that partners in a relationship must negotiate before settling into a more objective state of love not hindered by excitement. For indeed, excitement is intrinsic to romance—excitement plus: admiration, exultation, euphoria, passion—all centered upon another person. When analysts imply that romance cannot endure they further imply that its above-mentioned components will also shrink and, perhaps, disappear. Love in its other forms, whatever they may be and if they exist, must be called upon to sustain the relationship.

Is this what we are ultimately faced with in a permanent relationship—life without partner-centered admiration, exultation, euphoria and passion? Something about this theory stinks. How can the apparently instinctual drive to bond, which seems to be fueled by the romantic impulse, naturally lead to such apathy later which strains the bonds of the relationship? Does evolution have a purpose here, perhaps to force dissolution? Or, is the apathy not inevitable after all, but rather a symptom of a relationship ill-formed?

If a relationship contains the four ingredients I've described, isn't it natural for the partners to experience admiration, euphoria, exultation and passion? How can you fail to remain emotionally exhilarated when your partner constantly makes you feel visible; when you share the same goals; when you value and can therefore share the most important things in your lives; and when you see him/her as attractive. The aforementioned emotions seem to be positive reactions not detriments. They are the combustibles that fuel romance. And they tend to endure, often over lifetimes.

Some people (particularly in times past) have committed themselves permanently in order to have and raise children. Others, (particularly women seeking financial security) have come together for practical reasons to better position themselves in society. In both these scenarios each partner is using the relationship as a means to further personal agenda whether it coincides with that of their partner or not. The devotion is to personal ambitions rather than to the relationship. The positive emotional content that comes from sharing can only be very low, therefore these types of relationships certainly do need a great deal of conscious effort to sustain.

But must all relationships settle into this mode? Is the positive emotional content that surrounds the advent of most relationships inevitably doomed to deteriorate? I think not.

True, sexual chemistry can diminish, but it will most likely occur for biological reasons rather than because of an appetite for other partners. For if one still has a sex drive why would they want to share such an intimate experience with someone with whom they have little in common?

Granted, many people suffer from aberrant sexual appetites which draw them into relationships with others who do not share with them the three v's. But a vast majority of these people are prevented by their fixation upon sex from entering into any ideal relationship. They focus upon self-gratification and when self-gratification through sex is the binding force in a relationship the participants lose sight of the significance—both biological and psychological—of the act. For sex indulged in purely for self-gratification is not relationship oriented at all. Rather, it is an exotic form of masturbation in which one uses another person's body to flesh out the fantasy and free the hands.

The idea that romance is somehow a negative state flies in the face of reason. If one were to find a partner who fulfilled his/her real needs, that person would be justified in feeling euphoric and all the rest. And if that partner continued to fulfill those needs over time, the recipient would most likely find the euphoria sustained. How can this be negative?

Romantic love so often ends up in disaster because we are driven to fulfill the very genuine need for it even when the essential ingredients are absent. First, most of us have not dealt sufficiently with personal issues and thus do not know ourselves well enough to recognize what attributes in a partner would best harmonize with our own. Often, even when we do possess the inner security and self-awareness to fulfill our obligations within a relationship, no truly compatible partner is available. Nevertheless, the need for romance drives us and we either consciously settle for less, revise our image of an ideal partner, or distort our perception of our love object to make him/her conform to our ideal.

The result, of course, is frustration as the initial thrills of romance dissolve amidst waves of disharmony. But rather than blaming our own inner deficiencies or recognizing the dearth of potential compatible partners, many of us deprecate romance even as we are driven to continue our search for it. Pessimism is fortified by observing the high percentage of cases in which romance cannot be sustained. This increases the number of cases where parties enter into a relationship with lessened expectations and thereby increase the number of romance failures. Negative attitudes toward romance feed upon themselves.

I see romantic love being in the natural order of things—the strong urge to complete with the opposite sex. It is born of the cognitive mind—an anticipation of being able to blend the valid psychological need for recognition and acceptance by other human beings with the equally valid physical need for sex. It is essential for a fulfilling life.

What we see as "romance" in today's society is a distortion—emotions untempered by reason and ignoring cognition. Even true romance is afflicted in that manner partially because of patriarchal insistence on same gender identification. We find our natural urge to bond so afflicted by these unnatural gender concepts that our emotions become restrained. Ultimately they demand release and drive us to "fall in love" with individuals who fulfill these twisted gender concepts rather than with those who share a natural compatibility.

Homosexuality

Whereas years ago the topic of homosexuality would bring snickers and ridicule, today it has become a major issue of serious debate throughout society. Is homosexuality a legitimate, innate, genetically encoded sexual alternative?

Had we asked this question twenty years ago the vast majority of psychology professionals would have responded, "no!" Nearly all would have been prepared to give a lengthy dissertation as to what was "wrong" with practicing homosexuality. Today, however, many of them in their writings seem to shy away from the topic, leaving it to laboratory scientists and laymen. What has happened in the past twenty years to change this attitude? Has some great laboratory discovery been made to authenticate homosexuality?

When I talk about authenticating homosexuality I don't do so in a philosophical or religious moral sense. Rather I seek to determine whether this orientation is a distortion of humankind's instinctual sexual imperative. Even then it would not be morally wrong unless it worked against the best interests of the species.

Common sense would seem to say that if indeed homosexuality springs from a genetic imperative among certain members of a bi-sexual species, this imperative would likely be bred out over a period of time. Those members possessing this proclivity would not reproduce and therefore not pass along their genes. Pro-gay scientific opinion attempts to refute this by claiming the gene would be recessive and could be passed along through the female of the species. I personally find this explanation doubtful, especially considering the enormous number of people claiming gay sexual orientation. But I am not a geneticist and will therefore not try to defend this point.

Some geneticists have indeed come forth with studies that seem to hint that a genetic encoding may be responsible. But these studies remain highly speculative and have yet to be proven. Other scientists have brought forth explanations involving hormonal imbalances. But again, these await substantial proof.

So science has not yet brought forth irrefutable evidence to validate homosexuality. What then has driven so many psychologists to cover on this issue?

The answer would seem to be, social pressure—the fear of being classified as a bigot by various pressure groups. For no matter what side you take on this issue, you usually find yourself in a withering crossfire. Even homosexuals themselves disagree upon whether same-sex orientation has a genetic and/or hormonal basis. Many take issue with other gays, asserting that they have made a conscious choice to be gay. They feel that by attributing sexual orientation to biological hereditary factors homosexuals demean their power of volition in the eyes of others and get themselves classified as genetic distortions or aberrations, helpless to overcome an affliction.

With all the vitriolic rhetoric flying about on the topic it is easy to see why psychologists seem to steer away from the direct causes of homosexuality. Most, however, without saying so give the impression that they no longer consider homosexuality a problem. Whether this is to protect their status within the professional community or whether they truly believe this we can only surmise.

I find it important to examine homosexuality here for two reasons. First, homosexuals have stepped forth and organized in response to persecution, attempting to authenticate and proliferate their lifestyle. They seek a major change in society.

Second, the homosexual backlash has a detrimental effect upon the advancement of women's rights. Homosexuals would have us believe that somehow gay rights and women's rights are intertwined. They would have us believe that one must be "gay affirming" to be pro-feminist; that if one questions the legitimacy of homosexuality they are homophobic. The National Organization of Men Against Sexism (NOMAS), a men's group allied to NOW, has in its charter a commitment to gay affirmation. Indeed, in a recent letter from one of the organization's top spokesmen, I was told that a person could not be "pro-feminist" without being "gay affirming."

This attitude shuts out millions of men and women who might otherwise ally themselves with pro-feminist causes. They suspect that homosexuality is an aberration and do not wish to aid any movement that links gay affirmation with women's rights. This is not to say that gay rights are not as important as women's rights. But movements such as NOMAS are not talking simply about gay rights. They are demanding gay affirmation, a major step beyond. This tends to discredit the entire women's rights movement in the eyes of those who otherwise might be open to support it.

In the ensuing discussion I will be defining homosexuality as limiting oneself exclusively to same gender sexual experiences. Some members of both genders are able to become sexually aroused heterosexually as well as homosexually. I would not call these individuals homosexual, nor would I define their sexual behavior as homosexual even when it involves members of the same gender. I believe these individuals are basically heterosexual but because of deep gender identification confusion and, in some cases, heterosexual frustration, have found it necessary to express their sexuality with both genders.

My definition of the true homosexual is a sexually active person who finds no sexual attraction to members of the other sex. I do not wish to argue this definition. If others wish to define the term differently I grant them the latitude. However, with a different definition I would treat the subject differently.

I do not view same-sex sexual behavior as improper simply in its practice. Rather, its legitimacy becomes suspect when it is practiced to the exclusion of heterosexual behavior. Why? Because individuals who practice exclusively homosexual behavior do not reproduce. Nature gave them the sexual apparatus to reproduce but they are using it in a fashion which precludes them from doing so.

Nature provided sexual desire and pleasure in its fulfillment, to encourage reproduction of the species. I am not suggesting that sexual pleasure should be experienced only when one is trying to reproduce. However, for one to be able to experience sexual pleasure exclusively in situations where it is impossible to reproduce defies nature's imperative.

To abstain from sexual behavior because of lack of desire is not a course designed by nature. But it does not violate nature's laws. To choose homosexuality, however, is to admit that strong sexual desires exist while displaying a strong aversion to expressing them through the normal channels nature has provided. This is an indication that something in one's attitude toward sex has gone seriously awry.

Nature designed our sexual apparatus to perform in an optimum fashion. To try to legitimatize homosexual sexual intercourse (particularly between males) is to try to put forth that nature provided us with the wrong sexual equipment. The penis was never designed to penetrate the anus. If it had been, the anus would self-lubricate like the female's vagina and not bleed from penetration. The bowels would have the capacity to make use of the male sperm. And, the large intestine would not harbor bacteria that could easily gain access through the urethra into the other person's body.

Quite simply, the anus is the opening into a waste processing plant. This duct is specifically designed to expel material either detrimental, or no longer of use, to the body. Even doctors would never examine this area without gloves and then they would thoroughly wash their hands. And yet for centuries gay men have inserted their uncovered penises into these feces expulsion tubes and tried to claim they were performing a natural act. (The criticism holds true for heterosexual anal intercourse.) This is not only illogical—since the male body does not provide an opening designed specifically by nature to receive the penis—but it is also hygienically detrimental.

Homosexuals claim that we live in an ignorant, intolerant period and that in times past, especially ancient times, homosexuality was widely accepted. They like to describe sanctioned, ritualized male-male sexual activities in both ancient Greek and modern primitive societies. They also point to Roman times and the debauchery that occurred during the Imperial period.

The authorities on the Greeks and the primitives have to admit that the homosexual behavior was primarily driven not by the desire to participate in intra-sexual behavior to the exclusion of the other sex, but rather to bolster concepts of masculinity within a heterosexual society. Passing sperm from elders to youth was supposed to have fostered the growth of masculinity in young males. Once these young males reached "maturity," as defined within their society, they were expected to forego homosexual activity and focus upon the heterosexual pair bond. Homosexuality among "mature" adults, was generally frowned upon. Thus homosexuality in these societies would seem to have been culturally conditioned rather than biologically driven.

Those who look to the Romans to authenticate homosexuality glean their evidence from Roman writings and figures portrayed in various Roman art forms. They do not admit that this writing and art tended to portray the elite of those times rather than the views of common Roman citizens.

While indeed, homosexual activity might have been common among the elite—particularly among the entourages of various depraved emperors (I do not describe them as "depraved" because of their advocacy of homosexuality, but rather because of overall dastardly behavior—i.e. Caligula and Nero.)—indications are that overall social opinion disdained it. A case in point is the Consul Lucius Quinctius Flamininus, brother of the more famous Titus Quinctius Flamininus.

From the accounts of the Roman writers Livy and Plutarch we learn that Lucius was expelled from the Senate in 184 B.C. for, in Plutarch's words, being "low and dissolute in his pleasures and flagrantly regardless of all decency." Lucius kept with him a boy companion with whom he was frequently found "wantoning."

That a Senator and high magistrate could be expelled for this reason indicates Roman society's high intolerance for such behavior during that period. We are, of course, speaking of a period two centuries before Nero and Caligula. One might be tempted to assume that social mores shifted drastically during the intervening years, except that both authors, Livy (59 B.C.-17 A.D.) and Plutarch (c. 46-120 A.D.), lived during Imperial times, the latter during and, after Nero's reign. Their caustic criticism of Flamininus' behavior would seem to reflect the general mores of their times. This would seem to say that from the founding of Rome (c. 750 B.C.) to the death of Plutarch—eight and a half centuries—Roman society in general frowned upon homosexuality.

Only two more centuries transpired before the accession of Christianity—always a staunch enemy of homosexuality—to the status of state religion. So, if homosexuality ever carried social legitimacy in the Roman world it might, I repeat, might have occurred during that period. But that hardly would make the case for homosexuality being universally accepted during Roman times. Likely this was not the case since anti-gay patriarchal attitudes dominated Roman society just as they have dominated society in general throughout recorded history.

Homosexuals have found it necessary to defend their questionable behavior with clever arguments because they have been under ruthless attack. This is deplorable because homosexuals do not pose through their choice of sexuality any significant danger to society. I use the adjective "significant" because in certain cases homosexuality may appeal to a heterosexual who is confused about his/her sexual identity and thereby lead that person deeper into confusion. But this person is no more likely to be led astray by homosexuals than by the many "medics" I've discussed earlier.

If homosexuals pose any major threat to society, it is to its patriarchal nature. Gay men, by offering a male alternative to patriarchal attitudes, frighten patriarchs, who have always suffered deep insecurities about themselves as people and their position in society. Lesbians pose a similar threat by practicing behavior that completely defies the role patriarchal men have designed for women.

Homophobia is a disease that needs to be eradicated. With that in mind I'm concerned that my stand against the legitimacy of homosexuality may be used by homophobics to justify and strengthen their own aberrant attitudes. Even so, it does not serve the best interests of humanity, particularly women, to embrace negative behavior patterns just because people who practice them have been unjustifiably persecuted.

We have in our society two groups—homosexuals and

homophobics—whose attitudes are out of line. Homosexuals want approval for their sexuality; homophobics want to destroy them. Both use each other to justify their attitudes. We need to pull back and chastise both. We need to scold, restrain and in some cases punish homophobics for their attitudes and behavior, for sexual orientation should in no way deprive an individual of human rights. At the same time we need to outwardly reject the homosexual demand to have their sexual behavior canonized as legitimate.

All of us suffer to varying degrees from distorted behavior patterns that were initiated by inadequate or improper parenting during our formative years. (I shall discuss this in the next chapter.) We harm ourselves when we deny practicing deviant behavior, just as homosexuals harm themselves by trying to justify their sexual persuasion as natural. We don't serve our personal evolution or the best interests of society by ignoring the truth in order to make those who practice deviant behavior feel comfortable.

Homosexuals have used their mistreatment to instigate their own unreasonable, self-serving backlash. They have raised justifiable guilt in their tormentors. But they've used it to demand too much. They have been seeking affirmation and authentication for their lifestyle, not just equal rights. It is tantamount to saying, "because you have punished me for misbehavior that is none of your business, you must not only apologize but you must now declare my behavior to be legitimate."

Such social authentication is irresponsible because homosexuality is indeed a sexual aberration. It is the behavior of people who have gender identity problems which place them at war with their own bodies. It is behavior that deserves no punishment because its primary adverse effect is upon those who practice it. However, at the same time it deserves no authentication for it serves as a detrimental example, particularly for the young. Indeed, for society to embrace such an untruth only encourages others with gender identity problems to avoid addressing them directly and experiment with deviant sexuality. With gender enmity often making it difficult to achieve heterosexual fulfillment, homosexuality begins to look attractive. The gay lifestyle further adds to gender confusion.

The adjective "wrong" is often used by traditional society when discussing homosexuality. If indeed it is an aberration, does that make it "wrong?"

The misuse of that adjective has confused discussion on the topic. Homosexuality is not a threat (as it once could have been) to the reproduction of the species because we already have an overabundance of reproducing heterosexuals. It is not a threat to morality as long as each individual has the power to utilize their own conscience to embrace values. It therefore cannot be "wrong" in those contexts. But it is "wrong" for those who practice it, not because of the nature of the behavior, but because it is a symptom of a person at war with their true sexual identity. It is this type of "wrong," however, that is a personal issue over which society has no proper jurisdiction.

Heterosexuals in society should be seeking to help homosexuals find their lost sexuality and this can only occur by stopping the attacks and the gay bashing. It is this that has driven many gays to cling to their sexual orientation. Once they feel safe to seek out sexual fulfillment in any form they will also find it safer to explore the roots of their sexual orientation and perhaps make adjustments. If they still choose to cling to their homosexual identity that is their choice to make.

***

I have painted an idealized picture of relationships. Indeed, it would seem that if we follow the guidelines I have described, few would enter into relationships. Obviously this would not work because we would still be driven by the natural need to bond. Many people would feel far less fulfilled alone than in a fantasy relationship. Others just might get lucky and sustain a relationship that began on a false basis. Almost everyone has to pursue fulfillment and with people not being in touch with their true selves, we will continue to see a high rate of failures. But we can't demand that everyone who has not perfected their relationship approach be sentenced to the misery of loneliness.

Why then do I paint such a picture? Once again because we must aspire to the ideal, even if we fall short. What makes the vast majority of current relationships tragic is not that they have been based upon imagery and unrealistic aspirations. Rather, their participants try to rationalize the misery they encounter as normal. Counselors try to get people to settle for less. Instead of trying to encourage people to be more selective, they try to counsel partners regarding how to be more tolerant of negative situations. This snowballs, painting a negative picture for those who are aspiring to relationships. Disharmonious relationships ensue, fueling the divorce epidemic and increasing the flood of neglected children.

If no one ever pursues the ideal only a tiny fraction will ever achieve it. Many of us could achieve it and establish highly rewarding relationships if we make ourselves aware of what has been thwarting us.

Chapter Eleven
Children

As in all wars, conflict between the genders has left numerous innocent victims, most particularly, children. Those that survive the passage through a rapidly expanding mine field consisting of crib death, autism, hyperactivity, etc., find new pitfalls awaiting. Teenage pregnancy, substance addiction, gang affiliation and, ultimately, the attraction of suicide, inundate our "advanced" Western society. Child-related problems continue to proliferate in both numbers and complexity.

Advocates of patriarchy—both men and women—point to the erosion of traditional values as the main reason. They see the shifting of traditional parental roles as confusing to children especially in the formative years when parental guidance is crucial. They perceive feminist views as a major contributing factor to the deterioration of values in children.

Of course, feminists deny responsibility for these problems. Instead they point to patriarchy as the culprit. They maintain that in the process of resisting the liberation of women, many men have abdicated the responsibilities of fatherhood. They have left women to do most of the parenting as well as to provide for their families economically.

Feminists also claim that patriarchal families further set back children by raising them to accept values that exalt one gender over the other. They see traditional parenthood, which conditions males to seek domination—over other males (through competition) and females—as no longer acceptable. They adamantly believe that if a new set of children's problems have arisen as a result of the feminist revolution, we must address them without falling back on patriarchal approaches to parenting. We cannot use these problems as an excuse to maintain the gender hierarchy.

Both sides make cogent points. Traditional patriarchy did provide discipline and a form of parental guidance that prevented a great deal of the abovementioned difficulties. But it also exacted a price—rigidly controlled men and subservient women. Boys were impressed into a system which commonly led later to "mid-life crisis" and general dissatisfaction with life. Girls were taught to be subservient to boys and to hold themselves as inferior and less competent, thus dooming them to lives of underachievement.

Advocates of patriarchy can accurately point out that most serious youth problems attracting our attention today have arisen or intensified since the advent of "women's liberation." Prior to the 60s, substance addiction, organized gangs, childhood suicide, etc., were minimal compared to today. Divorces were the exception and the latch key child a rarity. Who can legitimately deny that the breakdown of the traditional family played a major part in fostering youth problems and that "women's lib" contributed?

But the women's revolution was not the only factor. Children also rebelled against the repressive lifestyle offered by the traditional family. The demand for blind obedience to patriarchal values (often in conflict with natural instincts) gave rise to painful psychological pressures. Many children swallowed these down, bravely enduring their ulcers until as adults they ended up in therapy or under medical care for stress related illnesses. Others protested in the only way they knew, rejecting everything associated with traditional society. Indeed, the women's liberation movement itself gained great impetus from the energy of the rebellious youth of the 60s.

The structure and focus of the typical traditional "nuclear" family of the 50s represented patriarchy at its zenith. In prior times the forces of patriarchy remained in rigid control. But in the 50s, particularly in the U.S., women and children reached their highest status under a patriarchal system. Men like to point to this as a high achievement—patriarchal men wielding unchallenged power generously, providing security and affluence for those inferior. Feminists, of course, see their fate differently.

Ironically the raising of women and children to higher status through education during the 50s and early 60s set the stage for the decline of the traditional family. Women began to recognize that the inferior status imposed upon them was in no way justified and that they had every right to pursue the world of accomplishment. Children, particularly male children, began to see that the patriarchal life they were expected to embrace held far fewer rewards and far more pitfalls than they had been led to believe. For the first time both groups found themselves with the conscious ability to make choices.

Patriarchy, however, remained all-powerful. Men had no inclination to listen to reason when it might demand that they modify their caste system. So women and children found themselves awakening but standing outside a fortress. In addition, their enlightened intellects could not heal the psychological insecurities imposed upon them by patriarchy as manifested through the nuclear family. Twenty years of being conditioned to be an "inferior" woman cannot be cast aside in a few years on a college campus. Nor can the results of browbeating boys to accept aggressiveness, fear femininity, and seek domination over others.

Both groups were faced with throwing off their conditioning even as they struggled against the aggressive forces being wielded by the patriarchal system to keep them in line. What resulted was a great deal of inner confusion and anxiety. This led to rage, the tool the psyche often employs to generate a sense of power and control one does not feel viscerally.

In the 60s both women and maturing children turned rage against the patriarchal system. In every bizarre manner possible they pointed out the repression, cruelty, greed, racism and hypocrisy that gripped our society. The force of their anger was just too powerful to suppress and the patriarchal system began to show cracks. Patriarchy still fought bitterly and today still wields its overbearing presence. Nevertheless, the rebels of the 60s point proudly to their accomplishments.

But what did they accomplish?

Like an indiscriminate gale, they blew down or away everything not firmly entrenched, no matter what its value. In the rubble could be found age-old institutions of repression alongside human values of dignity and responsibility. The nuclear family was among the major casualties.

And yet although the onslaught left patriarchy battered, the old system still stood in defiant strength. Today it uses the inability of feminists to replace many of those traditional values that served humanity well as a major argument against all premises of feminism.

It is important to examine what of value was lost during the 60s cyclone. 50s America was riddled with hypocrisy. Even as young children were taught at home and in school to embrace honesty, fair play, compassion for the downtrodden, equality of opportunity, citizenship responsibilities, marital fidelity, respect for family, and many other values that most of us today still regard highly, adults regularly behaved in a contrary manner. Most of this illicit activity was cleverly hidden, especially from children. But it could not be concealed indefinitely from an educated public with a growing access to information. Especially with our government involving us in questionable foreign activity that kept us on the brink of nuclear annihilation.

Without question, much adult behavior amounted to despicable hypocracy. But what of those values being taught children? Were they wrong? When the women and youth of America began to see that many adult activities taking place under patriarchy violated those values being taught in school, preached in church, idealized in the movies and advocated on TV, were they justified in disowning those values? Did the problem lie in the nature of the values, or in the substance of those who failed to live up to them? Was living true to those values too much to expect from normal human beings? Is it simply too hard to be honest, fair, responsible, faithful, compassionate, etc.? If not, then why was it okay to cast these values aside? Should not the adults of that time have been called to accounting for their failure rather than our scrapping our value system and drifting into aimless permissiveness?

It is easy for patriarchal men to blame feminists and rebellious youth for undermining traditional values. But men bear equal responsibility. Had they been better able to live up to the values they advocated and had they allowed their women and children the freedom to exercise free will and reach their full potential, the rebellion would never have occurred.

But six thousand years of patriarchal conditioning had hardened male views into cement. Many of the cleverest minds on the planet embraced the ages old system and were prepared to wield the full powers of their intellect to defend it. They were not open to rational, peaceful argument. They left the rebels no choice but to react forcefully.

At the same time, by not providing quality role models patriarchal men had cast doubt upon the importance of adhering to the values they preached. Young people without exemplary role models to emulate are left directionless. Therefore the youth of that time sculpted their own set of values, most of which were purposely contradictory to those of their parents. Through their own lack of integrity men set in motion those forces which have undermined society—both good and bad features.

Throughout this upheaval one question continues to be debated. Can we free women and provide a nurturing environment for our children while maintaining many of those traditional values we cherish? Both patriarchal men and feminists, by defending rigid positions in hostility to each other, seem to be saying, "no." I believe they are wrong.

To begin understanding why the two points of view seem so irreconcilable, we must once more go back to basics by asking: why do we choose to have children? We no longer live in primitive times where we must raise children to ensure the survival of the species. Underpopulation is certainly not a current problem. Instead, we either freely choose to raise children because we consider it a life enhancing experience, or we have them by "mistake."

In the latter case children face enormous obstacles to healthy growth. If one or both parents withhold love, or if they decide to take little or no responsibility for raising the child, it will suffer to varying degrees no matter what the remaining parent and/or the government does.

Already many feminists would tend to disagree because in order to throw off male shackles they have had to advocate the virtues of single parenthood. I will address single parenthood shortly. For now I wish to focus on the problems facing "wanted" children. I'm setting aside the problems facing "unwanted" children because neither traditionalists nor feminists advocate bringing "unwanted" children into the world. "Unwanted" children face devastating problems which lie beyond the scope of this book.

But why do parents "want" children?

Even among those parents who choose to have this experience we find a wide range of reasons. Some men, particularly patriarchal men, choose to have children to carry on their names and act as heirs. (Often these men find female children disappointing.) Some of these same men find the act of fertilization necessary to prove their manhood.

Patriarchal women, of course, face the same burden of proof

through conception and successful delivery. These same women will often seek children to provide them both companionship and a "career"—one of the few career options patriarchy offers to women. Many women, both patriarchal and "liberated," seek to bear children to experience a biological process they see as their birthright.

The most commonly stated reason we hear for having children is love of children. The term "love" has been pondered, debated, and written about for ages. The superficial view holds "love" as the exhilarating feeling one experiences when around another. Those who have examined the issue more deeply see it as much more.

What does "love" commonly connote in the adult/child context? Many of those who claim to "love" children display exhilaration when around them—that is, as long as they are playing with them or observing pleasing antics. But how many of these "loving" adults maintain that joyful feeling when the child becomes unruly and "misbehaves," or when its needs interfere with pleasant playful interludes?

Some adults carry this feeling with them constantly. Others sporadically, sometimes becoming bored with their little companions when other interests present themselves. Many experience children from a completely subjective perspective. They bask in their own joy without any consideration of what is in the best interest of the child they're relating to. They either indulge the child's every whim or they coldly cut off the child when it is no longer satisfying their need for pleasure. If asked, these adults would assure you they "love" children.

Sadly, most people who decide they "want" kids proceed to create them to adorn their lives. Very seldom do people become parents with full awareness that they have created a unique, separate human being with hopes, desires and rights that may be totally different from their own. Some don't acknowledge this at all while others accept it to a point and then proceed to fit the child into a preconceived mold. Rarely do parents commit themselves to providing a nurturing environment in which the child can find happiness in fulfilling those needs and drives that make it unique. This would entail the parents sacrificing needs and aspirations of their own.

Career-oriented parents often overlook their children's desires or neglect their children's needs when these conflict with the demands of career. The eventual result is that many adults end up in psychotherapy trying to unravel the twists and turns of a suppressed child-hood. And while doing so they are usually having and raising kids of their own who are being exposed to the same cruel pattern.

Joseph Chilton Pearce says it well:

> Childhood is a battleground between the biological plan's intent, which drives the child from within, and our anxious intentions, pressing the child from without.

Children are born helpless and only very gradually gain the ability to fulfill their own needs. Parents must assume the burden of fulfilling their child's needs along with their own. This is often difficult, since fulfilling one's own needs is often not easy in our society. However, that is the responsibility one assumes when having children.

Parents can only fulfill the emotional/psychological and physical needs of their children if they avoid succumbing to society's pressures and obey nature's plan as revealed through signals instinctively emitted by the child. But to do this parents must be willing to observe and listen, then subordinate certain of their own needs.

Unfortunately, the vast majority of children have been conceived to fulfill the needs of parents. The child's needs usually place second, a practice which does nothing but impair growth, create childhood anxiety, and lead to those problems we listed earlier, in addition to numerous others.

Psychologist Arthur Janov refers to such parents as neurotic. He says:

> One of the most common reasons neurotics have children is to produce someone who will be loving; someone the parents can have all to themselves; someone they can be proud of; someone who will need them. The child's value will lie in making his parents feel loved. This may not sound neurotic simply because it is so common. But the child conceived for these reasons has enormous—perhaps too much—responsibility before it even draws its first breath; it is to be its parents' world; to make two complex, unconscious human beings happy; to fulfill their needs in a world where it is hard enough just to get one's own needs fulfilled. However, newborns are themselves composed entirely of need, and so to conceive them out of one's own unfulfilled need is to invite disaster.

Many such parents would have difficulty identifying with the above description for they are even further removed from awareness of their children's needs. It is common to hear said, "I have my own life to live," or "my children must learn that I have needs too." This, of course, reflects an unawareness of their children's crucial bio/psychological needs as dictated by millions of years of evolution. Young children don't understand because, quite simply, they can't understand. Brain growth has not reached the level where they have the reasoning power to understand. To expect them to do so is unreasonable and cruel.

This common parental attitude also reflects a self-centered urge to accumulate possessions and advance their own needs at the expense of others. For these people children represent little more than complex ornaments, clever pets, or proof of biological prowess. The "love" they profess to have for their children is little more than the "love" one feels for their possessions.

If parents were to listen, seeking awareness of the biological imperatives that govern the growth of their child, what might they discover?

Nature designed the human species to be composed of two separate physical sexes which would provide separate ingredients necessary for the production of offspring. Man provided sperm; woman provided egg. Put these ingredients together and we have a child. Provide a nurturing environment and we have a well-adjusted child. Right? Well, yes. But what is a nurturing environment? This is where the big disagreement lies.

Our first problem lies in identifying where the child first experiences environment. Certainly not in the uterus as an egg nor in the testicles as sperm. And certainly not as a newborn in the outside world. The child's first environment is the womb. This places the mother in the special position of providing the child's first bond to the universe. (In fact, the word "mother" is derived from the word "matrix," the Latin equilvalent for womb.) Until the child is expelled from the womb its mother serves as its indispensable host. Its father, grandparents, pediatrician, all others, cannot affect it except through the medium of the mother.

Arguments abound as to at what age a fetus acquires consciousness. The behavior of the fetus itself indicates that beyond five months the brain has developed sufficient conscious capacity to begin compiling a "memory" of experiences. This may be primitive and operate on the level of "body knowing," but nevertheless it provides the child's first lasting impressions which will remain with it throughout its life. (Beyond seven months the fetus displays bodily reactions to sounds.)

To become a fully functioning being the child must eventually leave its first environment and emerge into the outside world. When one is forced to leave a safe bastion—indeed, the only environment one has ever known—to enter an alien world of bright lights, loud sounds and wildly fluctuating temperatures, high levels of stress are experienced. The environmental change is the most extreme that will ever be experienced because the known has so few points of similarity to the unknown.

Interestingly it is the release of hormones by the fetus which triggers the mother's birth delivery system. These indicate that the fetus is ready to exit. Thereupon the mother's hormonal system responds with secretions of its own.

The pertinent point here is that nature has spent a few billion years designing the process so that the child has control of its movement from one matrix to the other by making its needs known. If parents (in this case the mother) are not listening, or refuse to accept the child's signals as valid, nature's process has been violated and the growth of the child will be adversely affected.

The process designed by nature remains in effect throughout the child's journey through several matrices to adulthood. Brain growth—the increase in brain cells and how they are structured—follows a strict timetable and pattern. The level of physical brain development determines the level of intelligence a child is capable of achieving at any one time. It therefore also determines the types of activities that will best foster childhood intelligence. Physical brain growth rate varies little in all children.

Intelligence may seem to vary widely from child to child, but this is due to environmental stimuli. Various societies, and sometimes even segments of these societies, accent different aspects of intelligence. The type of intelligence we most commonly measure in Western Society—intellectual capacity—reflects only one aspect of brain development. We can often force-feed a child's intellect into a state of precocity, in the process leaving behind, or even destroying through overload, other mental capacities such as intuition and artistic ability.

In addition, higher intellectual capacity, which is supposed to begin functioning after age eleven when lower level brain capacities have matured, is impaired by the immature, undeveloped state of the lower brain. Usually this premature, overbalanced development in favor of the intellect is accompanied by high levels of anxiety which stunt the child's emotional growth and eventually drive it to therapy as an anxious adult. Had we not interfered with nature's timetable children's overall intelligence would grow at similar rates, easily catching up and passing intellectually the precocious child whose lower brain functions remain underdeveloped and thus a source of mental imbalance.

When we consider nature's plan we can begin to see where parenting, both traditional and modern, has gone astray. Let's look at single parenthood.

A career oriented pregnant woman who daily adheres to a rigorous schedule subjects her child to adverse tension. Just the urgent commute which leads to a stress-filled, noisy work environment subjects her fetus—certainly after seven months gestation and probably earlier—to an onslaught of disturbing stimuli that disrupts the intended placidity of the womb matrix.

Later, after birth, career women often ignore the biological necessity to maintain constant physical contact with their infant. This would allow for an anxiety-free transition from one matrix to another. The nightmare hospital experience, which often includes drugs that pass through the mother and stun the fetus into a state of unawareness, is followed by a shocking isolation in either an incubator (because the mother could not carry out the normal birth process, even under close supervision of an "expert" pediatrician) or a nursery. Subsequently, baby bottles, cribs, strollers, etc., fortify the infant's sense of isolation, preventing the crucial new matrix from properly forming. The result is an infant racked by anxiety whose growth is severely set back, if not permanently stunted.

Even as the child suffers, the mother is damaging herself. Not only has she robbed herself of the true psychological benefits of a natural birth, but she has deprived her body of crucial stimuli which would expedite its recovery from the birth process. For example, nursing a child immediately after birth triggers muscles that contract the distended birth canal.

Within a few months the baby, which has never had the opportunity to evolve in a proper mother-based matrix, is placed in the hands of a baby sitter while mother skips off to pursue her career. Thus begins day care, with parents eagerly awaiting the time when their children are "grown" enough to be enrolled in a nursery school.

In the case of the single mother, the crucial mother-child bond is further inhibited by the absence of the father. After fertilization, the father's initial role is to support the matrix provided by the mother. He must take away from her as many physical and psychological burdens as possible so that she can focus on providing the nurturing environment the child needs. After birth, in addition to supporting the family economically, father can help provide child supervision and carry out child related chores. He provides the first opportunity for a child to see that persons outside the original matrix (mother) can be safe to relate to. He can't, however, substitute for mother in providing the growth-enhancing matrix necessary for the child during its first years. As the child grows older the father will play a greater and greater role in its growth, helping guide it from one matrix to the next.

In a single-parent home, the mother is usually forced to economically support the matrix as well as provide its psycho/physical necessities. These two imperatives are often in conflict. In order to provide the material things the family needs often mothers must deprive their children of the attention needed to maintain an effective matrix.

I keep returning to the concept of matrices and their essential role in the growth of children. Growth takes place in stages. In order for it to progress effectively, a child must reach maturity in one matrix before moving on to another. Matrices must be experienced similarly to grades in formal schooling where a child must complete the work in sixth grade before being able to effectively move on to seventh. The child's inner biological program determines when the child's work within the matrix is complete and when the next spurt of brain growth will have prepared it for a shift into a new matrix. The parents, particularly in early years the mother, must be attuned to this carefully preprogrammed maturation process and be prepared to support it. This is the ideal approach to fostering intelligence.

Intelligence grows by reaching from the known to the unknown. A fetus reaches full 9-month maturity before secreting the hormones which trigger its mother's birthing mechanism. (Today doctors frequently interfere, causing severe psychological repercussions.) Up to the moment of birth, if properly cared for by mother, the fetus is secure in its environmental matrix—the womb. It has acquired both physically and mentally all that it could from this matrix and is ready to move on. Upon eviction, it must deal with an entirely alien matrix.

In order to avoid shock and confusion which will set back its growth, it needs a close bond to the preceding matrix—the known—so that it can reach out from there and adapt at its own pace. This means that mother must be prepared to provide whatever assurance the infant needs, especially close, continuous body contact, to remind the infant that it is still connected to the prior matrix (the womb) through a close bond to that which provided it (mother). Since the father did not provide the prior matrix he cannot provide the stable platform necessary to allow the child to fully explore the new matrix. In spite of caring fathers, motherless infants will be set back.

Joseph Chilton Pearce lists four great needs for bonding:
1. Holding (molding infant's body to mother's)
2. Prolonged, steady eye contact with mother
3. Smiling by mother
4. Soothing sounds uttered by the mother.

The maintenance of the mother matrix is crucial until around age four, when the next great matrix shift is due to occur.

If secure matrices are not provided, children experience insecurity which haunts them the rest of their lives. If children are wrenched out of a secure matrix the same result occurs. Mothers are most responsible for the earlier matrices. Fathers contribute more and more as the child matures.

Sadly, those women who claim they can balance child raising with a career and those who advocate single parenthood either lack awareness of or deny the importance of providing matrices. Some are innocently ignorant while others stubbornly ignore nature's biological plan. They don't seem to comprehend that the adult reality experience is a different order of logical structuring from child reality. Ideally, it is the child, based on its need for a matrix, which releases a woman to return to work or other responsibilities. A single parent, however, must return to work if she and the child are to survive. So to sustain them physically, she must sacrifice the child's psychological well being.

Many of these single mothers also see the tedious caring for a child's needs as additional "work" piled upon that of their occupation. This attitude, by itself, sabotages to varying degrees the essential mother/child bond. If this "work" is seen by a career-oriented parent as interfering with the pursuit of career or other interests, further frustration ensues and is communicated to the child. With the child under regular bombardment by this negative feedback, no secure matrices can exist. We see the results in our society today.

Nevertheless more and more feminists demand the "right" to become single parents. Ironically many advocate the return to a matriarchal society even as they seek to abdicate crucial responsibilities to children willingly embraced by devoted mothers throughout history. These feminists subscribe to the Murphy Brown philosophy which seems to say we can raise children any way we wish in spite of nature's plan. What they do not address is why parents choose to bring children into the world when they do not have the means to adequately care for them and must shuffle them off to the care of others.

I cannot emphasize this point too strongly. In our culture no one forces parents to have children. When one chooses to take that step they take upon a crucial responsibility. They have taken the life and psychological well being of a helpless human being into their hands. This human being has just as many rights as they do. Indeed, I claim the child has more right to consideration because it was brought into the world without its consent and will remain unable to care for itself or make intelligent choices for years. The parents knew, or should have known, what demands the child would be making upon them. If they were not prepared to fulfill these demands then they should have opted to remain childless.

Many medical professionals and parents can't accept the conclusions drawn by Pearce and others who support the matrix concept. Most often these scoffers are either people with a major investment in a traditional medical career, or they are anxious, unbonded parents without the commitment to parenthood or the courage to make the sacrifices necessary to carry out the matrix-honoring approach to child raising.

Dissenting professionals can cite studies by scientists who support the multi-billion dollar hospital birth industry. But these studies cannot discredit the importance of mother-child bonding. They usually say simply, "there is no scientific evidence" that it is crucial. In reality they have ignored what is really quite compelling empirical evidence in order to support their position in the scientific/medical community. This bastion is dominated by the male intellectual approach and committed to discrediting all others.

Amazingly, most feminists seem to ignore the patriarchal implications of the formal medical umbrella placed over the birth process. In order to advance their own agenda, which demands that they seek freedom from certain parental responsibilities dictated by nature, they are willing to enter an unholy alliance with what should be one of their most dangerous enemies—traditional Western medicine.

Over the past several decades the medical profession, largely controlled by men, has successfully discredited natural birth in the eyes of Western Society. Women have been led to believe that they are incompetent and largely helpless in the birth process. They are taught to fear the "likelihood" of terrible complications which could badly damage themselves or their child. They are bullied into placing themselves under the care of a physician who, whether male or female, has been trained in a male dominated system with patriarchal views. This system cannot accept that the knowledge born of women's instincts can have merit when weighed against that conceived by the male intellect. Men have "figured out" more about the birth process in this past century than women could possibly have been taught by millions of years of natural experience.

In *The Mismeasure of Women*, Carol Tavris points out:

> Medicine and law, based as they are on the male experience, fail to recognize the female viewpoint of what is distinctive about the experience of reproduction. The male perception of pregnancy consists of two steps: in goes a seed, out comes the result. In contrast, the woman's experience is continuous from conception to baby. By making the male experience the norm, we deny that continuity, the nine-month relationship a mother has with the fetus—calming it down when it's fussy, trying to sleep when it is too big, feeling it grow and change. By regarding pregnancy from the male perspective, and by celebrating high-tech prenatal technology over the continuous ma-

ternal relationship, law and medicine have created the impression
that women are merely containers for the fetus, and untrustworthy,
inefficient containers at that.

By relentlessly conditioning women to fear birth, men have
stripped women of perhaps their greatest power—the instinctual
knowledge of how best to bear and nurture human life. By attacking women's efficacy when they are most vulnerable, men have
robbed them of an important source of self esteem. In one more
way women are conditioned to accept patriarchy by accepting the
sanctity of the male intellect in regards to childbirth.

Why haven't feminists challenged this? Because many feminists
find that subscribing to modern medical practices furthers their
own cause. Many of them wish to repudiate their natural duties as
mothers in order to compete in the system against men.

To feminists the matrix system can't be valid. If it was, they would
have to sacrifice many of their personal ambitions when having a
child. And although they have no intention of dedicating their lives
to raising a child they refuse to give up the "privilege" of bringing
one into the world.

A typical such view was espoused by Sylvia Ann Hewlett in her
book, *A Lesser Life.* In it Hewlett does her best to discredit natural
childbirth. She herself had a negative experience trying to practice
it. During delivery she was unable to endure the pain and finally
submitted to drugs. She cites that the majority of other participants
in her Lamaze natural childbirth class also had negative experiences. Thus, she proceeds to use her case as well as other anec-
dotes to show that natural childbirth does not work for most women.

What makes Hewlett's childbirth experience suspect is her motivation for attempting it. She undertook the experience with the
understanding that women considered it "an experience to glory in
one's body and experience self-fulfillment." She quotes the declared
goal of one of the first natural birth centers in California as:

> to form 'a sisterhood concerned with birth and its process... We are
> finding out about the natural capabilities of women...and have taken
> our birthright, freedom, and decided for ourselves what our rituals
> of birth will be.'

Conspicuously absent in the above statements, as well as throughout Hewlett's remaining treatment of child bearing, is a deep concern as to what is in the best interests of the child. Two of Hewlett's own statements regarding her birthing experience are particularly sobering.

> I no longer cared what drug was administered as long as it was strong enough to produce relief from the appalling pain.

And,

> I could not bear any more and, after a particularly cruel contraction I implored Richard (her husband) to get me knocked out.

I do not mean to downplay the intensity of the pain Ms. Hewlett experienced. What troubles me is the total lack of consideration as to what the drug infusion would do to the fetus. It takes but 45 seconds for a drug to pass through the mother into the placenta. This means that the fetus would be "knocked out" during the birthing process and would be unable to participate normally. It would remain anesthetized during those crucial first minutes after being born. This apparently did not occur, or was of little concern, to Ms. Hewlett.

She did dig up quotes by a natural childbirth advocate, Dr. Robert A. Bradley to support her. First she admits that Dr. Bradley claims that the use of medication during labor produces "shortened attention span and memory, inability to handle stress, impaired reading ability and hyperactivity" in children. But then she attempts to debunk it with another of his quotes which she italicizes. "No scientific proof of any connection between medication during childbirth and subsequent child development."

This last statement may or may not have been true back in 1965 when it was made. However, much of the 30+ years research since points in a different direction. In any case, by embracing it Ms. Hewlett conveniently excuses her own dependence on medication during the process.

Any woman whose primary focus in a natural childbirth is to experience the expulsion of the fetus as a sort of personal "orgasm" and/or who seeks an infusion of self-esteem for having successfully carried out the process herself, is setting herself up for letdown and her child for a traumatic birth. Motivation is critical. To carry out the birth process properly one must not be focused upon selfish goals.

Birthing takes teamwork between mother and child. Mother's goal must be to transport the child with its experiencing minimum trauma from the inner to the outer matrix. To do this she must be finely attuned to the infant's signals. If mother is exclusively focusing on her own experience, her child, which is absolutely helpless at this point, cannot help but suffer. If she has focused on herself during her months of pregnancy, she will have failed to bond with the fetus and set herself up for a birth process lacking in harmony between the two participants. How could the experience help but be more painful?

Many women (including Ms. Hewlett) attempt the natural birthing process but must cease their efforts part way through because they find the pain unendurable. After drugs are administered the process continues relatively pain free and the mother is convinced that natural birthing is a sham.

No one can deny that a certain amount of pain or discomfort exists in birthing. But pain tolerance depends to a great degree upon focus. If a mother is completely focused upon her own rewards discomfort will factor in more heavily and likely be experienced as more intense than if she placed her child's needs on a par with her own.

Using Europe as an example, Ms. Hewlett tries to make the case that in times past before the advent of the modern medical approach, birth complications were more commonplace. Even if this was true, which is questionable, we need to examine to what extent these complex historical societies practiced truly natural childbirth. I suggest they were strict patriarchies which were infused with rigid religious superstition that precluded members from practicing anything instinctual.

Even Ms. Hewlett admits that today the infant mortality rate is considerably higher in the United States—arguably the most advanced country medically—than in Europe. One study says that childbirth related deaths in the hospital environment are six times more likely to occur here than in Europe. Does this not bring into question the effectiveness of advanced medicine's approach to childbirth?

I have taken aim upon Ms. Hewlett because she has so vigorously attacked natural childbirth and has defended the medical establishment by using her own experience. Her experience is valid as it pertains to herself, but is purely anecdotal in the discussion of the merits of natural childbirth.

Yes, I'm only a man. I've never experienced the physical process of birthing a child. How could I know?

And yet thousands of women have experienced the process successfully. Just because Ms. Hewlett and thousands of others who were focused on their own agenda during the birthing process could not carry it out, does not invalidate natural birthing.

Many women who are intently focused upon career and achieving success within the patriarchal system deny the importance of breast feeding. (Ms. Hewlett falls into this category, having had difficulty in this area as well.) So do many feminists, who not only defend the right to a career, but also seek gender equality in all other areas. They tend to look upon breast feeding as an imposition that men are precluded by anatomy from performing. Bottle feeding, by being gender neutral, exemplifies an egalitarian approach to caring for infants. This, of course, ignores the needs of the infant, but this is typical of the career-oriented more traditional woman as well as the radical feminist.

Many career women and most feminists further rationalize their position by maintaining that children can receive proper care and guidance even with the traditional family dissolved. Some don't even accept that the presence of a father is necessary. They offer universal, full time day-care and a quality school system as substitutes for parental presence.

But do we really believe that outsiders, who have tenuous bonds at best with our children, can provide the same quality supervision as loving parents? Not only common sense says no. Studies also agree.

Findings in research conducted by Phillips and Howe revealed that children who experienced day care from infancy were significantly less cooperative with adults, more physically and verbally aggressive with peers and adults, and more active. They tended to be less tolerant of frustration. Teenage boys who had experienced day care as young children tended to exhibit fearless, aggressive non-conformity to parental requirements with outgoing, active social interests which showed a peer-group orientation.

Another study found that compared to children cared for at home in a 6-month period, children in day-care homes are 25% more likely to contract infections. Those in day-care centers get nearly 50% more infections and are nearly 3 times as likely to need hospitalization.

Still another study showed that a majority of children under age four who attended day care regularly for extended periods were experiencing adrenal steroid secretions at near shock level. This shock was not being imposed by the day care environment itself but rather by separation anxiety at being "abandoned" by parents at a time when matrix integrity was crucial to growth.

One study, that by Dr. Patricia Arnold, should be particularly disturbing to feminists, who constantly demand equal treatment and who condemn gender roles. In nursery school classrooms taught by female teachers (how many male nursery school teachers do you know?), little boys and girls were treated differently when requesting help. Boys were given verbal instructions on how to do the project themselves. Girls were given direct assistance. This approach subjected these children to conditioning that accented gender difference and role playing. Boys were taught to be independent and to not share their feelings while girls were taught to be open but to accept themselves as less competent.

When the argument is made that subjecting a child to care from strangers increases the chances of its being sexually molested, some feminists counter with statistics that say a child is twice as likely to be sexually abused at home than in day care. The problem with the counter argument is that non-abusive parents can be 100% sure that their child will not be abused at home. Whatever the percentage of abuse in day care, for them the risk is significantly higher.

But is physical abuse the only risk facing children in day care? The above studies would indicate not. What is happening that is making children less controllable? The answer is that children in day care have been isolated from their matrix. A nursery school or baby sitter will not suffice. And even when the child is reunited with its matrix (mother), the bonds seem tenuous, the matrix less secure. Even in mother's arms, the child experiences anxiety, fearing the next separation.

Yes, after a time the child becomes conditioned to isolation from the matrix. But to accomplish this it must pay a price. Much of the energy it would focus upon exploring its universe, the task necessary to stimulate its intelligence, is expended steeling itself against separation anxiety. This it will suffer the rest of its life. It's like the Starship Enterprise directing energy away from its sensors in order to fortify its defensive shields to resist an attack that never ends.

Further complication comes from the onset of peer pressure. Children become vulnerable to peer pressure only to the extent that they are deprived of parental love, closeness and guidance. Extended absence of mother (30-50 hours a week) during the child's 2-4 year age period leaves the child particularly vulnerable to peer influence in its most impressionable years. Parents, particularly mothers, are supposed to be providing the primary role models and defining correct behavior patterns especially during those years.

But in day care the child is subjected to alternative role models that emulate behavior across a wide spectrum, much of it in the child's worst interests. Since parents have placed the child in this day care setting, this varied, aberrant behavior receives a measure of authentication by default. Sadly, even when a child has received a measure of proper love at home it often becomes victimized by other children's poor parenting when forced from a nurturing home environment into peer group situations.

Parents may try to undo negative learned behavior during their time with the child, but they will be fighting a battle daily. It is a battle they will later have to fight when they admit their child to formal schooling at age five. But by avoiding day care they have a full five years to develop the child's character and ability to resist peer pressure. Considering the child's rapid brain growth during those years the period is crucial. Especially with staggering peer pressures awaiting during the formal school experience.

Well meaning movements attempting to sterilize the environment of negative child influences such as war toys and games of violence are admirable but can only be marginally effective. To truly prevent children from embracing violent behavior we must immunize them against outside pressures by providing strong values through a proper matrix system.

Proper matrix development "inoculates" children against propensities to violence, not to mention the drug culture.

No one can legitimately deny that working mothers face extremely difficult problems balancing motherhood with a job. Keep in mind the distinction I made earlier between "job" and "career." The structure of our society demands that in every family at least one parent provide income. Obviously it would not be in the child's best interest to be sentenced to poverty by parents who refuse to work. Where children suffer is when parents make occupation their focus even when this is not crucial to providing necessary income. Parenting is a career all by itself and must take precedence over occupation. This applies just as strongly to fathers as to mothers.

To mothers who bore children with the intent of paying full attention to motherhood and then later were forced to work because of economic necessity, we can truly offer sympathy and seek to help them solve their child care problems. But those (men included) who have made work their focus and chosen to bear children as a sidelight deserve no aid from society (government or employee sponsored day care) to fortify their transgression. They, of course, would protest vehemently that they "love" their children. But this is belied when, to keep their career from suffering, they pass their children off to the care of others. Further evidence of their insensitivity to the needs of their children comes from their rejection of natural childbirth, breast feeding and the matrix concept when these approaches detract from their pursuing their profession.

The following statement by Ms. Hewlett is a classic example:

> The advice of child-rearing 'experts' is irresponsible and counterproductive in the modern world. It is irresponsible because there is no evidence that supports the notion that mother-intensive childrearing techniques constitute the only good way of bringing up children. And it is counterproductive because it impedes the development of sensible child-care policies in this country. The majority of mothers work, and the misguided notion that governments cannot and should not help provide a substitute for mother love and mother care has prevented us from creating high-quality day-care facilities. As a result, millions of children spend their waking hours in 'kennels,' and their mothers (and fathers) are subjected to high levels of strain and stress.

The thought of placing a child into a "kennel" should be abhorrent to anyone. Considering that this is the predominant day-care environment currently in existence, why would anyone choose to bear a child knowing that it would be subjected to a "kennel?" Ms. Hewlitt suggests that high-quality day care facilities, provided by the government of all things, can rise above this and provide a substitute for mother-love. I suggest that all day-care facilities are, to varying degrees, kennels. In order for any child-care environment to escape that label, mother must be present.

Parents who remain dedicated to careers which demand the use of day care always shortchange their children. Any prolonged parental absence or delay in parental response to a child's needs adds to a growing pool of child insecurity. In effect, this is mistreatment. If you leave a child to another's care while working and claim it turned out well adjusted because it behaves "normally" in society, I say, nonsense! It may be well adjusted comparatively, but consider how much more evolved it would be with full parental attention and proper guidance.

Once accepting the responsibility of parenthood, we must ask ourselves the question: what do we hope to accomplish when we raise our children? Do we wish them to reach their full potential? Or will we settle for them being "socially adjusted?"

The latter appears to be the majority view. If their children escape alcohol, drugs, gangs, jail, dereliction and insanity, and if they then assume a traditional role in society, modern parents tend to consider themselves successful. Whether their child is anxious, repressed, frustrated, or confused seems inconsequential since most other children suffer from the same ills.

Is that all is required of good parenting—steering children around catastrophic pitfalls? If that was true, so many adults who were considered "well adjusted" as children, would not be seeking psychotherapy to escape the horrors of deprived childhood.

Parents tend to rationalize their exposing their children to day care, peer pressure and other negative influences of society. They claim that shielding their children from these experiences only makes it more difficult for the children to cope later. They see their children becoming stronger for having experienced this negativity.

A certain logic accompanies this reasoning. However, shouldn't our goal in raising children be to provide them the means to achieve the highest quality life possible? Is our view of life so pessimistic that we accept painful experiences as normal and inevitable and find it productive to introduce our children to them?

Following that line of reasoning it is good parenting to verbally harass and even beat our female children since it is likely they will be so treated later in life. We will have prepared them to endure domineering husbands and domestic violence. If we treat them with nothing but love and kindness they won't be able to cope with the many brutes they will eventually encounter. Of course, in the process of conditioning them in this way we will have infused them with their own quantity of brutishness. And we will have done our part in perpetuating the cycle.

If we are to reverse the negative direction in which most children are heading, both genders must accept that the traditional family under patriarchy failed. At the same time they must recognize that the bi-gender family provides the best environment for raising children. Both patriarchal men (and women) and feminists must retreat from their positions. Many of the values that characterized the traditional family must be resurrected. At the same time, the patriarchal hierarchy and resulting philosophy must be scrapped.

Those who choose to bring children into the world must make children the focus of their lives. "Careers" must be sacrificed and replaced by occupations. Fathers must take a larger part in family life, including chores and overall child supervision. At the same time mothers must cultivate closer bonds to their children, both physically and psychologically, especially in the early years. This prohibits using day care except in absolute emergencies.

Anyone who finds the constant presence of children an imposition should reexamine their reasons for having them. Truly "loving" parents are dedicated to parenthood. Those who commit themselves to following nature's plan will find that much of the unruliness they have been taught to expect in young children will not appear. The behavior of infants depends greatly upon how they experience birth and its immediate aftermath. The modern hospital-based birthing process will produce infants with far different behavior patterns and dispositions than children whose parents follow nature's process religiously. To base behavioral analysis on surveys of infants born in hospitals distorts the picture of natural child behavior. What is considered "normal" unruliness is the child's way of rebelling against not having its needs met.

Child raising is a major challenge, especially in our modern, fast-paced, complex society. If you really love children you must be ready to meet nature's challenge. Otherwise, don't have them!

Chapter Twelve
Gender Polarization

Gender enmity has existed for aeons. Humanity has come to accept it as natural, the result of two vastly different gender identities pursuing separate, diverse goals. Even today, you constantly hear men and women referring to members of the other gender saying, "I don't understand them."

Other than among those holding the most extreme gender views, the vast majority of men and women seem to desire gender rapprochement. Generally women want to feel closer to men and vice versa. But how does a male and a female achieve true closeness while clinging to gender identity concepts that accent differences and advocate different priorities?

Both sides, like adversarial nations with different values and cultural goals, seek to forge a treaty through which we can establish peaceful relations and take advantage of products and services the other has to offer. Yet while doing so we cling to our national boundaries—our gender loyalties. It remains "us" and "them." Is that what nature intended?

As men and women, how different are we? Do our goals naturally conflict with each other's? Do you see yourself as a man or woman with the other gender as vastly different from you? Do you see yourself in that gender role, identifying with those of your gender while feeling far less than akin to the other gender and thereby to the species as a whole?

The vast majority of people feel this way. We've been conditioned from birth to see ourselves this way. We seek out members of the other gender not because we value them as an equal member of a more important group—humanity—but because of psycho/biological imperative. We often resent this need for its having shackled us with responsibility and pulled us away from gender focused interests.

Even where people have committed themselves to personal intergender relationships, these exist in an uneasy atmosphere haunted by the need of both parties to cling to gender identity. They do not see themselves as equal, interrelated components of a greater whole (the relationship), but rather as "the man" and "the woman" in a partnership from which they can extract elements to satisfy their own personal needs. Thus they regularly find themselves perplexed by each other and feel more akin to members of their own gender than to their partner. This often drives them to seek counsel from members of their own gender when trying to solve relationship related problems. The effect is to trivialize the relationship, downgrade the value of the other gender, and prevent the intimacy necessary for a deep bonding.

One of the earliest lessons taught to us as children is to identify with our gender. Can you remember a time when you were not forced to define yourself as male or female?

The pressure to identify with one or the other began when we were infants. Even when we couldn't recognize on our own any significant difference between ourselves and a sibling of the other gender (During the first years of childhood the sex of an individual can only be truly determined by examining the external genital organs.), our parents were incessantly talking and behaving as if major differences did exist.

Naturally the relentless gender identification pressure met little resistance from the relatively undeveloped infant mind. After all, at birth the human mind is similar to an empty computer disk and lacks masculine or feminine identity concepts. It awaits the coding of data that shapes identity, looking to parents as the primary source of that data. If the parents have been conditioned to live out traditional roles common to their society, they will imprint traditional gender behavior patterns upon their children that might not otherwise develop. So already in the infant stage a child will begin acting out common "boy" or "girl" roles almost as if born with that propensity.

As adults, defining our identities as masculine and feminine has become a fixation overriding our affiliation to our species. We see ourselves as men and women first, human second. Thus we are only willing to serve our species in roles that preserve our gender concepts. In those endeavors we see members of the other gender more like allies with whom we have a common interest, than siblings or devoted comrades with whom we've developed a permanent bond. Once these endeavors conclude the genders tend to distance themselves from each other, limiting association with the other while gravitating to gender exclusive groups which seek to fortify their gender identity. Too often their diverging goals place the genders in conflict.

Primarily the responsibility for this volatile situation must be laid upon men. By classifying women as inferior and excluding them from the power structure; by raising daughters to feel inferior to sons; men turned the genders into caste groups divided by imagined differences that went far beyond the biological.

This was not an organized conspiracy. It didn't have to be. Males saw other males treating females as inferior and, seeing advantages to themselves, copied this behavior. Inevitably within the caste structure, males saw themselves having more in common with other males than with females.

Women, because of a comparative physical strength deficit in a physical world, have been forced to accept this model. Over the millennia their conditioning has been so effective that most have never even questioned their role. They could only seek solace from others who suffered similarly, virtually all of whom have been females. This fortifies gender identification on the female side. Until recently few women (or men) have ever considered that another path was not only possible, but essential for long-term fulfillment and, ultimately, survival.

Current men's philosophy remains loyal to gender polarization. Men naturally see themselves as the dominating pole. They have used attacks by the feminist movement to organize and fight for their concept of male separateness and superiority. Even the so-called "Men's Movement," in spite of its claims to seeking a more feeling, compassionate nature for men, nevertheless remains a strong advocate of gender polarization.

Men in men's groups have shown no inclination to dismantle the gender caste system. Men's movement leaders—not directly in words but in the structure of their gatherings—emphasize that men bonding with men holds primacy over inter-gender bonding. They claim that men do their "deepest work" (and thus by implication can only self-actuate) in the presence of other men. At group gatherings attendees are reminded that when they disperse and return to the everyday world of gender interrelation, they will be leaving a safe, positive environment for one of gender conflict. "Brothers" are encouraged to remember the powerful bonds that exist in their group, an impression which tends to make the all-male group environment the ultimate sanctuary—"home."

Likewise feminists, in their vigorous efforts to advance women's rights, have become strong advocates of polarization. And in doing so they have embraced the basic tenet of patriarchy even as they have fought against it. For patriarchy exists both as a direct result of, and to foster, gender polarization.

When feminists advocate gender duality and separateness, then seek to topple patriarchy in a quest for equality, they take upon both an impossible and hypocritical task. Division into genders only breeds rivalry and the urge in each to seek domination over the other. This is inevitable, for each gender in the very act of separating from the other, defines priorities which it values above those of the other. When these priorities conflict the option is: sacrifice or dominate.

It is not easy to sacrifice for those you consider different than you. Loyalty is always focused on one's own gender with the other gender being seen as less important and therefore potentially adversarial. Eventually, areas of conflict occur and ultimately, because this is a physical world, the male gender usually employs its greater strength to prevail. These dynamics brought the advent of patriarchy. Only when the genders bond will patriarchy disappear and a truly egalitarian society ensue.

So, in the process of wresting away control over their lives wielded by men (a positive development in itself) the feminist movement has widened the breach between the genders and strengthened the female pole of the bi-polar gender system. This has placed the axis binding us together under extreme tension.

Instead of the two genders blending into a closely interrelated system, they keep revolving around each other trying to act as sovereign forces, each trying to pull the entire system in the direction they see as best for their gender. They try to satisfy each other's biological needs—an act that demands closeness—even as they seek to maintain the distance necessary to maintain gender exclusivity. It doesn't work. Biological fulfillment eludes them just as does fulfillment of their gender-centered aims. Both have been thwarted by the forces of resistance the genders have exerted upon each other.

For much of history the male planetoid remained at the center of this gravitational system with the female revolving around it. Only recently has the female planetoid begun exercising a stronger gravitational presence, forcing the system's center of gravity to shift towards the female pole.

Some radical feminists seek to reverse polarity completely, making the female pole dominant. However, the stated goal of most feminists is to create a balanced system, with the center of gravity halfway between.

At first glance the effort seems admirable and constructive. But if it is successful we will be left with a system of separate genders, equal in power but isolated by distrust and different agenda. Women will still see men as adversaries and vice versa. The result, of course, will be competition rather than cooperation between genders.

History shows us that competition has always led to subjugation, domination, hierarchies and the division of people into classes, whether they be racial, economic or gender. This appears to be the nature of competition—the separation of the participants into winners and losers. Therefore women rising to equality with men and using this status to compete against them cannot serve the species any more than aggressive men have in the past. Rather, with both genders participating, the urge to dominate will likely proliferate, spilling over from the gender conflict and further poisoning relationships between races and cultures. The urge to dominate will continue to exploit the environment as dominators seek to expand their physical power through exploitation of physical resources.

Relatively few people advocate domination. But virtually all fail to see that our urge to dominate grows as a matter of course from our need to identify with our gender. In his study of the relationships established between the sexes, one noted gender researcher observed that "sexual dualism is the paradigm of all dualisms—the paradigm of the history of the world." Is it a history to be proud of?

Throughout, we have justified polarization by defining various characteristics as gender exclusive. We have sorted out these behavior traits into two piles which we have assigned different roles. Aggression is masculine; nurturing is feminine. Hard is male; soft is female. The list of dichotomies seems endless and the cultural pressure to adhere to them and thereby act out acceptable gender roles, relentless. Only males are allowed to act out one role; females the other.

We have attempted to attribute these roles to innately programmed psychological motivation, behavioral patterns and emotions. We are conditioned to believe that if we do not embrace the slate of traits society has assigned to our gender, we are less than fully human. Naturally, each gender seeks to behave more "ideally" in their role so they tend to accent the more extreme behavior of their roles. To be more "masculine," males must be more aggressive and dominating. To be more "feminine," females must be softer, less physical and more nurturing. Because over time this gender exclusive behavior has become nearly universal, we have tended to accept it as normal.

To imply that the worldwide prevalence of the seeking for gender identification serves as proof that biology drives us in this direction overlooks the fact that patriarchy dominates the world. Children everywhere receive patriarchal parenting from both parents thereby causing this gender identification need.

Even psychologists who have researched the gender identity issue and accept that gender identity is a socialized phenomenon are trapped by their personal conditioning into accepting the concept of distinct "masculine" and "feminine" behavior. Typical is the view that to properly assess a client careful observation of behavior is necessary to determine whether "gender is congruent with anatomy."

But the terms "masculinity" and "femininity" refer primarily to behavior—to a lesser degree, appearance. What determines which behavior is "masculine" and which "feminine?" "Masculine," as defined by the pacifistic Balinese studied by Margaret Mead, has little resemblance to "masculine," as defined by the misogynous, bloodthirsty New Guinean Sambians studied by G. H. Herdt. Yet within their societies, except in unusual cases, each man practicing "normal" male behavior is comfortable with his "masculinity." A psychologist treating "abnormal masculinity" in Bali would have a far different view from one treating "abnormal" male Sambians. Each might be seeking to determine whether "gender is congruent with anatomy," but each would define those gender characteristics differently. This divergence would be found to be true in comparing many societies, pointing to behavior not being determined by bio/genital factors.

Aggressive and/or passive propensities would seem to be equally

available to both sexes prior to the imposition of cultural conditioning. Thus it seems that by seeking to determine whether "gender is
congruent with anatomy," we define gender identity according to
specific behavior patterns even as we define these specific behavior patterns as attributable to gender identity. But logic demands
that one must proceed from the other. They cannot beget each other.

The concept of defining the "masculine" and "feminine" as distinctly different characteristics has been strongly fortified by the
work of Carl Jung. He was a strong advocate of codifying behavior
and behavior propensities as belonging exclusively to one gender
or the other. It was he who made popular the concept that each
person has both a "male and female side." He called them the anima
and animus—the anima being the female side of man; the animus
the male side of woman.

Upon superficial examination this view seems to conceptually
bring the genders closer together. It authenticates men acting at
times in ways normally attributed to women, and vice versa. It has
allowed men to excuse their behavior when acting "intuitively" or
"nurturing." According to Jung they had not lost their masculinity
by acting so, but rather were accessing their "feminine side," or
anima. Similarly women could rationalize their acting "masculine."

Both genders found this concept easy to embrace. Jung's theory
allowed men, who had difficulty relating to behavior impulses which
seemed to come natural to them yet were classified as strictly feminine, to salvage their concept of masculinity exclusive of femininity. Women were affected slightly differently since they were not as
deeply resentful of the characteristics attributed to other gender.
(In our culture masculinity meant having access to power. Thus
many women would have gladly embraced masculine traits if they
had been so allowed.) Nevertheless, many women gravitated to Jung
because he authenticated femininity by asserting that it was valuable as an aid to masculinity. Before Jung, the status of femininity
was distinctly lower therefore women were grateful for this uplifting.

Yet Jung's theory fell far short of raising women to equality. Jean
Baker Miller ably points out:

> Jung's woman 'hidden inside the man' is not the same as its re-
> verse. Instead we have to ask who really runs the world and who
> 'decides' the part of each sex that is suppressed. The notions of Jung
> and others deny the basic inequality and asymmetry that exists; they

are also ahistorical. The question is one of what has been suppressed and what can begin to emerge at this time in our history—and who is able to bring forward the suppressed parts? Who has declared what is to be labeled masculine and feminine? Finally, these formulations are themselves a reflection of the whole dichotomization of the essentials of human experience. The present divisions and separations are, I believe, a product of culture as we have known it—that is, a culture based on a primary inequity. It is the very nature of this dichotomization that is in question.

Jung's theory served the field of psychology by providing a release of pressure. Psychologically speaking, men and women had been so repressed by rigid gender codes of behavior, plus guilt ridden when they couldn't measure up, that they were on the verge of blowing apart. Jung gave them slack even as his clever personality design preserved gender duality.

Jung himself wrote prolifically on the subject of the anima and animus. His students and critics have produced hundreds of other volumes on the topic. I will not try to address it at length here. However, one point is particularly pertinent.

Jung's anima/animus concept fortifies the concept of classifying roles as being exclusive to one gender or the other. When he speaks of the anima and how it acts upon men, he claims that it is ingrained and then proceeds to describe it as an outside force. Granted, his words seem to say that it exists "within" all men. But he always discusses it as a force exclusive of the male identity. According to Jung, man must "deal with" his anima. This presentation objectifies the anima and makes it a house guest rather than a member of the family. And since the anima is considered the "feminine side" of man, his "feminine side" is conveniently relegated to a subordinate position. His "masculine side," which he identifies with subjectively, remains the valued side. His "feminine side" is there to give him an excuse whenever he feels or behaves in a less than manly fashion. (The same process holds true for women and the animus.) Thus, Jung's anima/animus model has aided and abetted sexism.

Although a large segment of modern psychology does not accept Jung, it nevertheless embraces the concept of "masculine" and "feminine" character sides to each gender. If interpreted properly this could be a step toward gender healing. Unfortunately, behavior that was once considered exclusively masculine or feminine has been legitimatized for practice by what continues to be viewed as two distinctly separate genders. It has become okay for men to nurture and women to aggress—that is, as long as each gender continues to act out traits traditionally assigned to it. (A man who always nurtures and never aggresses begins to look suspiciously feminine.) The bottom line remains—masculine is distinct from feminine. These classifications are sacred and inviolable.

A subtle, yet very critical distinction needs to be pointed out here. When psychology restructured the human psyche by claiming that both genders have legitimate aspects of the other gender in their makeup, it was simply trying to explain away the existence of identical behavior traits in both genders. It was not attempting to retract the idea that the two genders are distinctly different. It has restructured its view of the male and female psyches so that both can, without being considered aberrant, embrace traits most commonly practiced by the other. In this way psychologists can cling to the view that maleness and femaleness remain exclusive of each other. In psychology aggression remains a masculine trait, even when practiced by women. Likewise, nurturing remains a feminine trait.

The crucial aspect of gender confusion lies in the driving need to find identity through one's gender. The vast majority of published psychologists emphasize the importance of finding one's own "masculine" or "feminine" identity. Obviously it is important to establish a personal identity. But why is it so important to be gender based?

These same authors respond to this question as if it advocates androgyny or, indeed, asexuality. Not so. Patriarchal conditioning, which encourages the gender classification of behavior, fosters this misconception.

While one's sexual nature is an aspect of one's identity, many other aspects and personal attributes contribute even more. Once we come to recognize that these other non-sexual aspects have no gender basis (e.g. aggressiveness is a human rather than a male behavior pattern), one is free to establish a large portion of their identity without concern for their gender.

Yes, sexual identity is an important dynamic. But only in defining one's role and attitudes toward reproduction and child raising. In all other aspects of life gender identification only tends to divide and undermine the species.

Generally, feminists have followed the lead of psychology, many taking it to the extreme. They seek to eliminate the list of traits traditionally attributed to each gender. They want all behavior viewed as acceptable to both genders.

This appears to be a constructive view which would further remove stifling restrictions from both genders. However, a closer examination casts doubt on the motivation behind it. Feminists have found that the traits formerly attributed to women have kept them straightjacketed and in less than equal status to men. By seeking legitimatized access to masculine behavior patterns they hope to raise their status.

Yet even as they seek to genderwise declassify traits such as aggression, feminists cling to their own gender classification as females. They want a new gender role authenticated for females but they seek no bonding with men. Once again, gender identification remains sacred.

The New Age man has taken much the same approach. He has serious differences with his macho brothers, who disdain all softer traits traditionally attributed to women. New Age man values those traits and would like to exercise many of them, but he too is ensnared by the need to identify with his gender. The thought of being less than "masculine" frightens him, just as it does his macho brothers. This means that in order to experience a strong sense of masculinity he must embrace many of those traits that typify machismo.

To escape the quandary he finds himself in, New Age man has eagerly accepted the Jungian concept of possessing a "feminine side." In this way he can exercise his natural urge to nurture and soften his machismo approach, even as he retains many traditionally masculine attributes. He seems softer and therefore draws women closer to him even as he retains power over them.

Is it valid to declare behavior traits as natural to only one gender? Take for example aggression. This is considered a male trait linked to testosterone. And yet, as I indicated in an earlier chapter, cases have been found where unusually aggressive males lacked testosterone and that injections of it lowered their level of aggression. Indeed, some researchers have begun questioning whether behavioral urges may trigger hormone flow rather than the reverse. So it would seem that the jury is still out on the effect of hormones.

Meanwhile our society has begun to see vastly increasing displays of aggression from females in business, politics, and especially in competitive sports. Why? Is women's "masculine side" strengthening, or do they innately possess as a part of natural femininity an aggressive capacity equal to men's?

In the past, female aggression lay suppressed under the threat of male retaliation. In general, superior male physical strength made it impractical for women to successfully attack men physically. Simply, few women could prevail in fistfights with men. And since men employed physical force as the ultimate arbitrator (taken to its extreme in trial by combat), women had to seek other means to obtain power. Thus for the most part, aggression was not employed by women and it became stamped as being exclusively male. Even today, although female aggression has become acceptable it is labeled as male behavior practiced by females.

Likewise intuition/empathy has always been considered a female skill. And yet if one looks at it in more depth, intuition/empathy is another self-protective, survival skill available to both genders. Men tend to exercise it less frequently and thus lose touch with this skill because their greater physical strength allows them to effectively address more problems in a physical manner than can women. Men also have greater cultural authority which allows them to address more cultural issues assertively without resorting to the aid of their intuition. However, men do tend to develop empathic skills when they must regularly deal with others who are equal or more powerful. A good example in today's world is when a man must "read" his boss to maintain his security or gain economic advantage.

Nurturing is yet another trait that has undergone a similar classification as exclusively female. Nurturing is most often looked upon as exercising a soft approach. I will take issue with this later. In any case, softness is more often practiced by females than males and therefore is attributed to femaleness. Once again, what is overlooked is the survival need that brings this about. The needs of infants, who demand soft handling, are most often met by females and therefore females by necessity have learned to practice the soft approach. When males are asked to perform these or similar tasks that demand softness, they have proven to be just as effective as females.

Cultural pressure has also forced the dubious gender-oriented classification of many other traits. Most of these have no proven genetic linkage with one gender or the other. Their characterization as gender based is the effort of gender-duality advocates to maintain the artificial rift between the genders.

Why is it important not to classify human traits as exclusively masculine or feminine? Why can't we use this approach simply for the purpose of discussion?

Because this method does not remain a tool to further discussion, but rather, soon becomes concept. It fortifies the misguided gender-based search for personal identity. The very act of referring to these traits in this manner fosters the concept of gender separation. It implies differences in the genders that do not exist. Many of these commonly perceived "differences" have evolved because of social conditions. To attribute them to innate gender differences distorts reality and fortifies aeons of gender misconception which has fostered polarization.

The same approach is used by racial bigots. In many geographical areas social conditions have deprived minorities of educational opportunities equal to those of whites. As a result, minorities from these areas tend to score lower on knowledge and intelligence tests. The bigot would like to use these tests to prove that minorities are generally less intelligent than whites. Fortunately more enlightened opinion recognizes that social conditions are responsible for these lower scores and that basic intelligence does not vary because of race.

Now ask yourself: would this latter, unprejudiced group, simply for the purpose of discussing comparative intelligence, create Jungian-style archetypes, using the fact that minorities have generally scored lower on tests and refer to low intelligence as a "minority trait?" Would they say that any white person of low intelligence was accessing their "minority side?" Or that any minority person of high intelligence was accessing their "white side?" Would they use this technique even metaphorically, hoping that somehow people would better grasp the workings of intelligence by attributing high and low intelligence to the groups in which each is most commonly displayed? They wouldn't do this because it would be inaccurate and it would further polarize the races and foster racism.

This, however, is what psychologists and gender-duality advocates do all the time when using the terms "masculine" and "feminine sides" in trying to sort out gender issues. The big question should not be: what's wrong with attributing behavior traits to a "masculine" or "feminine" side? Rather it should be: why is it so essential to classify traits as male or female? Why do we have such an enormous investment in gender identification?

The concept of male/female dichotomy has become a Gibraltar, looming as the unchallenged foundation of human relationships. Few have even thought of the above question, much less had the courage to ask it.

No one would argue that except for a tiny percentage of us we all have the physical structure of either one sex or the other and thus can be classified as either male or female. Because of these physical differences some physical tasks may be better performed by one gender or the other.

But does task specialization call for us to conceptually split the human species into two autonomous parts? Must we find identity with and pledge allegiance to one, thereby segregating ourselves spiritually from the other? It would seem that our basic physical differences have been blown far out of proportion to their real significance. An entire behavioral etiquette has been established for the genders that has nothing to do with biological imperative.

A woman bears and suckles children of both sexes. A man wields his physical strength to both provide for and protect members of his family, be they male or female. Nature designed us as a species with two distinct but interrelated parts. Without that interrelation, the species cannot even survive, much less achieve psychological and spiritual fulfillment. Therefore our primary identification and loyalty should be with our species, gender playing a minor role.

Elisabeth Badinter states it eloquently:

> That the One (gender) should have different attributes (and attributions) from the Other, that each should do something that the Other cannot do, should not be seen as opposition, but as a mutual exchange that does not depreciate the One in order to ascribe more value to the Other. The androgynal myth reminds human beings that when the two sexes are united, they form such an image of completeness that the One separated from the Other becomes mutilated and incomplete.
>
> Clearly this lesson has not been learnt by the patriarchal ideology which has too often replaced the symmetry of the sexes by a radical asymmetry. Perhaps it was obliged to do so in order to establish its

domination, without realizing that at the same time it was producing the seeds of its own death.

If we set aside our gender prejudices, we can see that in its own way nature designed humankind to function as a team, with the two genders playing different roles (positions) with different responsibilities. I'm no longer an advocate of competitive sports but since they command such encompassing attention in our culture, consider the following metaphor.

More than any other major sport, basketball exploits two physical dimensions during play—vertical and horizontal. To get from one basket to the other players must move horizontally; and in order to score they must address a goal that is vertically beyond their normal standing reach. To be successful, teams must be able to move swiftly across the court as well as control the vertical space near the baskets. Since players have varying physical attributes, they are divided into positions which ask for specialized skills.

Two of these positions—those which demand the most widely contrasting physical skills—are that of center and point guard. The center position calls for a tall person, usually the tallest on the team. He operates near the basket and is expected to focus primarily on the vertical aspects of the game. The point guard is usually the most dexterous player in handling the ball and the one most likely to be able to transport it quickly and safely horizontally from one end of the court to the other.

Both players must operate in the medium the other person excels in. The center must run from one basket to the other to get into position to exercise his primary skills. At the same time the point guard must be able to cast the ball successfully through vertical space if he is to pass to teammates or score.

Few centers, because of their greater statures and their tendency to develop strength rather than speed, can transport the ball effectively from one basket to the other. Few point guards, because they are usually of shorter stature, can control the vertical space at each end of the court. Both need the other's skills to be successful in game situations. This need resembles the need facing the human genders as they try to relate and turn the human endeavor into a successful one.

Although basketball players are classified by the positions they have been assigned, they primarily identify themselves as belonging to a team, not a caste group as identified by their position. They may on occasion practice together by position, but primarily practices are held for the entire team together since the team must function as a unit to be successful.

Players do not wear different uniforms to designate their positions. They don't shower separately by position. They don't socialize separately by position. They don't see game-related problems as issues to be addressed by individual positions without input from the rest of the team. On those rare occasions when the center personally transports the ball up the court he is not said to be practicing "guard behavior." Nor when guards get rebounds are they said to be practicing "center behavior."

All team members relate to each other as equal human beings. Each position provides its separate skills, but all are valued and provide a distinct crucial worth to the team. Against certain teams or during certain parts of the game, the skills of one position may be more crucial than those of the others, but no position is exalted over another as in a caste system. (In fact, any position can provide the Team Captain.) The team effort would seriously suffer if a player lorded his skills over teammates, dominating them and demanding subservience. Classification by position serves no function except to more easily define role division which overall enhances the team.

To be successful all teams in all sports or all other pursuits must define roles based upon the varying skills of the members. Often because of major physical differences these skills are very diverse. The secret of success is to blend these diverse skills into a homogenized effort. In the process, successful teams do not create caste systems. Participants who play the same role do not primarily identify as a group and isolate themselves from others playing other roles. They respect each other's roles, working, living and socializing together with a common goal creating a common bond that overrides all role differences.

On the human team, men bring certain distinct physical skills to the species that women possess in lesser degree, and vice versa. Since both male and female skills are essential for the well being of the species, neither gender can remain exclusive of or exalted over the other. At the same time, the species cannot experience as much success if one gender is trying to downplay the differences and usurp the areas in which the other gender is more skillful.

Since women throughout the ages have been discouraged from exploring the full extent of their physical potential, modern athletics give us a unique opportunity to examine just how different physically men and women really are. On this topic Anne Fausto-Sterling in her book, *Myths of Gender*, has numerous pertinent observations to make.

She acknowledges that men and women have different reproductive systems and organs which lead to women experiencing three unique physiological processes: menstruation, menopause and childbirth. Hormones, however, are shared by both genders, differing in amount, not in kind. She points out:

> These differences may be small or large, depending on biological rhythms, life cycle rhythms, stress, and both lifelong and immediate individual experience. These factors, not genetic gender difference, explain why, on average, men are slightly taller and stronger.

The key hormone in the human growth process is secreted by the pituitary gland, which probably responds to a different biological clock in males than in females, although this has not been proven. Some studies suggest that exercise can affect the short-term synthesis of the growth hormone and that physical training stimulates more vigorous growth in children. It therefore follows that different exercise levels in boys and girls could alter growth hormone metabolism and explain the ten percent height difference between men and women.

Fausto-Sterling admits that although height and shape differences are not absolute, strength differences just may be. She says:

> The number of muscle fibers in each individual becomes fixed during the first few years of life, and subsequent muscle growth consists only of increases in the length and width of such fibers. Much of the muscle size differences between males and females result from disparities in fiber growth rather than fiber number. Both hormones and physical activity play a role.

The question remains, however, what would be the average difference in muscle strength between men and women who received the same level of exercise? In the past, girls were not allowed anywhere near the activity levels of boys and therefore compared poorly.

The margin has closed in recent years but a wide disparity in favor of boys still exists.

We return to Fausto-Sterling:

> Strength is the ability of an individual to exert force against some external resistance, and different parts of the body have different strengths. The average strength differences between men and women result at least in part from men's larger size. The upper body strength of the average female (that is, strength derived from arms and shoulders) is about half that of the average male although, when matched for size, a woman has 80% of a man's upper body strength. The lower body strength of the average woman reaches 70% of the average man's, and when the comparison is made between individuals of the same weight a woman's lower body strength approaches 93% of a man's. Leg strength measured relative to lean body weight actually shows women's legs to be 5.8% stronger than men's. One implication is that sports emphasizing upper body strength will probably always offer males an advantage. Advantages accruing to men in other sports such as running, however, may be due only to differences in leg length, rather than strength.

The gap between men and women in athletic performance has been steadily narrowing. Still, it is not likely that women will ever gain parity in those sports designed by and for men. Nevertheless athletic training is beginning to show us that innate physical differences between the genders have been exaggerated.

It seems highly likely that the height and strength dimorphism between males and females would narrow in a culture where from infancy girls engaged in the same amount and kind of physical activity as boys. This would prove that the gender difference as represented in patriarchy is a sham. For that reason patriarchal men must defend their concept of gender roles and thereby keep women "feminized"—that is, relatively inactive physically.

By keeping women "feminized" patriarchy also is able to justify its claim that mothers hamper the development of "masculinity" in boys and that boys must break with mother in order to become men. For traditional "feminine" behavior under patriarchy has always been viewed as a sign of weakness and thus anathema to males.

But this soft, passive behavior pattern has been bred by patriarchal conditioning. From infancy children in patriarchal societies are subjected to relentless conditioning to conform to gender behavior standards. Girls are taught to be soft and passive; boys to be hard and aggressive. Females who have been victimized by this childhood conditioning will naturally present a role model to their male infants which is contrary to the one necessary to mold these boys into patriarchal men.

Thus, patriarchal men are correct when they charge that the average patriarchal woman serves as a detriment to boys seeking "manhood" as defined by patriarchy. Patriarchal men have created the weak, passive behavior pattern and molded their female children into it. In effect, patriarchal men have conditioned their female offspring to become a detriment to patriarchal "masculinity" and then blamed women for it as if it occurred naturally.

If women had not been so conditioned they could be every bit as tough as males and, through example, instill necessary toughness into their sons. Detrimental "softness" (I make this designation because many attributes that would be described as "soft" are just as desirable in men as women) is as much an anathema to a woman as it is to her son. She is unable to raise a boy to his full potential by herself because she has been prevented from self-actualizing and is less than a full person. She has difficulty facilitating her son's growth to real humanhood because she herself cannot perceive what that is. She also fails to mold him into a patriarchal man because by herself she cannot provide him with an example to emulate.

Gender conditioning under our patriarchal system has become so universal, traditional and ritualistic that generation after generation passes without anyone questioning. Gender behavior has become so standardized that evidence for its legitimacy seems overwhelmingly empirical. However, if we do examine the patriarchal concept of gender roles more closely, major flaws become apparent.

Studies indicate that at a very young age children begin to identify with their gender. As the years go by they tend to spend more and more time with members of their gender. This tendency seems to fortify the argument that gender identification is instinctual and normal.

What is not considered is that from the child's earliest cognitive moments it is exposed to strong gender-biased input.

In her book *Gender Blending*, Holly Devor points out:

> The adults who welcome newborns into the world have well-established genders, personalities, and belief systems by the time they find themselves in attendance at a birth. They invariably, and often

unintentionally, communicate their gender beliefs to newborns through the medium of their own personalities and actions. One way that this is manifested is in adults' strong social need to attribute membership in a sex status, and sex differences, to newborn infants. This tendency is so strong that they will often do it even when they have no concrete information on which to base their actions. Adults seem almost unable to relate to an "ungendered" child. When adults are presented with a baby whose sex is not specified, they will generally want to know the sex of the child before commencing social interactions with it. If that information is not forthcoming, they will usually proceed to decide for themselves what the sex and gender of the child are. These sex/gender attributions then form a basis for their subsequent understandings of, and interactions with, the child.

Thus as infants we found ourselves referred to by our parents as "he" or "she," "boy" or "girl," "son" or "daughter," "brother" or "sister." Consider studies described by Elisabeth Badinter:

Zella Luria and Jeffrey Rubin questioned fathers and mothers twenty-four hours after the baby's birth about their impressions of their child. The fathers had seen their baby through a pane of glass, the mothers had held it in their arms once. The babies, boys and girls, weighed the same and were the same size, they were all normal and born at term. The results of the interviews with the parents were eloquent.

The parents used the word 'big' for sons more than for daughters, and 'beautiful,' 'cute,' 'sweet' for the latter. The little girls had 'delicate features' and the little boys 'strong features'; the little girls were 'small,' while the little boys, who were the same size, were 'big.' Both parents tended to stereotype their babies, but all the research has shown that this tendency is more marked in the father.

All these studies show the extreme importance of the viewpoint of those associating with the baby. As soon as it is born, we teach the baby through gesture, voice, and choice of playthings and clothes which sex it belongs to. But we are not truly aware of the influence of this phenomenon of teaching until the sex of the child poses problems.

Badinter stops here, but gender conditioning does not. The infant is subjected to relentless bombardment driving home the significance of the pronouns "he" and "she." It soon sees that its parents and all other adults divide humanity into two separate groups which have distinct behavior requirements. The parents have assigned the infant to one of these groups, thereby imposing gender-oriented behavior demands.

The infant gradually comes to see that boys carry names taboo for girls. The color blue is associated with boys; pink with girls. Males wear pants, females dresses. Boys don't get scared or cry; girls don't fight. Usually it sees its mother and father dressed and groomed differently and playing different roles. When taken outside it sees other evidence of defined gender difference, e.g. gender exclusive bathrooms.

Once in nursery school it begins to be taught society's view of gender difference. It learns that the genitalia must be kept covered, especially from the other gender. Teachers often refer to children as "boys and girls" rather than "children." It is exposed to sexist nursery rhymes and fairy tales. Older children, who have been indoctrinated with gender bias, serve as examples of "proper" gender-exclusive behavior and trigger the onset of gender oriented peer pressure.

Robert J. Stoller, a physician who broke much new ground on the gender identity issue through his work with transsexuals, makes this statement:

> The sense of sexual identity is essentially culturally determined, i.e. learnt after birth. 'This process of apprenticeship comes from the social milieu... But the knowledge comes through the mother, so that what actually reaches the child is the mother's interpretation of society's attitudes. Later, the father, the brothers and sisters...influence the development of the child's identity.'
>
> Everything begins at birth, when the doctor declares the child's sex and it is officially registered. Parents and society then consider it a boy or a girl. It is not some innate force that tells the baby that he is of the male sex and will become masculine. It is what his parents teach him, and they could equally well teach him something else. From the moment they know they have a boy, they start on a process which, depending on their idea of masculinity, will make them encourage some kinds of behavior and discourage others. The choice of name, the style of clothes, the way the child is carried, the kind of games, etc., constitute the greater part of the child's training in the development of its gender identity. In most cases, what our society considers masculinity will be encouraged, and by about the end of his first year the little boy's behavior has a distinctly masculine character.

Those social scientists who wish to put forth that gender identification is instinctual ignore the constant bombardment of gender oriented signals the child begins receiving from infancy. Find me a child whose parents did not play out patriarchal gender roles in front of it; who was not spoken to or of by parents as if it belonged to a particular gender; who was not dressed as a member of a particular gender and given gender-oriented playthings; who was not subjected to an early school environment which fostered gender difference; and in spite of this developed a strong gender identification, and I will surrender my point.

To once more borrow a quote from Holly Devor:

> Femininity and masculinity can best be understood as ideological constructions whose human manifestations (women and men, girls and boys) are recreated in each generation according to the intermeshing requirements of social, cultural, economic, and biological necessities. The apparent naturalness of femininity and masculinity does not stem from an inevitable and overwhelming biological imperative, but rather from the pervasiveness of a patriarchal social structure founded on the division of humanity by sex; a division which a patriarchal society demands must be at all times, and under all circumstances, unequivocal and obvious.
>
> The imbededness of members of society within this belief system leads them to experience themselves and those around them as verifying the 'intrinsicness' of femininity and masculinity. They can transfer not only their beliefs but also psychological and physiological reproductions of those beliefs to the infants in their care. In this way, the 'universality' of gender as the primary organizing principle of all human endeavor is continuously reinforced and reconstituted within, and between, each succeeding generation.

Nature has assigned men and women together three interrelated goals: physical survival, species reproduction, and cerebral (intellectual and spiritual) evolution. These triune goals cannot be achieved unless men and women bond and deemphasize gender. This would seem obvious in considering the first two goals. But what about the third: cerebral evolution? Is that not an individual pursuit?

It is and it isn't. I have purposely used the word triune and mean its definition to closely parallel its usage in the religious context. All three goals, although seemingly pursued separately, are closely linked. In particular, cerebral evolution can only fully take place when an individual has placed him/herself in proper relationship to the first two goals. They provide testing grounds for our minds and psyches.

A major part of cerebral evolution involves learning to subordinate oneself to the needs of the species even as we maintain our individuality. To reject bonding with the other gender in order to maintain loyalty to our own, robs us of the crucial challenge to address the responsibilities of our physical humanness. It is only after we have completed this basic course successfully, that our minds are prepared to move on to greater challenges that lie beyond the physical.

The biological imperatives appear plain. The human race cannot exist as a single gender. If it is to remain a viable species it must seek perpetuation and this is best accomplished with the two genders working together. Healthy members of both genders accept this. Indeed, they recognize that they cannot achieve personal fulfillment without bonding with the other gender and pursuing species perpetuation.

Am I suggesting that the human race should seek a state of androgyny? Absolutely not. A masculine and feminine identity completely distinct from each other definitely exists. But these distinctions rest purely on the biological. Only to the extent that biology assigns distinct roles to the sexes can we legitimately define masculinity and femininity. And these blend together as integral parts of an integrated whole.

Many animals live much of their lives as separate genders, coming together purely to reproduce. Why is that not natural for humans also? Because humans have been given advanced intelligence and a sophisticated psyche that experiences feelings of compassion, love, etc. The fulfillment of these makes bonding essential. In addition, the human young need more care and for a much longer period of time. The best way to provide this care is with both parents harmonized in a pair bond.

Mankind is currently in the midst of an adventure—the quest for our continuing evolution. Millions of other species have set out on this same quest and have ultimately failed and suffered extinction. Perhaps ultimately all creatures reach the extent of their potential and die out. All seem to face crossroads where one path leads to relatively abrupt oblivion while the other promises extended life. Even when the species takes the former path, their life can go on for a time. We too face the same circumstances.

In effect, when we gave membership in our respective genders primacy over our relationship to our species we disengaged our autopilot. We chose a specific fork at the crossroads—that to a patriarchal approach which features competition and domination. To this point we have survived and can defend our choice on that basis. But a few dozen aeons is but an instant in evolutionary time; and a few centuries—the tenure of modern science—but a tick of the clock. Just because we have survived this relatively short period proves nothing. Rather, our sudden crisis of disharmony with nature seems to indicate that we have taken the wrong fork.

A friend suggested to me that to try to link overpopulation and pollution to gender conflict was "a real stretch." My response is that most social problems occur because people are confused about their identity and therefore have difficulty identifying constructive goals and positive behavior.

Specifically, traditional gender roles demand that males establish identity based upon social status linked to power and wealth. This mindset has further driven our male-led society to "thing orientation" which has led to overproduction and overconsumption, making the environment a source of personal exploitation rather than an honored matrix which supports us all. It has also led to destructive wars.

In addition, men and women who cling to distorted gender views usually respond to the biological mating urge confused about their role, their goals and their responsibility in having children. Not only is this a major factor in overpopulation, but it adversely affects child-raising. The parental drive to establish gender identities in infants undermines the matrix system. Pressuring infant boys to assume "masculine" traits, only tends to foster adversarial attitudes toward the crucial infant matrix—mother. Those children not provided effective matrices, in their lifelong attempt to anesthetize the pain of neglect and the frustrated hunger for parental love, commonly become self-centered adults obsessed with possession and consumption.

The negative influence of identifying with gender cannot be over-emphasized. It has fostered all the gender conflict we find today. It has suffocated both men and women, making them afraid to explore their full potential for fear of violating the rules of the group they have been assigned to. It has led to women's subjugation while engrossing men in a frustrating, futile search for "masculinity."

Even as women continue to fight for and gain more freedom they will face deepening frustration as long as the cost of their freedom is isolation from men. Men will continue to endure haunting insecurity regarding their manhood because the "masculinity" they are seeking—a deep, overwhelming inner sense of the masculine—is not natural and can only be attained by distorting their natural instincts.

Once more, Holly Devor:

> 'Masculinity' might be characterized as a cluster of psychological needs which vibrate with the conflict between a largely unconscious need for emotional submersion and a continuously socially reinforced gender role need for independence.

No simple solution to the complex problems of gender relationships exists. However, our first step must be to acknowledge that our link to our species as a whole supersedes any allegiance to gender. Men and women must see each other as "we," not "them" and "us." I think most men and women would welcome this. But to achieve it we must first shed our need to base our identities upon—and gain our feeling of self worth from—belonging to a gender. We must recognize that the essential relationship dictated by evolution is man/woman, not man/man or woman/woman. Only then can men and women truly bond, take full advantage of each other's inherent qualities and evolve together to the level nature intended.

Chapter Thirteen
True Masculinity

What makes a man? What is masculinity?

It wasn't until the last few decades with the advent of feminism that men even pondered these questions. The answers to them had always seemed self-evident. Strength, aggressiveness, competitiveness, leadership, success, athleticism, iron control of feelings, the ability to settle disputes physically, the ability to control women. Men's symbols of masculinity have been: a large penis, the gun, the athletic trophy, the cigarette, liquor, horsepower, the fist. The bottom line was that "real men" were winners who knew how to use force and the threat of force to prevail. They measured their success against other men, competing to accumulate the most money, power and glory, and to possess the most desirable women.

Few men or women challenged the image of virile manhood that was considered ideal and the goal of all boys growing up. Even mothers (and later, wives and girlfriends) supported the males in their lives in pursuing these standards.

Those unfortunate men who found this image unnatural and had difficulty measuring up, had to hide their "inadequacies" to escape disdain. Some tried to fake it, acting out bravado and exaggerated aggression to look manly. Others hid in groups, which "real men" classified as "wimps" and "fags." Still others hid, period, immersing themselves in activities that kept them away from the public.

Even many of those who found the concept of a "real man" easier to emulate, suffered an inner distortion to their natural character as they tried to fit the mold laid out for them. The rewards they received by conforming blinded them to an inner conflict they had triggered. Later many of them would complain of mid-life crises or burnout. Still others would sustain their effort until a nervous breakdown, stress-related heart attack or stroke finally felled them.

Even after suffering one of these serious setbacks, few, if any, of those who try to conform to their image of a "real man" are willing to question their concept. Many entrust their well being to medical professionals who patch them up through surgery, drugs and/or mental reconditioning to return to the "rat race." Some of these men may modify their behavior to compensate for the stark onset of stress induced physical frailty. But few are willing to change focus. Status and power must be maintained and, if possible, increased. This is what makes a "true man."

A small minority of those who have bought into the traditional patriarchal view of manhood do make major adjustments in life focus once tragedy strikes them. Many of them are willing to acknowledge that their lifestyle and ambitions within the system were dragging them down. They admit that the system needs major modification to keep men from destroying themselves. However, they are not willing to go so far as to admit that the concept of true manhood portrayed by the patriarchal system is largely fallacious and primarily responsible for creating men's difficulties. Instead they seek to define some new system which will allow them to maintain their position as patriarchs without having to participate in ruthless competition.

Men cannot find true manhood within our patriarchal system because patriarchy demands male dominance—an unnatural relationship between men and women. Until a man is willing to purge himself of this insecure need to dominate, he will never be able to completely define himself. For he must do so—indeed, the only way he can do so—is in a healthy relationship with a woman (partner, spouse, wife, etc.).

I know that statement will freak out many members of both genders, but I stand by it. As I've emphasized before, nature did not design the human species as two genders with distinct physical differences so that each could find its fulfillment by living alone or with its same gender.

Yes, many of both genders live successfully by themselves. But most of these have had to struggle in order to justify their isolation from the other gender. Some have sought to satisfy the bonding imperative by retreating into homosexuality. Some, after many relationship failures and bad experiences seeking out the other gender, have steeled themselves against further attempts to bond by convincing themselves they have overcome the need. Nevertheless, the seeking is the proof that bonding is a necessary ingredient of total fulfillment.

Nature designed us to operate at optimum in pair bonds. (Even

Sam Keen goes so far as to admit: "A man or woman without an abiding investment in family, children and generations yet to come is a straw blowing in the wind.") That is why instinct drives both men and women to seek out each other. I believe it is also why married men, statistically, live significantly longer than single men.

In those rare moments where men participate in a discussion of true manhood, the first issue usually considered is the role of men's physical strength. Most men take pride in possessing physical strength that exceeds that of the average woman. They see it as the primary justification for their exercising dominance.

Sadly, the level of self-esteem in many men is directly linked to the level of physical force they can wield, especially in the level of violence they can direct against fellow men. These men feel competent when they can conceive of themselves as being able to win fights against other men; incompetent otherwise. I grew up in a neighborhood where one of the most common topics of conversation among all young men was who could "take" who in a fight. Older men, once past their physical prime, tended to talk about who they had "taken." Never, of course, who had "taken" them.

When it is suggested that men misuse their physical strength; that they should learn to address problems using other means, men often feel threatened. They look upon such a shift as a sacrifice that would emasculate them. They see the ability to wield physical strength as an attribute that determines their identity as men. They see it as a measuring stick to judge themselves against other men. And, they see it setting them apart from, and above, women.

Therefore, to begin defining genuine masculinity we must first address the issue of greater male physical strength and its proper use in enhancing the species. I can best do this by using another sports analogy.

In the 60s Elgin Baylor played basketball for the Lakers. During that time he earned a reputation as the greatest player to ever play his position—an assessment some feel is still valid. He stood 6'5"—an unimposing height even in those times—while weighing 225 pounds. If any of those pounds was fat it was not apparent to the observer. While nowhere near the biggest, he was certainly among the strongest players in the NBA.

In addition to his strength, Baylor was blessed with ballet-like co-ordination and grace. He could jump higher than most competitors and gave the impression of being able to "hang" in the air in defiance of gravity. At the same time he could control the ball with uncanny skill, being able to cast up accurate shots from all sorts of unorthodox positions that seemed to defy both the imagination and the defender's efforts to stop them.

Baylor's physical tools allowed him to employ any style of play he chose. His strength was so great that no one could use strength to stop him. No one could prevent him from going anywhere on the court he wanted or from releasing an accurate shot. Quite simply he could have pushed people around, humiliated and then ridiculed them as many players now do. But Baylor played a truly masculine role on the basketball court.

Often the opposing team would assign a player with gorilla-like physique to guard him. Neither intimidated nor outwardly angered, Baylor would use just enough of his strength to attain the position he wanted and then would cast up his graceful, often unorthodox, shots in defiance of the desperate attempts to stop him. He never sacrificed his gracefulness or met aggression with aggression. In many cases he could have "dunked" the ball, a gesture of defiance to opponents that is universal today. But Baylor so seldom employed that tactic that observers often wondered whether he was capable.

I too wondered until one night when I saw him "dunk" against perhaps the greatest defender to ever play the game, Bill Russell. In that situation Baylor quite simply could find no other way to score the basket against the taller Russell. So by using brute strength he defied even the great Russell's efforts and jammed the ball in the basket. But his "dunk" was not an act of defiance or an attempt to humiliate. It was the only solution to his problem.

Baylor ultimately made use of all of his exceptional physical strength to contribute to his team. But in most circumstances he used only enough to perform the necessary task. He didn't need to flaunt his skills or humiliate his opponents. As a player he felt secure. That in contrast to today's players who find it necessary to flaunt their superiority whenever they can, expressing self-adulation and disdain for opponents through "dunking" and other violent gestures. They personify the distorted male attitude that has prevailed throughout the centuries—exult in one's strength over others. In that context male strength is ugly and unmasculine.

Strength wielded in a truly masculine fashion is used constructively. One can violently swing one's arms in order to knock some-one down and impose dominance or one can do so to drive nails into wood and raise buildings. One can use the strength in one's back to wrestle someone to the ground and prove superiority or one can use that same strength to carry someone to safety. (I am reminded of Jimmy Dean's old pop song "Big Bad John" which praises a powerful miner who, using the raw strength in his back, held up shoring beams during a tunnel cavein, giving his life so that his fellow miners could escape.) The flaunting of physical strength for the purpose of intimidation is a reflection of insecurity, not healthy masculinity.

A true man does not ignore or deny his masculine strength, for it is a gift given to the species. The species would be impoverished and perhaps, in times past, hard pressed to survive without it. But it is to be used to the benefit of both men and women, not misused in the pursuit of domination. Men have been given that strength to protect, construct and yes, nurture, not to intimidate and destroy.

This relates not only to men's relationship to women and the environment, but to other men as well. True masculinity does not need to compete with and establish superiority over other men. It is not about being able to destroy or subdue adversaries (although a true man might have to do this on occasion). Rather it is about being able to build, nurture, create and cooperate with other men and women for mutual benefit.

The competitive instinct is a normal one that has enabled the human species to survive. But it becomes misdirected when turned upon other men. Sadly, in modern society we see competition between human beings encouraged and worshipped in a ritualistic manner.

Originally the undistorted competitive urge grew from having to wrest the means of survival from indifferent natural forces. Survival demanded that we vie with these forces to gain sustenance or resist the threat they posed to us. Occasionally humans might compete with each other, but primarily the competitive urge was utilized to deal with nature.

Today the environment does not present the varied threats it once did but humankind still clings to the competitive instinct. We have distorted competition by viewing it as something which occurs exclusively between humans.

Humanity's best interests dictate that competition should occur only rarely between humans. Cooperation is what fosters the highest level of human productivity. Humans, however, have not found this to be the case because without competing with others they lack motivation. Instead of being driven by an inner desire to operate at optimum, humans depend on measuring themselves against others to drag them out of their doldrums. It would seem that if one needs competition with another in order to direct full energy toward a constructive project, he is psychologically handicapped.

Those who advocate competition as a crucial motivating force behind human achievement tend to overlook the negative aspects—namely, the accompanying animosity and the fate of the loser. Some anthropologists would claim that competition has fostered a virile species, weeding out the weak. Does that mean we should abandon the elderly or disabled because they can no longer keep up with the rest of us? I suggest that compassion for others is one of those characteristics that make us uniquely human. To preserve our human nature we must be willing to share with those less fortunate, not disdain them as "losers" to be left to their fates while we continue engaging in our cruel competitions.

A true man (and true woman) first defines a goal as worthy in itself and then pursues it with his full energies without concern for what others are doing or how others see him. Those who are outwardly motivated by competitive instincts become slaves to those they compete with. If these others choose not to compete or don't compete effectively, our competitive male is not provided the energy to express his full potential. Indeed, he may not choose to pursue the goal at all. And if he loses in the competition he is suddenly beset by deep doubts about his abilities, which may be quite exceptional, if not quite as good as his competitor's.

The competitive mania that grips our society can be no better illustrated than with our addiction to competitive sports. A true man does not focus upon sports because he has healthy self-esteem which does not need artificial bolstering. He wishes to focus his energies upon activities that have utility. He would rather invoke the same enthusiasm others devote to sports toward organized efforts that enhance mankind.

What if all those sports fans changed focus and dedicated themselves to projects that would improve conditions in the world? Just imagine the 100+ million Americans who watch the Super Bowl annually, directing all the energy they've focused upon that game to some environmental project. It couldn't happen because it couldn't generate the same or greater level of pleasure these viewers experience when watching dozens of physically mutated giants crashing into each other. Why, because most of us have never learned to access pleasure through creating and nurturing? We have become a society with an infantile approach to pleasure and therefore we find little satisfaction in being constructive.

Even as millions follow the games, more millions are swallowed in recreational pursuits which, by challenging the environment, generate the thrill of facing danger and experiencing unusual physical sensation. By accepting and overcoming the challenges offered by these activities the participants (both men and women) seek identity and feelings of self worth.

Everywhere we turn we see new sports and recreational activities which seek excitement. Jumping from airplanes, gliding from cliffs, scaling sheer walls, skiing over precipices, plowing through river rapids, riding mountainous waves, mountain biking, motorcrossing, jetskiing, snowboarding—the number of thrill-seeking activities seems to be growing daily.

Adults spend hours of their free time toning their bodies and perfecting equipment in order to experience the exhilaration of these and other unique physical experiences. No sooner is some new sport developed than some form of competition is devised to pit participants against each other. Play is the order of the day and for many, success at this play denotes manhood.

This is tragic because play is the function designed by nature to foster the growth of children. Boys legitimately play. Men hide from themselves in play. What we are currently seeing are adults trying to recapture growth experiences they were prevented from experiencing as boys.

Psychologists defend this behavior by claiming we all have an "inner child." Thus they imply that adulthood is all serious and dull—maturity a burden. In order to fully enjoy oneself one must be able to act childlike and play. This, of course, encourages men to involve themselves in sports and recreation.

Modern psychology's assessment seems vindicated when we examine which pursuits bring men the most pleasure. Sports sit at the top of the list. Most men cannot achieve nearly as much pleasure in constructing something, or creating a work of art, or successfully teaching a child. Why do these activities hold such little fulfillment for most men? Why do these things seem dull and tedious, almost like work? Because they indeed are dull and tedious—to children. And sadly, children are what most men have remained.

But psychology's pessimistic view of the prospects for pleasure offered by adulthood does not reconcile with nature's plan. Each successive matrix offers fulfillment. Each provides pleasure in the seeking of that fulfillment. Frustration and boredom in a matrix only occur when biological necessity thrusts an individual into that matrix without his having completed proper mental preparation in a previous one. This leaves him unprepared for dealing with the challenges of the new matrix.

So, those who cannot find pleasure in adult pursuits tend to be locked into their childhood. Their bodies have matured but their psyches have been left behind, trapped in a childhood matrix in which they failed to achieve completion. They still seek the fun they experienced while pursuing fulfillment in that matrix. But now, having been denied that fulfillment, they are not prepared to experience adult pleasure because they lack the foundation from which to explore adulthood confidently.

What evidence of this do we find? Look at the environment. Only a crazed or immature mind allows one to destroy the place one lives. Self-centered, inconsiderate, consumption-oriented behavior is normal for young children exploring a childhood matrix. Fortunately in their very natural explorations most of these children have adult supervision which prevents destruction of the house. Today's "adults" have little of that supervision. In addition, they have adult physiques and intellects with which to pursue fulfillment of their clinging childhood needs. This combination threatens the earth.

What is the nature of adult pleasure? What makes true man happy?

The adult matrix opens up vast horizons of the mind previously inaccessible. With proper preparation in the lower matrices, the mind enters adulthood hungry to be fed. In the adult matrix the mind finds the sustenance it needs—the opportunity to explore mental capacity to its optimum. As it continues searching successfully it is rewarded with pleasure and contentment, not burdened by the boredom so many of us have come to attribute to adulthood.

The quest for expanded consciousness conducted by the properly prepared adult mind is not limited to the intellectual level. (Many brilliant intellectuals suffer from deep insecurities and low self-esteem related to failing to achieve mind balance and physical fulfillment in a previous matrix. That's why we have been victimized throughout history by so many twisted, destructive intellectual viewpoints.) Expansion in all aspects of the mind—intellect, psyche, intuition and physical consciousness—brings pleasure. Physical sensations without assimilation into context that fosters mental growth is unfulfilling. Thus the pursuits that bring elation to children leave a true man bereft of satisfaction because he finds in them no completion.

Does that mean a true man would shut himself off from the aforementioned recreational activity?

No. But a true man has entered the adult matrix seeking mind expansion. He can find genuine pleasure in sports and recreation when he uses them as tools to expand his mind as well as to provide occasional exercise and relaxation.

For example, he might participate on an athletic team to explore the dynamics of teamwork or to sharpen his mental focus in physically demanding situations. He might downhill ski or skydive to perfect body discipline and to examine the feelings generated by high speed and the fear of falling. Winning or losing a competition would not matter. Exotic physical sensations by themselves would not thrill him. His pleasure would come whenever these activities triggered an exhilarating sense of consciousness expansion. That would not likely be abundant in these contexts so he would not set aside a large portion of his time for them. Not with so many other mind-stimulating pursuits available.

A true man might use these sporting activities as teaching tools for children. But he would most certainly downplay the competitive aspects and make sure all the participants are having fun. For play is nature's way of teaching children and fun is the sign that children are being fulfilled.

Fun, however, has no fulfilling quality for a true man. A true man seeks pleasure. I define the terms differently.

To adults, "fun" usually refers to escape from anxiety or boredom. ("You need to go and have some fun.") It amounts to anesthetizing oneself against prior negative experience rather than creating a positive new one. "Fun" is often linked to excitement (the anticipation of pleasure), which also serves as a powerful anesthesia. (How often the excitement, or "fun," of planning a trip is as much, or more, "fun" than the trip itself.) Pleasure comes from excitement being fulfilled. It is followed by contentment—a mind/body experience. Pleasure may provide escape from pain, but it is more than a state of painlessness. It is an exuberant feeling of well being at having accomplished or experienced something positive.

Most adults are dominated by the pursuit of "fun" because they are seeking escape from the haunting frustration of being trapped between two matrices. Physical maturity—body, glands and brain mass—have propelled adults into a matrix which offers pleasures to the mature mind even as the psyche is still seeking completion in prior matrices.

One major "fun" pursuit of an immature male psyche residing in an adult body is sex. A true man sees sex as an act of bonding. To do so he must be fully involved mentally with his partner. Only then can he recognize her pleasure even as he experiences his own in a mind/body context. In comparison, a man locked into a childhood matrix experiences only his own pleasure, and that usually in a purely physical context.

A major misconception has for ages been driven home to children and continues to haunt adults that are trapped in the childhood matrix. This is, that evil controls a large percentage of human beings and that the greatest service one can perform is fighting it.

While one might correctly assess that many people regularly practice behavior that one might classify as "evil," such behavior is instigated by a distortion in human nature rather than natural instincts. Thus the need to resist human "evil," even when necessary, draws men away from the path to self-realization. These "defenders" must seek to return to that path as quickly as possible.

We damage ourselves when we choose a life path focused upon the avoidance and resistance of "evil." The sword may be necessary, but except in an emergency it is always best kept in its scabbard locked away and far removed from consciousness.

This brings to mind a comparison between General Patton and ancient Roman citizen Lucius Quinctius Cincinnatus. Cincinnatus was busy plowing the fields of his small farm when a group of frantic citizens asked him to take command of the army and repel an invasion of a hostile tribe. Cincinnatus had previously commanded but had settled down to the life of a simple farmer. Still, loyal to his duty as a citizen, he dropped the reins of his oxen, took command, and ultimately defeated the invaders. At this point the grateful citizenry offered him the office of Dictator which he promptly refused, returning to his farm to finish his plowing.

Unlike Patton, Cincinnatus needed no war to motivate him. He recognized life's true priorities. He fought when he had to, but found himself more akin to the peaceful, obscure life of a farmer. He returned to that life at the earliest possible moment, preventing the conflict he had just endured from damaging his spirit.

To its terrible detriment, humanity throughout its history has viewed the world as hostile. We see the environment and other humans as threats that we must deal with. We measure our efficacy as human beings in terms of our being able to deal with these threats. The most common reaction has been for us—particularly men—to face these threats in a combative, or "warrior" mode.

Even those devoted to peace tend to view the world as threatening and other humans as hostile and in need of pacification. The difference is that while the warrior seeks to pacify his/her world through physical force or threat of same, the pacifist seeks peace through discussion, generosity, etc. The problem is that both sides share the same view of the world. Both see a distinctly innate hostile (sometimes even "evil") element in humanity that must be dealt with. This prioritizes the need for an individual to develop his/her abilities to deal with evil.

The fictional heroes we are encouraged to embrace as children are mostly evil-fighters. It used to be Dick Tracy, Captain Marvel and Flash Gordon. Now it's Power Rangers, Hercules and Xena the Warrior Princess. All of them receive their identity from fighting evil. And thus those children who idolize them tend to embrace the view that evil fills the world and the ultimate service they can perform for themselves or humanity is to fight evil. The concept of universal evil comes to control their views and aspirations, sending millions of them to martial arts studios where they learn to punch and kick as a primary means of self expression. All this training to fight evil tends to blind them to the realization that human beings are most productive when they are creating, nurturing, building, learning, etc. No one emphasizes to them that it is these latter pursuits, rather than the practice of warriorhood, that exemplify the highest nature of mankind.

Granted, many humans are controlled by hostility and seek to dominate others. And these must be resisted even to the extent of using force. But once this evil has been successfully resisted, those who fought should follow the example of Cincinnatus and eagerly return to a normal life within a peace loving society. The need to use force to subdue aggressors must be regretted, not idolized. It is this tendency to idolize those who use force that spawns the physical aggression which leads to conflict.

Men today, just as they always have, find themselves facing an identity crisis. Why has the search for "masculinity" been so frustrating to men? Because there is very little to find. Men expect to exult in the great discovery but they can never seem to make it. Refusing to admit failure, they continue to search, assuming they've been looking in the wrong place. New books—guidebooks to aid the search—are written, describing new techniques for searching and new places to look. But alas, no discovery. It is like the Spaniards searching the southwest for the Seven Cities of Gold. They could never find them but their lust for riches drove them on for many decades. Man's lust to find the anticipated riches of "masculinity" continues to drive him similarly.

The lust for "masculinity" arises from men's lack of basic self-esteem. Inadequate parenting has prevented them from gaining respect for their own basic essence. Some have never been encouraged to look within. Instead they have been taught to identify with gender, race, nationality, culture, religion, heritage or any number of other superficial characteristics. The myth of masculinity is presented to males in their earliest years, becoming their first fairy tale.

A true man finds his identity in his consciousness. Not as his consciousness perceives his being objectively, as it would from an external point of view. Rather, how it perceives his being subjectively—from an internal viewpoint which blends thought, emotions and body impulses. This point is crucial and must be clarified.

We experience life subjectively rather than objectively. We sit inside a vehicle—our bodies—and experience life through the instruments it has provided us—eyes, ears, etc. The stimuli provided by our senses trigger our mind which generates images which in turn trigger emotions. Emotions serve as a barometer measuring the quality of our lives and at the same time mobilizing body responses.

Much has been written to stigmatize emotions. Puritanical philosophies have branded them as destructive hungers to be wrestled into submission. Super intellects have classified them as impulses not to be trusted. A large segment of our society sees them as negative, especially in relationship to our objective consciousness. What these viewpoints fail to see is that emotions are the lifeblood of consciousness.

Our motivation for living lies in the pursuit of positive emotional experience. If you were told that in your life you would experience nothing but sadness, anxiety, frustration and despair you would have no desire to live. Even those who lead lives in the most miserable circumstances either find some pleasurable activity to momentarily divert them or they continue to toil in anticipation of a pleasurable time in the future, perhaps in some nirvana after having died. Pleasure is like breathing. We must have it, whether in reality or by deceiving ourselves. I suggest that those few who seem to have accepted a life without pleasure have done so because they lack the courage to kill themselves, not by choice.

Emotions are directly linked to the body through the glands. Fear stimulates the adrenals; desire the sex glands; etc. However, if we did not recognize a physical threat through the thought process, the adrenals would remain at rest. Likewise, if we perceived a potential sex partner as unattractive, penis and testicles would not respond. Even infants, whose brain mass has grown little beyond the reptilian stage, react to primitive brain impulses when their emotions prod them to cry out their needs.

Emotions never misguide us. Emotions respond to thought. It is thought that misguides us. What complicates the issue is that when a thought triggers an emotion which stimulates the body the entire three-fold process gets locked into a psycho/physical awareness that cannot be altered simply by later generating a new thought.

For example, a barking dog might trigger terror in a child who perceives it as life threatening. Terror activates the adrenals so now we have the experience locked into the psycho-physical structure. We may even see evidence in the musculature with certain muscles remaining tense long after the experience is over. (See the work of Wilhelm Reich and Alexander Lowen.) Years afterward a barking dog will still trigger the same emotions and physical reaction, even though the current conscious thought will seek to convince the grown up child that no threat exists.

The "improper" reaction to the dog is not the fault of the fear emotion which is only reacting to a prior thought which has become an engram, encoded into the system by the prior experience. Spontaneous conscious thought doesn't automatically erase engrams.

The point here is that emotion is a tool the human organism uses to further its best interests. Nature designed emotions to tell us when we are doing well and when we are doing poorly. Only they (not thought) can do this on a visceral level. However, to serve the organism rather than undermine it, emotions depend upon proper cognition by the consciousness. If our minds perceive and classify something innocuous as a threat, our emotions will respond accordingly until our minds reclassify and override the prior thought.

Yes, emotions can be evaluated objectively. But no matter how perceptive our thinking may be, emotions can only be experienced subjectively. We tend to overlook this because our consciousness can exit our vehicle (our body) through exercising imagination. By doing so we can assess the direction we have been following. This is akin to studying a road map. By doing so we can choose course corrections based upon what we imagine the road holds ahead. But this is only an image based on the picture and data presented by the map. In order for us to continue our journey and experience the road as it really is we must reenter our vehicle and direct it forward down the road. Of course, as we continue on, many unimagined sights and experiences will surprise us.

While moving down the road we are experiencing the journey (life) subjectively. While reading the map we are assessing our journey objectively. To get the most out of our journey we need to exercise both states of mind. But actual living takes place subjectively from within the vehicle. If we were to spend all of our time in the objective state our life would be an imagined one, not truly experienced.

Most of us cannot effectively drive this bumpy, curvy road and read our road map at the same time. A few have been working to overcome this problem through meditation and other mind control exercises and to the degree they have been successful their lives have been enhanced. However, one cannot live effectively in this physical world completely outside the subjective state. Thought can tell us what to do and what direction to take, but we must direct the vehicle from inside. While there, we seek verification of the proper nature of our actions by experiencing our emotions.

Man's lack of trust in his basic essence is comparable to his lack of confidence in being able to drive his vehicle. While behind the wheel he doubts that he is making progress. He is consumed with fear of road hazards and of getting lost. With this sense of insecurity dominating him his journey is miserable.

He attempts to fight this misery by making objective evaluations. By taking himself out of his vehicle and assessing his journey he can see how far he has come without catastrophe and he can compare himself to others trying to make the same journey. By measuring himself against them he can console himself and continue on, even though the doubt and fear continue to nag.

The crucial factor determining your level of self-esteem is the ability to be all right with yourself without comparing yourself with others. This refers to a subjective (emotional) rather than an objective (thought) evaluation. True inner security (one might even use the term "faith") rests upon confidence in that inner essence that gives us the potential to "be." In other words confidence in our ability to be an effective person.

The effect of distrusting that basic essence is to doom ourselves to haunting feelings of insecurity—engrams resulting in physical tension. For how can you live comfortably in such intimate contact twenty-four hours a day with something that exerts such a powerful control in your life when you don't trust it to serve you?

All feelings of self-worth dependent on comparisons amount to pseudo-self-esteem. These may help cover over the painful cavity formed by an absence of self-esteem, but they do not satisfy because they cannot be experienced subjectively. Pseudo-self-esteem is manufactured in the objective mind.

This takes us back to why men identify with gender, race, nationality, culture, religion, heritage, etc. All of these are contrived, objectively perceived classifications which allow us to compare ourselves with others. Naturally we wish to compare favorably so we must downgrade all those who are not members of our own various groups. Only then can we elevate ourselves sufficiently to feel a measure of self-worth.

This form of pseudo-self-esteem serves as an anesthetic to the excruciating absence of subjective self-worth. We therefore must maintain this objective concept of superiority to others through bigotry in its various forms. The bottom line is that sexism, racism, patriotism, religious prejudice, etc., can all be attributed to a lack of personal self-esteem.

A true man is one who possesses subjective self-esteem. He feels all right with himself without comparing himself to others. Gender, skin color, national origin, philosophy—all may raise his curiosity, but none affect the level of his self-esteem. The only classification that matters to him is his membership in the human species. Biologically he has an obligation to serve the well being of his species. Even so, he respects other species and the environment which serves as matrix for all.

Once during a lecture Sam Keen took issue with the concept put forth by Carlos Castaneda that we must "erase personal history." Keen proceeded to explain that it was valuable to him to acknowledge his roots and the heritage he came from. He felt this important in order to understand himself.

I acknowledge Keen's point, for our past experiences do shape us to a great degree. And yet from his comments I believe Keen misunderstood Castaneda. I see a major part of the term "personal history" encompassing membership in the various classifications I've just mentioned. I believe that our real identity waits to be realized not through any affiliation, but rather through our subjective reaction to experiences as they occur. Each moment the slate is clean and we are a new person.

Consider: if you were to base your entire feeling of self-worth on your personal history and later found out that your heritage, based upon your own objective standards, failed miserably to measure up, would that sabotage your chances for a positive future?

Those who grasp for identity and self-esteem based on personal history are victims of self-deception. A concept of one's personal history is the creation of the mind and will have an effect on current experience only to the degree we allow it. Naturally, if we allow past experiences to condition us personal history takes on significance. But that is a game the objective mind is playing. Whether intentionally or inadvertently, anyone who advocates maintaining a strong connection to one's personal history fosters bigotry.

(For this reason women hurt themselves when advocating development of an exclusively female history. We certainly need to know the full range of women's experience in history, but not exclusive of men's experience. Only a gender neutral human history can reveal women's contributions to humanity and men's mistreatment of women.)

A related activity is the practice of ritual. Those who lack genuine self-esteem reach out to ritual to provide them guidance and motivation. They cannot trust their own judgment or discipline and therefore reach outside themselves to others.

A true man finds no value in being locked into a pattern of behavior designed in and for another time. The key word is "locked." A true man might choose to practice behavior learned from others, but only after he has evaluated it, understood it, and authenticated it for himself in that moment. At that point it no longer is ritual, but rather a mode of behavior that belongs to him personally.

The aspect of true manhood most difficult to comprehend by today's males is their membership in a species rather than in a gender group. A true man has no loyalties to his gender which supersede those to his species and thus he feels just as much camaraderie with women as he does with men. He sees no major gender distinctions and wishes to see all females reach their full potential.

A true man accepts his need to bond, and upon finding the right woman, sees himself as an equal member of a two person team. He recognizes specific biological roles to be played by each, but does not place any power significance in those roles. In all areas where biology has not determined that one or the other gender has an advantage, he sees himself and his partner as interchangeable. She has an equal right to determine the path their pair bond will take. Both have an equal obligation to perform tasks and chores they will encounter along the way.

When a true man desires children he is willing to sacrifice his career to care for them. He will work whatever job necessary to support his wife—physically with his presence, and financially—so she is free to provide the proper matrices for the infant. If that means sacrificing a career he has pursued all his life, he will do so because he willingly accepts the responsibility of his decision to bring another precious, and initially helpless, being into the world.

As the child grows older and the boundaries of its matrix shift to include the outside world, true man will be prepared to assume even more responsibility. His focus will remain upon the child, subordinating his own desires and providing the fertile ground it needs to reach fulfillment as an autonomous individual. He does this willingly because he recognizes the raising of a child as a sacred duty that he has voluntarily initiated.

First and foremost a true man is a nurturing being. The word "nurture" has always been associated with femininity and scares many men. This is a cruel misconception. In addition to performing the many nurturing tasks ordinarily performed by women, men nurture when they build things, raise crops, teach their children to value the rights of others, speak out against oppression and defend the helpless from attack. Nurturing is an attitude as much as a physical act.

True men exult in seeing things evolve and grow. They abhor destruction, except for that which is necessary to clear the way for constructive projects. And in those situations where they must employ violence to protect high principles and the helpless, they do so with regret, not exultation. They do all these things without sacrificing their physical strength, but rather harnessing it.

Perhaps the greatest test of true manhood comes with being tempted to use physical superiority over another in order to get one's way in a dispute which could easily be settled peacefully. This situation occurs most often in relating to women. Physical superiority can be a potent intoxicant; knowing that one can control others through physical intimidation a great high. A true man finds it unthinkable to bring his physical strength into such a situation.

In reality, true manhood doesn't differ that much from true womanhood. Set aside the biological differences—which aren't as many as patriarchal man would have us believe—and the roles are interchangeable. I have only surrendered and discussed "true manhood" because we live in a gender-focused society. If my arguments are to have any impact they must address the bastion of power which is male identified.

Achieving true manhood will be very difficult, even for men who are willing to change to seek fulfillment. It will be virtually impossible for the rest, for it's very difficult to give up what you have identified as your basic essence. Those who cling to patriarchal concepts are doomed to remain less than true men.

All men who wish to change face a struggle with lifelong negative conditioning and relentlessly hostile social pressure. Perhaps many of us who wish to make a positive impact on our society cannot, for now, completely overcome the obstacles that separate us from true manhood. Even so, let us acknowledge our failings, admit that we are currently too weak to surmount them, and repent of them to those we adversely affect. In that way we can begin smoothing the way to both true manhood and true womanhood for the children who will follow.

Conclusion

A female friend of mine has suggested that I am asking men to give up an awful lot. She asked what I was offering to convince men to make the sacrifice and share their power equally with women.

I saw her point. Men haven't reached this self serving level by being conscience driven. They have been driven by the pursuit of power and gain. To men, most of whom are thus focused, does the offer of a clear conscience, thriving womanhood and enriched children mean anything when weighed against a loss of wealth and power to dominate? It hasn't until now. Is that because of ignorance or stubborn greed? I've always hoped it was the former, but I have my doubts.

We asked the southern slaveowners to give up a lot when we abolished slavery. We had to fight a war to get them to acquiesce. But there was a lot more to consider than just the selfish interests of slaveowners. The rights and quality of life of a large segment of the human community was at stake.

We face a similar situation when assessing gender privilege. Perhaps it is a "sacrifice" for men to give up their privileged position. But what about the sacrifice of rights women have endured the past several thousand years? As one feminist put it, "While some men face mid-life crises, women face entire-life crises."

I have never had wealth or status. But as a white male in our society I recognize that neither my gender nor the color of my skin has stood in my way to achieving any rational goal I set for myself. I also recognize that those aspects of society which do hinder my aspirations are male imposed—particularly white male. Furthermore I see that me and my white-skinned brothers have the most authority and opportunity to change this system which abuses us as well as all others.

We males are the princes in a long history of royal tradition. Most of us embrace this tradition and seek the crown. While only a few succeed in assuming it, the rest assume a lesser, albeit exalted, status as dukes, counts, barons, etc. Often the king and other high nobility make unreasonable demands upon and thereby abuse the lower nobility. Nevertheless, these lesser nobles maintain a level of power bestowed by their genetic heritage that is not available to the other gender. This lesser nobility has far more power to change the system than women who must make their protests from an imposed zero status. Some of these women may be held in high regard by their benefactors, but female protests against the system carry little impact. The caste system may have changed to degree, but it remains entrenched, class determined by gender.

In this book I have been asking all of us—men in particular—to measure ourselves against the ideal. And while the ideal may seem to be an elusive goal to most of us, by accepting less than the ideal we not only accept a lifestyle of lesser quality but we set in motion forces which further undermine us. By refusing to pursue the ideal we allow those forces to condition us to a way and view of life that has brought on the problems we complain about today. Perhaps we are not capable of instantly transforming into the ideal. Major transformation such as this takes major work. But by measuring ourselves against the ideal and committing ourselves to taking significant steps in that direction we break the chain of behavior that has fostered gender conflict and created disenchanted, self-centered beings whose inner confusion has led to many of our most serious social problems.

Bibliography

Ardrey, Robert—*The Hunting Hypothesis*, Bantam, 1977

Badinter, Elisabeth—*XY, On Masculine Identity*, Columbia, 1995

" "—*The Unopposite Sex*, Harper & Row, 1989

Bahr, Robert—*The Virility Factor*, Factor Press, 1992

Baird, Robert & Katherine (ed.)—*Homosexuality*

Bakan, David—*And They Took Themselves Wives*, Harper & Row, 1979

Barash, David—*The Hare and the Tortoise*, Viking, 1986

Batten, Mary—*Sexual Strategies*, Putnam, 1992

Benderly, Beryl Lieff—*The Myth of Two Minds*, Doubleday, 1987

Blankenhorn, David—*Fatherless America*, Basic Books, 1995

Bly, Robert—*Iron John*, Random House, 1990

" " — *The Sibling Society*, Addison-Wesley, 1996

Branden, Nathaniel—*The Psychology of Romantic Love*, Bantam, 1981

Brownmiller, Susan—*Against Our Will*, Simon & Schuster, 1975

Bullough, Vern—*The Subordinate Sex*, Penguin, 1974

Bullough, Vern & Bonnie—*Contraception*, Prometheus Books, 1990

Calvin, William H.—*The Ascent of Mind*, Bantam, 1991

Campbell, Joseph (ed.)—*The Portable Jung*, Viking, 1971

Capra, Fritjof—*The Tao of Physics*, Bantam, 1984

Cardelle, Frank—*Journey to Brotherhood*, Gardner Press, 1990

Castaneda, Carlos—*Journey to Ixtlan*—Pocket Books, 1974

Close, Ellis—*A Man's World*

Corneau, Guy—*Absent Fathers, Lost Sons*, Shambala, 1991

Davis, Elizabeth Gould—*The First Sex*, Penguin Books Inc., 1972

Davis, Flora—Moving the Mountain—*The Women's Movement in America Since 1960*

Dawkins, Richard—*The Selfish Gene*, Oxford U. Press, 1989

" "—*River out of Eden*, Basic Books, 1995

De Beauvoir, Simone—*The Second Sex,* Bantam, 1961

Debold, Wilson & Malave—(Elizabeth, Marie & Idelisse)—*Mother/ Daughter Revolution,* Addison-Wesley, 1993

Dench, Geoff—*The Frog, The Prince,* Neanderthal Books

Denfeld, Rene—*The New Victorians,* Warner, 1995

Devor, Holly—*Gender Blending,* Indiana U. Press, 1989

Diamond, Jared—*The Third Chimpanzee,* HarperCollins, 1992

Douglas, Carol Anne—*Love & Politics,* ISM, 1990

Dworkin, Andrea—*Our Blood,* Harper & Row, 1976

Eisler, Riane—*The Chalice and the Blade,* Harper & Row, 1987

Eisler & Loye, Riane & David—*The Partnership Way,* HarperCollins, 1990

Elshtain, Jean B.—*Women and War,* Basic Books, 1987

Fagan, Brian M.—*The Journey from Eden,* Thames & Hudson, 1990

Faludi, Susan—*Backlash,* Crown, 1991

Farago, Ladilas—*Patton: Ordeal and Triumph,* Dell, 1965

Farb, Peter—*Man's Rise to Civilization,* Avon, 1971

Farmer, Steven—*The Wounded Male,* Lowell House, 1991

Farrell, Warren—*The Myth of Male Power,* Simon & Schuster, 1993

Fasteau, Marc—*The Male Machine,* Dell, 1981

Fausto-Sterling, Anne—*Myths of Gender,* Basic Books, 1985

Firestone, Shulamith—*The Dialectic of Sex,* Bantam, 1971

Fisher, Elizabeth—*Woman's Creation,* McGraw-Hill, 1979

Flexner, Eleanor—*Century of Struggle,* Harvard, 1975

Fox-Genovese, Elizabeth—*Feminism Without Illusions,* Univ. of North Carolina, 1991

Fraser, Antonia—*The Warrior Queens,* Knopf, 1988

French, Marilyn—*Beyond Power,* Random House, 1985

" "—*The War Against Women,* Simon & Schuster, 1992

Friedan, Betty—*The Feminine Mystique,* Dell, 1963

" "—*The Second Stage,* Summit, 1981

Frueh, Langer & Raven (ed.)—*New Feminist Criticism,* Icon Editions, 1994

Gilligan, Carol—*In a Different Voice,* Harvard, 1982

Goldberg, Herb—*The Inner Male*, New American Library, 1987

" , "—*The Hazards of Being Male*, New American Library, 1987

" , "—*The New Male,* New American Library, 1980

Goldberg, Steven—*The Inevitability of Patriarchy*, Morrow, 1973

" "—*Why Men Rule,* Open Court, 1993

Gould and Gunther—*Reinventing Fatherhood*, Tab Books, 1993

Grant, Toni—*Being A Woman*, Random House, 1988

Gray, John—*Men are from Mars, Women are from Venus*, HarperCollins, 1992

Greenstein, Ben—*The Fragile Male*, Carol Publishing, 1994

Hagan, Kay Leigh (ed.)—*Women Respond to the Men's Movement*, HarperCollins, 1992

Harris, Marvin—*Our Kind*, Harper & Row, 1989

Harrison, Beverly Wildung (ed. Robb)—*Making the Connections*, Beacon Press, 1985

Hawley, Richard A.—*Boys Will Be Men*, Paul S. Eriksson, 1993

Hewlitt, Sylvia Ann—*A Lesser Life*, Warner Books, 1987

Jaggar & Rothenberg—*Feminist Frameworks*, McGraw Hill, 1984

Janov, Arther—*The Primal Scream*, Dell, 1973

Johanson, Donald & Lenora—*Ancestors: In Search of Human Origins*, Villard Books, 1994

Johnson, Sonia—*Going Out of Our Minds*, The Crossing Press, 1987

Jones, Steve—*The Language of Genes*, Doubleday, 1994

Kanowitz, Leo—*Women and the Law, The Unfinished Revolution*, University of New Mexico Press, 1973

Kaschak, Ellyn—*Engendered Lives*, Basic Books, 1992

Keen, Sam—*Fire in the Belly*, Bantam, 1991

Kimmel, Michael S.—*The Politics of Manhood*, Temple U. Press, 1995

Kipnis, Aaron—*Knights Without Armor,* Tarcher, 1991

Klein, Ellen R.—*Feminism Under Fire*, Prometheus, 1996

Kurten, Bjorn—*Our Earliest Ancestors,* Columbia U. Press, 1993

" "—*Not from the Apes*, Random House, 1972

Leakey, Richard—*The Origin of Mankind*, Basicbooks, 1994

Leone & O'Neill (Bruno & Teresa)—*Male/Female Roles*, Greenhaven Press, 1983

Lerner, Gerda—*The Creation of Patriarchy*, Oxford, 1986

Levant, Ronald—*Masculinity Reconstructed*, Dutton, 1995

Lewin, Roger—*Bones of Contention*, Simon & Schuster, 1987

Liddell Hart, B. H.—*The Real War 1914-1918*, Little, Brown & Co., 1930

Livy—*The Early History of Rome*, Penguin, 1971

"—*Rome and the Meditteranean*, Penguin, 1976

Lowen, Alexander—*The Language of the Body*, MacMillan, 1971

Maslow, Abraham—*Toward A Psychology of Being*, Van Nostrand Co., 1962

Mead, Margaret—*Sex and Temperament in Three Primitive Societies*, Wm. Morrow & Co., 1963

Meade, Michael—*Men and the Water of Life*, HarperSF, 1993

Mellaart, James—*Earliest Civilizations of the Near East*, Thames and Hudson Limited, 1965

Messner, Michael A. & Donald F. Sabo—*Sex, Violence and Power in Sports*, The Crossing Press, 1994

Miedzian, Myriam—*Boys Will Be Boys*, Doubleday, 1991

Miller, Jean Baker—*Toward A New Psychology of Women*, Beacon Press, 1986

Millett, Kate—*Sexual Politics*, Ballantine, 1978

Moore & Gillette (Robt. & Douglas)—*King, Warrior, Magician, Lover*, HarperCollins, 1991

Moraga & Anzaldua, Cherrie & Gloria (eds.)—*This Bridge Called My Back*, Kitchen Table Press, 1983

Neely, James C.—*Gender, The Myth of Equality*, Simon & Schuster, 1981

Nelson, Mariah Burton—*The Stronger Women Get, The More Men Love Football*, Harcourt Brace, 1994

Paglia, Camille—*Sex, Art and American Culture*, Vintage, 1992

Pearce, Joseph Chilton—*Magical Child,* Bantam, 1980

" " "—*Evolution's End,* HarperSF, 1992

Pleck, Joseph—*The Myth of Masculinity,* MIT Press, 1981

Plutarch—*Lives of the Noble Greeks and Romans,* Modern Library

Pomeroy, Sarah B.—*Goddesses, Whores, Wives and Slaves,* Schocken Books, 1975

Pruett, Kyle D.—*The Nurturing Father,* Warner, 1987

Richards, Janet Radcliff—*The Sceptical Feminist,* Penguin, 1980

Rothblatt, Martine—*The Apartheid of Sex,* Crown, 1995

Ruether, Rosemary Radford—*Gaia & God,* HarperCollins, 1992

Sanford, John A.—*The Invisible Partners,* Paulist Press, 1980

Seidler, Victor J.—*Recreating Sexual Politics,* Routledge, 1991

Silverstein, Olga & Beth Rashbaum—*The Courage to Raise Good Men,* Viking, 1994

Sommers, Christina Hoff—*Who Stole Feminism,* Simon & Schuster, 1982

Spelman, Elizabeth V.—*Inessential Woman,* Beacon Press, 1988

Stoller, Robert J.—*Sex and Gender,* Science House, 1968

" "—*Presentations of Gender,* Yale U. Press, 1985

Stoltenberg, John—*The End of Manhood,* Dutton, 1993

" "—*Refusing to be a Man,* Meridian, 1989

Tavris, Carol—*The Mismeasure of Woman,* Simon & Schuster, 1982

Tiger, Lionel—*Men in Groups,* Marion Boyars, 1984

Towery, Twyman L.—*Male Code,* Glenbridge Publications, 1992

Vlahos, Olivia—*New World Beginnings,* Fawcett, 1972

Wehr, Demaris S.—*Jung & Feminism,* Beacon Press, 1987

Whyte, Martin King—*The Status of Women in Preindustrial Societies,* Princeton U. Press, 1978

Wolf, Naomi—*Fire With Fire,* Ballantine Books, 1994

various—*Male/Female Roles* (Opposing Viewpoint Series)

"—*Violence Against Women,* Greenhaven Press, 1994

About The Author

Born and raised in Chicago, as a teenager Russell S. Dynda moved to Los Angeles, where he still lives. A non-conformist who graduated high school a year ahead of his class, he decided to forego the typical impersonal, structured college regimen. Instead he chose to study writing with a specialized school while conducting comprehensive research on topics of interest to him. Thusly he gained significant expertise in subjects such as anthropology, psychology, and social, political and military history. His expertise in the natural sciences allowed him entrance into the achaeological community and he has worked on major excavations in Southern California including Spanish explorer Portola's "Lost Village of Encino."

Even while continuing his academic research, he explored opportunities in the business world. But after reaching management status in a large international insurance corporation, he gave up his promising business career to seek deeper fulfillment in his first love, writing. As a free-lance writer he has had numerous articles published on social issues and and has written four books.

Competitive team sports have played a major role in his life. A skilled basketball and baseball player, in twenty-five years as a hoopster he regularly competed in top leagues and tournaments against many of the finest players in Southern California. In addition he served four years as a basketball referee and baseball umpire.

Throughout his athletic endeavors his primary interest remained the study of social and cultural issues. Eventually negative experiences in sports helped lead him to his current focus—an exhaustive study of the issues that stifle gender harmony. In addition to exhaustive academic research on the subject, he has attended men's groups as well as co-ed self-improvement seminars. In that setting he was befriended by Dr. Barbara DeAngelis who once referred to him as a "visionary."

Even as he continues his research he serves as a civilian interviewer chairing entry level interview boards for candidates seeking to join the Los Angeles Police Department. In that capacity he is asked to grade the attitudes and character of those who would be entrusted with carrying the power of life and death in their role as law enforcers. The position gives him access to the expertise of many highly experienced officers who deal daily with serious social problems in the natural setting. He is single and currently uses his athleticism to explore the possibilities of modern dance.